What others are saying about …

GO&TELL

I love this book! The testimonies will inspire you. The call to missions and evangelism will challenge you. And the Holy Spirit fire burning inside Shawn will remind you that now is the time to seize the Gospel Baton and *Go & Tell*!

STEPHEN EVANS – PRESIDENT, LIGHT OF LIFE INTERNATIONAL

"*Go & Tell* is a shocking reminder of the price so many people who passed the Gospel Baton in the past! In this book Shawn Brann forces us all to look inward to the magnificent work Jesus has done inside us as followers of Christ, and dares us to stay silent with so much good news to shout about to all the world!"

DR. RON LUCE – FUTURIST AND GLOBAL CHURCH STRATEGIST; FORMER PRESIDENT OF TEEN MANIA

"Shawn Brann was my student 20 years ago at the Brownsville Revival School of Ministry. But now he is my friend. In his book, *Go & Tell*, he has masterfully addressed all the reasons we don't share the Gospel—the excuses we make. I've made them all. Shawn addresses these, not with a stick, but with story, history, humor, passion and powerful insights from the Scriptures. You will come away equipped ... and excited to share with others your testimony of this man, Jesus."

RON CANTOR – PRESIDENT, SHELANU TV, ISRAEL; ISRAEL DIRECTOR, GOD TV

"I read Shawn Brann's *Go & Tell—This Is Your Moment to Run*, and I was moved by such a powerful, passionate, targeted book that addresses some urgent needs in the Body of Christ. Shawn clearly convinces us of the dire need for all serious believers in Jesus to take seriously our individual callings to fulfill the Great Commission—to go, share our faith, and make disciples. He does so with a rare combination of sound biblical story-telling, modern and relevant illustrations, and recollections of some of the greatest heroes and heroines in the history of Christianity. Inspired by these spiritual fore-parents who did not allow the reality of persecution or even martyrdom to prevent them from sharing the Good News, with Shawn's help we can all summon up courage, take steps of faith, and offer our own expressions of the greatest story ever told."

DR. DAVID COLE – PROVOST AND DEAN OF GRADUATE STUDIES, THE KING'S UNIVERSITY

"This book is hard to put down. *Go & Tell* immediately captured my attention with its exciting actual stories of believers from Christian history, each chapter representing a different century. This book is jam-packed with inspiring Scriptural insights and contemporary illustrations, many of which were taken from the author's own ministry encounters. In an age of coffee-bar churches and armchair Christians, *Go & Tell's* refreshing and motivating message offers the potential of raising up an army of modern believers passionately in love with Jesus and armed with the strategy to share the Gospel with power and effectiveness. *Go & Tell* is ideal for group study and discipleship training."

DAVID W. DORRIES, PH.D. – PRESIDENT AND FOUNDER, KAIROS MINISTRIES INTERNATIONAL; FORMER CHURCH HISTORY PROFESSOR AT ORAL ROBERTS UNIVERSITY

THIS IS YOUR MOMENT TO *RUN*

GO & TELL

SHAWN BRANN

FOREWARD BY DANIEL KOLENDA

GO & TELL—THIS IS YOUR MOMENT TO RUN

Details in some anecdotes and stories have been changed to protect the identities of persons mentioned.

Trade paperback ISBN 978-0-9822876-0-6

Cover design and layout by Micah Conger. Edited by Allison Griffin.

Published in Dallas, Texas, by Zürich House Publishing.

Zürich House Publishing
P.O. Box 92366
Southlake, TX 76092 (USA)
www.zurichhousepublishing.com

Printed in the United States of America
1 2 3 4 5 6 7 8 9 10

ACKNOWLEDGMENTS

Thank you, Jesus, for your life, death, and resurrection. You are my savior, my king, and my best friend. My life for your gospel. Tanja, your encouragement and love throughout the writing of this book carried me when I wanted to quit. I love you. Bailey and Zoé, this good news is for you, too. A life that is sold out to Jesus has nothing to lose, nothing to regret, and everything to gain. Daddy is so proud of you. Micah Conger and Allison Griffin, you two ladies are incredible. I could not ask for a better designer and editor for this book. *Go & Tell* looks and reads exactly how I had wanted. Thank you for your patience and professionalism. Thank you, Daniel Kolenda, for taking the time out of your busy schedule to write the forward for this book. You are an exceptional leader and gift to the body of Christ. Thanks to the many of you friends who gave endorsements for *Go & Tell*. Many of those endorsements didn't make it into this book, but they were of great encouragement to me and have been useful in other places beyond this printed book. Finally, thank you all who supported the writing of this book through your prayers, finances, and encouragement. You know who you are. I love you all. Thank you.

CONTENTS

FOREWARD

I'm so excited you've picked up this book. I know it will encourage you greatly.

If I had to choose just one thing this book's author, Shawn Brann, and I have in common, it would be that evangelism burns in both of our hearts.

Beyond that, we have other things in common as well. Shawn and I both attended the Brownsville Revival School of Ministry in the late 90s, where God ignited our love of evangelism and set us both on the course of our lives: to tell anyone and everyone who will listen about Jesus.

Over the years (now decades!), many people have watched Shawn in his personal life and in ministry. Whether as a student, husband, father, or serving as a pastor, chaplain, or the founder of his own evangelistic ministry, he's a blessing to those he works with and serves.

And now, with this book, *Go & Tell*, you'll be blessed by his ministry as well.

The great evangelist and author Leonard Ravenhill said, "The opportunity of a lifetime must be seized during the lifetime of the opportunity." In *Go & Tell*, Shawn reminds us that this is our opportunity of a lifetime—our moment to run with the gospel!

Years ago, I was preaching at a conference in Germany with my mentor Reinhard Bonnke. When we met for breakfast one morning, he was unusually silent. I could tell something was stirring in his heart. Then he said, "I had a dream last night. Actually, I'm not sure if it was a dream or a vision—it was so vivid. I was projected years into the future, and

I heard two personalities talking about things happening in the world in their time." All of what he had heard was significant, but it was the final question and answer that most impacted him. "I heard one ask the other 'what ever became of Reinhard Bonnke?' He replied, 'oh, Reinhard Bonnke was just a forerunner for a whole new generation of Holy Spirit empowered evangelists.'"

The last decade of his life, Reinhard lived with a burden to see that new generation of evangelists birthed, equipped, and launched out. He foresaw them not only preaching on platforms, but on street corners and permeating every corner of society. I believe we are going to see the fulfillment of that vision in our day—an army of laborers unleashed on the world to bring in the end time harvest. Indeed, as Jesus said, the harvest is plentiful, but the workers are few. Every believer must be equipped to run the race of sharing Jesus with everyone around them. But, as I've found in my own work as a pastor and evangelist, some believers don't know how, don't know where to start, or have a million excuses and reasons for not sharing the good news.

In *Go & Tell*, you'll find the antidote to apathy, the courage to overcome fear or hesitancy, and the tools you need to be an effective evangelist in your context. This book is packed with practical applications, powerful stories, and valuable insights into the Scriptures. Page after page is filled with humor, passion, solemnity, sound doctrine, and vivid stories from believers throughout the centuries, making it not only rich in theology and history but enjoyable and exciting to read.

Shawn masterfully reminds us of what it has cost for the gospel to advance through the ages. You'll be inspired as you walk through each century and meet great heroes of the faith who laid it all down (often including their own lives) in order to fulfill the Great Commission. Then it gets real, and hits the heart of the modern-day believer, because all believers are evangelists, sent into the world to share the good news of Jesus. Whether in a stadium or street corner, a corporate office or a daycare, the gospel should be proclaimed by everyone who follows Christ.

I know you will love reading *Go & Tell* as much as I did. It's a game changer for all believers and churches wanting to be equipped to share the gospel. I highly recommend you (and your church) not only go through this book and the companion workbook, but let the words of the book to go through you. We are on the brink of a worldwide harvest, and the Gospel Baton is in our hands.

Be encouraged, brother or sister, this is our moment to run.

Daniel Kolenda
President
Christ for all Nations

PREFACE

Maxima crouched in the middle of the arena. Her body vibrated. Her teeth clenched in fear. Her heart pounded. The breeze from the Mediterranean sea gently breathed through the stone archways. Ninety short feet in front of her the metal cage rocked forwards and backwards. With every leap of the caged lions, Maxima could see the teeth that would soon sink into her flesh.

Flashes of the fond memories of her family snapped through her mind. Although she was alone on the dirt arena floor, she felt the presence of another with her. Naked and humiliated, Maxima whispered to God for comfort. The crowds roared, delighted that this rebellious teenager was soon to meet her punishment. They couldn't understand why Maxima was so passionate about some guy named Jesus who lived two hundred years earlier or why she constantly talked about him and his message even though it was illegal. No excuses would stop her. People were drawn to her loving kindness, though they considered her ill or rebellious due to her constant talk about Jesus. After all, teenage, virgin girls were supposed to talk about a prince they would ride away with forever or dream of their future children.

Sure Maxima thought about these things, but she became consumed by the message she heard in her village, which overshadowed any dream of romance. A message of a king, his kingdom, and the hope for every man to know him for eternity. Just a few miles away in Utica, days earlier, three hundred other believers were killed for sharing the gospel. Together, they were placed along the rim of a burning fire pit. They were told to sacrifice to the god Jupiter or be thrown in the pit. All refused. The gospel meant more than life to them. That day, all three hundred gladly gave their lives up in the flames.

Now, authorities had captured Maxima and her two friends, Donatilla and Secunda. It was Maxima's time to recant her message or face a premature death. Donatilla and Secunda would follow. And, who knows when the other two million Christ followers around the empire would be condemned to death?

"Stop spreading the lies of this gospel and give up this Christ!" shouted the procurator over the roar of the crowds.

"The truth is too good, my honor. I can't help but speak of Jesus!" Maxima pleaded.

"Enough with you, Maxima!"

The procurator pointed to the soldiers. Maxima burst into tears. They forced her to drink gall and vinegar, imitating the soldiers at the cross of Jesus. As they laughed, they beat her with whips, raking the flesh from her muscles. With each strike, Maxima called out to God for help. Another soldier, who had enough of her yells, poured lime juice over her naked, bloodied body.

Maxima could barely keep her eyes open. Her strength was quickly fading.

"Lions! Lions! Lions!" the crowds chanted as the caged cats paced ferociously from side to side.

Maxima pleaded in agony to the crowds to please stop and hear about her Jesus, to no avail. They hung her weakened body to the gallows and continued to beat her.

Unsure of how she could be so bold yet still loving people in her final seconds puzzled the gladiators kneeling on the top of the cage of the lions. They had seen this perplexing faith and audacity from dozens of believers over the years in these same kinds of circumstances. They knew how this would end. They knew Maxima's last words and pleas would haunt their dreams, just as the other dozens had. But, right now, they had a job to do.

As the soldiers jogged away from Maxima to safety, the procurator looked at the gladiators and gave them the nod. They lifted the cage doors.

The lions charged out.

Maxima squeezed her eyes shut, gripped the rope that tied her to the gallows, and let out a scream.

It was the year 258 A.D.

1

B.C. to A.D.–THE GOSPEL BATON
But ... I Don't Know What the Gospel Is

"The gospel is like a baton in a relay race." — *Reinhard Bonnke*

The king had come. Jesus emerged into the darkness—the light of the world. For thirty years, he worked in general obscurity, employed at his earthly father's carpenter shop. He fixed broken tables and chairs, but he was focused on fixing something much greater. Four thousand years earlier, Adam and Eve disobeyed God. Evil was introduced to a once-utopian paradise where God and man lived together. It destroyed everything.

But in the midst of the darkness, came a promise from God. A savior, a conquering king, a lover would come one day to cure the sickness of sin, the brokenness it brought, and restore the relationship between God and man. God himself would come. And, that time had arrived.

Jesus traveled around Israel proclaiming a simple message packed with power and love. The Kingdom of God is here. The results of that kingdom manifested. Entire villages were healed, demoniacs were set free, the dead were raised to life, and great multitudes began to follow him.

Three years after his public ministry began, Jesus reclined with his disciples to celebrate Passover. This Passover celebration would be much different than prior years.

Instead of pointing backward to the miracle by which God had saved his people from slavery, this meal pointed forward to the great sacrifice through which God would save the entire world from the ultimate slavery, death, and the evil that had broken paradise. This would be the

Jesus' entire public life was an unfolding of the deep, wonderful, and precious mystery of redeeming love

real exodus—the establishment of a new covenant. The bread would be his body, the wine his blood. He would save the world with his life, death, and resurrection.

After his ascension back to heaven, it was obvious that Jesus' entire public life was an unfolding of the deep, wonderful, and precious mystery of redeeming love. He came to restore, rescue, and ransom man. He came to defeat evil. And, that is exactly what he did.

Over the next two thousand years, followers of Jesus would overcome every excuse, using every means possible, full of love and with all the authority given to them from God to proclaim the good news of Jesus throughout the world.

This is their story.

This is his story.

This can be your story, too.

Each chapter in this book highlights an excuse that holds us back from sharing the gospel and how to overcome them, a story from each century of believers on a principle necessary for evangelism, and biblical insights to help you run with the great multitudes of believers in the global advancement of the good news of Jesus Christ.

KING JESUS

I was speaking at a national youth conference in Europe when, after the meeting, a teenager approached me at the front of the stage. He was wearing a Superman muscle shirt and was a typical mid-adolescence, testosterone-overloaded teenager. It was obvious he had a serious question for me.

"So, tell me, who's your hero?" his voice cracked as he questioned me.

It wasn't the deep theological question I thought he'd ask, but I could tell he was quite serious. So I responded, "Oh, that's simple. Jesus."

"No, for real."

"I am for real."

"OK, take the Bible away. Now who is it?" he replied.

"It's still Jesus," I confirmed.

"How? What makes him so special besides what it says about him in the Bible?" he qualified, as though he wanted to pick a comic book superhero he liked.

"Oh, that's easy. There are three things that can be said about Jesus that can't be said about anyone who has ever lived," I replied.

His brow furrowed and eyes widened a bit as he tried to think of what three points I would give him.

I continued, "First, he is the only person in history who was prophesied about by many people for many centuries and who actually arrived, fulfilling the prophecies. That can't be said about anyone. Not Muhammad, not Buddha, not Einstein, not Newton, and not even you or me.

"Secondly, Jesus came with such power that he split time in half. Everyone from that moment on counted time based on the life of Jesus. Including you! You base the date of your birth by the life of my hero."

"That's cool," he whispered as a grin grew on his face.

"And, thirdly, he was born to die. That's why he came. We are all born to have life, he came to give his life."

"Wow. That's pretty awesome. I've never thought about that."

"Now let's talk about what the Bible says," I answered and then shared the gospel with him.

When the conversation was over, it was clear that his Superman was no match for Jesus. He left with a new hero to follow—a real God who happens to also be the king of the world.

> *Jesus came with such power that he split time in half. Everyone from that moment on counted time based on the life of Jesus. Including you!*

Can I state the obvious? The three descriptions about Jesus really do not do him justice.

I love how Charles Spurgeon wrote about Jesus, "Christ is the great central fact in the world's history. To Him everything looks forward or backward. All the lines of history converge upon Him." Twenty centuries have come and gone, and today Jesus is still the centerpiece of humanity. All the great men and women who ever ruled combined have not affected us as powerfully as has this one solitary life.

Those who have known Jesus the closest have typically been the ones burning with passion for others to know him too—no matter the cost.

Just start with the first followers who shared Jesus everywhere they went after his ascension. We know from Acts 12 that James was put to death by King Herod. But what about the other disciples?

Andrew went throughout modern-day Turkey and Greece as well as an unspecified area of Eastern Europe known as the "land of man-eaters" to tell as many people as possible about Jesus. He was eventually crucified like his savior.

Thomas went to an area east of Syria and possibly as far as India. Although Thomas is often remembered for initially doubting Jesus, he lived out the remainder of his life in full devotion to him. Thomas was stabbed to death for preaching Jesus.

Philip went to North Africa and there saw many people come to Jesus through his preaching. Later, he went to Asia Minor, where the wife of a Roman proconsul would hear the gospel and follow Christ. Her husband had Philip put to death.

Matthew went to Persia and Ethiopia. He, too, was possibly martyred.

Bartholomew was martyred after faithfully sharing the gospel throughout India, Armenia, Ethiopia, and Southern Arabia.

James, the son of Alphaeus, went to Syria. The Jewish historian Josephus reported that he was stoned and clubbed to death for preaching about Jesus.

If those who had first-hand knowledge of Jesus, witnessing him in flesh, were so driven, shouldn't we be too?

Simon the Zealot was likely killed in Persia. Tradition has it that he was sawn in half.

Matthias was likely burned to death.

John survived after being cast into boiling oil at Rome. He was exiled to the island of Patmos where he died of natural causes.

Peter and Paul were both martyred in Rome around 66 A.D. during persecution under Emperor Nero. Paul was beheaded. Peter was sentenced to crucifixion. He asked to be crucified upside down as he did not feel worthy to die the same way as his Jesus.

And, these are the people we know about. Only eternity knows the other stories of the dozens of believers at Jesus' ascension or the three thousand who were converted on the day of Pentecost. If those who had first-hand knowledge of Jesus, witnessing him in flesh, were so driven, shouldn't we be too?

Shouldn't we be so focused on loving Jesus and sharing his good news that anything that distracts us from this be eliminated from our lives?

I'm sure you've seen *The Last Supper* painting by Leonardo da Vinci. In real life, it is quite spectacular. The 23- by 35-foot painting covers an entire wall inside the Convent of Santa Maria delle Grazie in Milan, Italy. It took Leonardo da Vinci three years to finish his masterpiece. He painted the disciples in groups of threes, two groups on either side of Jesus. Jesus sat in the center—his arms stretched before them. In one hand, he held a glass of wine painted with incredible realism. A little too real, in fact. Upon completion, da Vinci's friend remarked that he couldn't keep his eyes off the marvelously realistic glass.

The story goes that da Vinci grabbed his wet paintbrush and wiped across the sparkling cup and said it could not remain. Nothing should distract those who saw the painting from Jesus. Like da Vinci's friend, we, too, let life's distractions pull our eyes from what is most important—Jesus and his gospel message.

We sometimes forget how critical it is that we keep Jesus on the throne of our hearts, the focus of our passion, and the commitment of our lives. We can lose our wonder and awe of Jesus. Why is this? If Jesus is God, and he is, then what is it that keeps us fully focused on him?

I think when many people hear the word "God," they picture a monolithic dictator. A bully in the sky ready to strike someone dead for disobedience. They assume that if God, Jesus, really does exist, he is distant, dull, and dangerous. They tend to think that due to evil all around, this God doesn't have a grasp on managing our world.

Yet, Jesus is everything but this. He's full of compassion, truth, hope, forgiveness, nearness, and love. A classic hymn tries to capture this eternal love of God:

> *"Could we with ink the ocean fill,*
> *   And were the skies of parchment made;*
> *Were every stalk on earth a quill,*
> *   And every man a scribe by trade;*
> *To write the love of God above*
> *   Would drain the ocean dry;*
> *Nor could the scroll contain the whole,*

There are not enough positive descriptions to define who Jesus really is, how valuable he is to every person, and the way he rescues each of us.

Though stretched from sky to sky."[1]

There are not enough positive descriptions to define who Jesus really is, how valuable he is to every person, and the way he rescues each of us. He is continually involved in every detail of every life. His miracles are numerous—his activity is infinite. If we are not careful, we can identify Jesus with only the stories in the Bible, forgetting these are only a glimpse of what he did and can do. Have you ever read this amazing verse by John?

"Jesus did many other things as well. If every one of them were written down, I suppose that even the whole world would not have room for the books that would be written." — John 21:25

It's impossible to put into a book the true description and workings of Jesus in our lives and what he has done for mankind. They are measureless. The adjectives for Christ cannot be numbered.

However, there's one description about Jesus that is important to understand as a believer. It is one of the most frequent descriptions and themes about him throughout all sixty six books of the Bible. It's this. Jesus is a king. Better yet, he is the King of Kings.

Every day, we read headlines about wars, political scandals, economic doom, or the spread of a deadly virus. Our broken, fallen world can be a place with little to no hope. No matter how much we try to fix our problems, there seems to be no end to the daily evil and bad news. Such problems make our hearts yearn for a wise, righteous leader. A king that can give us hope, address root causes of our problems, defeat our enemies, and lovingly protect us from wickedness. The Bible tells us of such a king—King Jesus.

When I was learning German in Switzerland, there was a guy in the class who was agnostic. After one of the classes, I asked him to join me for lunch. I had one purpose. I wanted him to know my hero and become a follower. I shared the gospel with him. Early on in the conversation, he stopped and said he didn't like that I called Jesus a king. He didn't like the images he thought of when he heard this word.

And, I understand. Many people don't like to view Jesus as a "king." Like the word "God," it, too, can paint an idea of a dictator in someone's mind. A person who sits on a throne, far away from ordinary people, full of hate, anger, revenge—an arrogant tyrant who has no problem flexing his power to destroy anyone against him. Or, conjures images of now-meaningless figureheads; a historical office held over from the past that no longer wields any real power.

King Jesus is not this way. He is a perfect, righteous, and victoriously loving king who is sovereign in his authority and eternal reign. His kingdom is not one of this world—it's one of love, of hope, of life.

I told my friend that I understood his concern. However, I had good news for him. I went on to explain why Jesus is described as king, why I stand in awe of him, and the gospel. When we finished our lunch, he looked me in the eyes and said, "I want a Bible. I want to know Jesus. Can you teach me more about Jesus?" I did. The gospel was preached and the journey of discipleship had begun.

CAESAR, JESUS, AND GOOD NEWS

I want to ask you a basic question that I used to have a difficult time answering. However, it is vitally important you understand the answer to this one question as you proceed through this book.

The question may surprise you. Are you ready? I'd like to know what you think the answer is. Here we go …

What is the gospel?

Do you have difficulty articulating the answer, too? I used to stumble over my words when answering this question. I think this may help you.

To answer this question, we could look at the word. It comes from the Greek word *euangelion*, which is a message one is glad to hear, particularly in regards to a military victory that would directly affect the trajectory of the hearer's life. Simply put, gospel meant, and still means, good news.

Or, we could look at verses in the Bible like John 3:16 or Romans 5:8.

Although both of these verses are powerful and are a part of the gospel message, it still may not clear up the question.

So, let's rewind to when it became a popular saying in the days before the birth of Jesus and during the time he was on the earth.

On September 2, 31 B.C., off the western coast of Greece, Octavian's navy defeated Mark Antony and Cleopatra in a critical battle for who would be the sole leader of the Roman empire.[2] This news of Octavian's victory quickly arrived in Rome. Emissaries were sent around the towns and villages announcing this life-altering news: *"Euangelion!* Octavian has won!"

It wouldn't take long for the word to spread like a wildfire from one home to another.

Octavian's supporters celebrated. The civil war, which had raged on since 44 B.C., was over. Rome had its leader. Within a few short days, everyone in the region, and eventually around the ancient world, was abuzz. This unpopular slogan, *euangelion,* became the trending word throughout the Roman Empire. Those in favor of Octavian rejoiced. Those opposed didn't find the news so good.

This *euangelion* took some time to materialize. Octavian, who changed his name to Caesar Augustus, went around the Roman Empire bringing his new kingdom rulership to the areas of the empire that were committed to Antony and Cleopatra. Finally, two years later, he sailed into Rome as the sole ruler of the empire.

What does this have to do with Jesus? I'm glad you asked.

The Jews living in Israel took little comfort in Caesar Augustus' victory. This was not particularly "good news" to them. They would be thrust under the rulership of Octavian, but pray with more fervency for the real king they read about in Scriptures to come, bring forgiveness of sins, and rescue them all.

Then, Jesus was born.

> *"In those days Caesar Augustus issued a decree that a census should be taken of the entire Roman world."* — Luke 2:1

Have you ever wondered why Jesus was born when he was? Why wasn't he born three hundred, five hundred, or seven hundred years earlier or later? The timing of his birth was not coincidental. It was part of God's plan. It was chosen by God. Check out this fascinating verse:

> *"But when the set time had fully come, God sent his Son."*
> — Galatians 4:4

Jesus strategically came onto the scene in world history when he did for a reason. One of those reasons may have been directly related to Caesar Augustus' victory and this popularized idea of *euangelion*. This buzzword was still on everyone's lips. They understood exactly what it meant. The stage was set for the ultimate king, his victory and his story—history—to be made.

The believers during this time understood this concept. Sixty times, Paul mentions the gospel in his letters but never once had to define what he was talking about—they knew. So what exactly was it?

The good news is not that Jesus lived and died, but that he died and lived!

To sum up the entire gospel in a few words is both simple and impossible. It's like someone asking directions from NYC to London. A simple response is to go directly east. But we all know there's a lot more to it than that. A simple statement on what the early believers meant when they said "good news" can be summed up in a few words:

Jesus won!

He is the king--the savior of the world.

The way to eternal life is through faith in him.

This is the gospel.

This all-encompassing declaration packs eternal power and possibilities. Through Jesus' life, death, burial, and resurrection, man can be forgiven and become part of his eternal kingdom, on earth and for all eternity.

The good news is not that Jesus lived and died, but that he died and lived! He is victorious, ruler over all. And, as a result, we can be saved, healed, and set free. All who encounter him should be radically changed and passionate for others to experience the same. We have hope for today and for all eternity because of Jesus. "The good news was, and is," according to theologian N.T. Wright, "that all this has happened in and through Jesus; that one day it will happen, completely and utterly, to all creation; and that we humans, every single one of us, whoever we are, can be caught up in that transformation here and now."[3]

RESPONDING TO A KING

On a cloudy Saturday evening in 2002, I looked down at the field from my seats in Texas Stadium. I was one of eighty-two thousand in attendance who had just heard a beautiful gospel presentation from Billy Graham. As he closed his message, Graham invited everyone who wanted to make a first-time decision to follow Christ to come to the front of the stage. Thousands came forward.

The movement of the crowd was an unspoken reminder. The gospel demands a response—first loyalty to the king and then an expectation.

Do you remember when Isaiah saw King Jesus? Here it is:

> *"In the year that King Uzziah died, I saw the Lord, high and exalted, seated on a throne; and the train of his robe filled the temple. Above him were seraphim, each with six wings: With two wings they covered their faces, with two they covered their feet, and with two they were flying. And they were calling to one another:*

> *"Holy, holy, holy is the Lord Almighty; the whole earth is full of his glory."*

> *At the sound of their voices the doorposts and thresholds shook and the temple was filled with smoke.*

> *Woe to me!" I cried. "I am ruined! For I am a man of unclean lips, and I live among a people of unclean lips, and my eyes have seen the King, the Lord Almighty." — Isaiah 6:1-5*

Isaiah's immediate response was to fall on his knees in hopes of mercy and awe of the king. His life was fully placed in the mercy and control of the king. He saw his sin and his need for the forgiveness of rebellion towards the king. Even the angels covered their faces, shielding themselves from the king's holiness.

In Revelation, when John sees the resurrected Jesus in heaven, he too, responds like Isaiah.

> *"When I saw him, I fell at his feet as though dead. Then he placed his right hand on me and said: "Do not be afraid. I am the First and the Last. I am the Living One; I was dead and now look, I am alive for ever and ever! And I hold the keys of death and Hades." — Revelation 1:17–18*

Like Isaiah and John, our response to the good news is to fully give our lives to King Jesus in adoration, worship, and obedience. We no longer live for the gods of this world, but wholeheartedly devoted to him.

GO & TELL

I've seen many "believers" stop at this point. Imagine if those on Mark Antony's side only congratulated Caesar Augustus on his victory, but never submitted to his new kingship. Chances are, they wouldn't have been around much longer either.

Initial worship and admiration is not enough—more is required. Not only are we expected to be a disciple of Jesus, being committed followers to everything he taught, but we're also to tell others about his victory, his Good News.

This is what happened throughout the Bible. Paul, Timothy, Silas and Luke traveled across the Roman empire telling everyone about Jesus and, as Luke recorded in Acts 16:17, "showing people the way of salvation." Peter, Barnabas, and the early believers did the same. Or, again, take John for example. The entire book of Revelation is his response to get the message out. What about Isaiah? Look what happens immediately after he worships and receives forgiveness for his sins:

> *"Then I heard the voice of the Lord saying, "Whom shall I send? And who will go for us?"*
>
> *And I said, "Here am I. Send me!"*
>
> *He said, "Go and tell this people ..." — Isaiah 6:8-9*

After Jesus' victory on the cross and his resurrection from the dead, he gathered his disciples to him on the Mount of Olives. These would be his final words:

He said to them, "Go into all the world and preach (tell) the gospel to all creation. Whoever believes and is baptized will be saved, but whoever does not believe will be condemned. And these signs will accompany those who believe: In my name they will drive out demons; they will speak in new tongues; they will pick up snakes with their hands; and when they drink deadly poison, it will not hurt them at all; they will place their hands on sick people, and they will get well."

After the Lord Jesus had spoken to them, he was taken up into heaven and he sat at the right hand of God. Then the disciples went out and preached everywhere, and the Lord worked with them and confirmed his word by the signs that accompanied it. — Mark 16:15-20

What were some of Jesus' final words? Go & Tell. And, that is exactly what they did.

And, when would he return? After this gospel of the kingdom is preached in the whole world as a testimony to all nations.[4]

THE GOSPEL BATON

One of my favorite events during the Olympics is the relay races. A runner sprints a quarter of the way around the track where he meets another runner on his team. When his leg of the race is completed, he enters into the exchange zone where he passes the baton to the next runner. This passing of the baton continues with each runner completing his part of the race, until the final runner crosses the finish line with the baton in hand. It's one of the greatest team accomplishments in sports.

The late evangelist Reinhard Bonnke wrote, "The Gospel is like a baton in a relay race."[5] Why?

We are to tell, but we are also to "go." This is a powerful and comforting word that Jesus gave his disciples. You see, the Greek word for go is *poreuō*. This word means to transfer one thing to another. It is the same word used when a runner passes a baton to the next runner.

Poreuō portrays the picture of Jesus handing the advancement of his kingdom and gospel message to those new believers and all who would follow. The Gospel Baton they were receiving had the same

> *"The Gospel is like a baton in a relay race."*

authority, the same power, and the same anointing as it did in the life and on the lips of Jesus. It was their time to replicate everything Jesus was, taught, and did. It was their moment to run. There was a race that they had been enrolled in—to get this good news to the rest of the world.

Every believer was to grab onto this Gospel Baton and share the message of Jesus to the whole world. This was the chief task of everyone who encountered the life-changing message of King Jesus.

Many excuses surely flooded the minds of those believers as they do for us today. But what if? … What about? … How will I? … I don't feel … . That's where the comfort of this word comes in. The disciples were not supposed to do it alone. They would all have different methods, callings, and places in the race, but they all had a common message to proclaim. It wasn't their kingdom they were building but rather Jesus was going to build his kingdom through them. And, it would be Jesus helping them do it! As he ascended into heaven, he said this last sentence to them:

> *"And surely I am with you always, to the very end of the age."*
> — *Matthew 28:20*

The disciples had entered the exchange zone. The Gospel Baton was being handed off. The race for the whole world to hear about Jesus had begun.

2

THE FIRST CENTURY–THE HOLY SPIRIT
But ... I Don't Feel Comfortable Sharing the Gospel

"You might as well try to hear without ears, or breathe without lungs, as try to live a Christian life without the Spirit of God in your heart." — D. L. Moody

The first one hundred and twenty followers of Jesus were eager to run, but they knew they could not effectively share the gospel until the full exchange of the baton had been handed to them. Just ten days earlier, Jesus had told them to wait for the gift of the Holy Spirit. This final exchange of the baton would give them the power to be "his witnesses in Jerusalem, all Judea and Samaria, and to the ends of the earth."[1] These were his last words on earth before ascending back to heaven as the king of all kings.

Suddenly, it happened. As they all sat in a room praying, a sound like the blowing of a violent wind and what appeared to be fire rested on their heads. This was the grand entrance of the Holy Spirit coming just as Jesus had promised. God had once again come to reside on earth. This time it was not just to live with men, but to live in them. The Holy Spirit, God, would be available for all mankind—for every century that followed. The Gospel Baton was now in their hands and the Holy Spirit in their hearts. It was their moment to run.

Peter stepped out of the room where several thousand people had gathered in bewilderment. He had to Go & Tell them of the good news of Jesus. Flashbacks of his life must have raced through Peter's mind. Just three years earlier, he and his brothers were part of a fishing guild in the sprawling, fertile city of Galilee. His life was ordinary. Day after day, his boat would take him across the eight-mile wide Sea of Galilee catching tilapia, sardines, and any other fish that would find itself captured in Peter's nets.

Then, one historic day, Jesus gave him an opportunity of a lifetime. No longer would he catch live fish, kill them, and send them to the market—now he would go to the market, catch dead men, and make them alive.

No longer would he catch live fish, kill them, and send them to the market–now he would go to the market, catch dead men, and make them alive.

Jesus told him that he would "be a fisher of men"[2] and that the "kingdom of heaven had come."[3]

He left everything and followed Jesus. What a three years it was! The miracles. The crowds. The stories. He walked on water, saw Jesus transfigured while being visited by his Old Testament heroes of Moses and Elijah, and saw Jesus raise his friend from the dead. The king of the world had truly come. The Messiah was here. Peter's friend, John, would write in a letter that, "if every one of the things Jesus did were written down, the whole world would not have room for the books that would be written." (John 21:25) Yet, in his witnessing, he was missing something. Peter lacked the power to boldly tell others about Jesus.

At one of the most critical times in Jesus' life, Peter denied Jesus three times. Warming himself by the fire the night of Jesus' arrest, Peter could not share his faith in Jesus to a servant girl or even a small crowd. How would he ever follow the command to share the gospel to the world? In that room, his answer had come.

Now, something was different. Bold, with a message to now share, he addressed the crowds. Perhaps that same servant girl looked on in disbelief. That timid Peter, filled with the Holy Spirit, was a different man. Along with the other disciples, they boldly declared the gospel. "Brothers, what must we do?" the crowd responded.

Peter replied, "Repent and be baptized, every one of you, in the name of Jesus Christ for the forgiveness of your sins. And you will receive the gift of the Holy Spirit."

Peter paused as he looked at the crowd. Then, the Holy Spirit brought the future centuries to Peter's heart and mouth. As if Peter was thinking specifically about you, he continued, "The promise is for you and your children and for all who are far off—for all whom the Lord our God will call!"[4] The Gospel Baton would be passed through the centuries in the future to come.

Over three thousand people accepted Peter's message and grabbed on to the baton that day. The global spread of the gospel had begun!

SEND IT ON DOWN

I became a follower of Jesus while attending a Pentecostal church as a teenager. And, to say it was a wild church is an understatement. It was like something out of the movies. Do you know what I mean? Dancing, shouting, and speaking in tongues was routine. The services were long, the preaching was full of passion, and we had a choir fully decked-out with purple robes. A few times I even joined the choir to the dismay of all who heard me sing.

We affectionately gave the nickname "Flying Squirrel" to one of our friends. Chris was in the choir. Somewhere in the middle of the second song, Chris would get "touched by the Holy Spirit," take off running, and in full stride he would jump off the stage with his arms fully extended outward. As Chris flew off the four-foot stage to the ground, the effect of his choir robe made him look like a squirrel in flight. As fun as the church was, there were a few things that made me uneasy; some things I didn't understand. One of those was the Holy Spirit.

We would sing songs with lyrics like "send it on down" and "send the fire." The preacher would often say that the Holy Spirit was about to "come down" into the room and "fall on us." I was very confused. Who or what was this Spirit, this Ghost, and how was he/it going to show up? I would stare at the ceiling in anticipation for what was to come. Nothing happened.

I thought the Holy Spirit was too confusing to spend time thinking about and did not want these mysterious teachings to get me distracted on my relationship with God. I was simply ignorant of this indispensable understanding of God and the life of a believer. As a new believer, I was unaware that to be effective in advancing the kingdom on earth and living the Christian life is and has always been dependent on the Holy Spirit.

What about you? Is the Holy Spirit, Holy Ghost, a bit of a mystery or something weird that you have preferred to tune out rather than understand? Let's untangle a few critical facts that will unlock a life of spiritual fruitfulness and freedom.

First, throw out the pronoun "it." The Holy Spirit is not an "it" or some kind of mystical force.

The Holy Spirit is God—fully God. Not an expression of God, but God. He has been with man on earth since our creation. He's never left. He doesn't come and go. He is always here. And, amazingly, he wants to be known by us and desires to be in fellowship with us daily.

The Holy Spirit is wholly and a part of the great mystery of the composition of God. Three in one. One in three. The Trinity: Father, Son, and the Holy Spirit. An infinite God who's beyond our finite understanding.

The Holy Spirit is not an "it" or some kind of mystical force.

Attempts have been made to explain the Trinity nature of God. Every attempt is a futile, but noble try. In the fourth century, a theologian named Augustine tried to explain the trinity like love and its three parts: he that loves, that which is love, and love. They are not the same nor are they separate. In the next century, a young man named Patrick in Ireland (more on him later) would use the three leaf clover as a way to explain this mystery—three leaves but one flower. Modern commentators use water as a metaphor. Water is H_2O but can take on three different forms: ice, water, and vapor. The Father is like ice, Jesus like water, and the Holy Spirit like vapor. All are different but all are H_2O.

Either way, what is important is that the Holy Spirit *is* God.

Unlike the songs we would sing and the expressions we used at that Pentecostal church, the Holy Spirit is not an *it*, not fire, and not something that falls from the sky like water on a rainy day. Don't sing to God to send "it" down and expect a mystical experience. This is absurd and degrading language to God. The Holy Spirit is God and wants us to fully be in his loving embrace.

But, wait … doesn't the Bible say that the Holy Spirit fell on the people? Well, kind of.

> *"Even as Peter was saying these things, the Holy Spirit fell upon all who were listening to the message." — Acts 10:44 (NLT)*

The word for *fell* in this text portrays a passionately beautiful image. The Greek word is *epipito*. This word implies more than just falling. Fell is more accurately translated as being seized, taken full possession while falling in one's embrace.

When my daughters would come home from kindergarten, I would be waiting for them at the front door. Often, they would walk through the door and I would lean down, give them a big hug, and while in my embrace I would gently but affectionately "fall" on them. We would both fall to the floor. And, while on the ground I would give them a big kiss, hug them, tickle them, and tell them how much I loved them. This is *epipito*.

This is what the Holy Spirit did that day to those listening to Paul. As they heard the word, the Holy Spirit embraced them. God affectionately loved them. And, this is what God, the Holy Spirit, does for us today. He loves us. He fully embraces us ... and, like those in Acts, he desires to fill us with his presence.

GOD IN US

Somehow, as Tertullian would say two hundred years after Christ, we had chased the Holy Spirit into a book. The Holy Spirit was never meant to live in a book but inside us. Centuries later, Welsh evangelist Evan Roberts would declare "You can get to heaven without being filled with the Holy Spirit, but without being filled, you will lose much on the way." What were these men talking about? And, what does this have to do with evangelism? Put on your seat belt, and let's race through a Cliff Note's seminary degree.

One main thesis of theology is how a perfect God can live with sinful man. How can light and darkness co-exist? And, if he does live with us, where does he live?

For the first four thousand years, God would consistently appear to one man (high priest), once a year, in a specific location (the most holy place in the temple). In this small room, the two worlds would collide. Holy God and unholy man. The two could dwell together.

In a few random cases, God, the Holy Spirit, would come on or in an individual and use them for a specific task. Think of a hand in a glove. The hand would be a person in the case of Othniel in Judges[5] and the glove

"You can get to heaven without being filled with the Holy Spirit, but without being filled, you will lose much on the way."

would be the Holy Spirit coming over him. At other times, the glove would be man and the Holy Spirit would work from within him like with Joshua.[6] However, these were very rare cases.

But God's plan for the spread of this gospel message was about to make a radical shift. He had spoken to the prophet Joel of this new shift that was soon to come.

> *"I will pour out my spirit on all people."* — *Joel 2:28*

Pour? What does this mean? And, how does this relate to theology and especially my life as a bringer of the gospel? Let's keep going.

When Jesus rose from the dead, the Bible says he remained with his disciples another forty days, speaking about the kingdom of God (Acts 1). Matthew, Mark, Luke, and John did not expound much on what happened during those days. However, there are a couple of things we do know. Jesus was adamant to remind the disciples of their calling and the way it would happen. He was about to hand the Gospel Baton to them. It was about to be their moment to run. They were to preach the gospel and make disciples. This was not their chance to become popular, celebrities, or entertainers. The calling to run with this mandate was the greatest opportunity ever given to man, even if it would cost many of them their lives. And as we will soon find out, for many it did.

At the end of those forty days, on a hill in Galilee, Jesus met with his disciples one last time. I'm sure Jesus *epipito* each one of them that day and told them how much he loved them. Even though he was leaving, he wasn't fully leaving them. The Holy Spirit, also God, was about to not just be with them but something even greater. Jesus looked at each of those disciples and gave them this final command. This was not an option. This was the shift; the new way God would live with man.

> *"Do not leave Jerusalem, but wait for the gift my Father promised, which you have heard me speak about. For John baptized with water, but in a few days you will be baptized with the Holy Spirit...you will receive power when the Holy Spirit comes on you; and you will be my witnesses in Jerusalem, and in all Judea and Samaria, and to the ends of the earth."* — *Acts 1:4–5; 8*

And like that, Jesus was gone.

The disciples immediately ran down the hill shouting to everyone the gospel. Right? Wrong.

Thankfully for the generations that followed, these first believers obeyed Jesus until the proper transition of the Gospel Baton from Jesus to man had taken place. Had they not received what was coming, their running would have been in their own strength, and they would have quickly burned out. They would have had no authority to properly represent Jesus and see his kingdom come. Unfortunately, many believers live this way today. But for the next ten days, they waited. Then it happened. The shift. Pentecost.

> *If Christmas is God with us and Easter is God for us, Pentecost is God in us.*

If Christmas is God with us and Easter is God for us, Pentecost is God in us.

On the day of Pentecost, ten days after Jesus left, a hundred and twenty disciples waited in prayer for the transition of the Gospel Baton. Suddenly, the Holy Spirit made his presence known with a mighty wind and a fiery visual. In that moment, the Holy Spirit entered man and "filled" them up with his presence as Joel had prophesied. The believers in the room that day had received the promised gift, the Holy Spirit, just as Jesus said. God was now in them, with all the authority of heaven included. The world was about to be radically changed. The Gospel Baton had been successfully passed off from Jesus to us.

The mystery of theology is now solved. The thesis completed. Congratulations on finishing seminary. Paul said it like this:

> *"...the mystery that has been kept hidden for ages and generations, but is now disclosed to the Lord's people. To them God has chosen to make known among the Gentiles the glorious riches of this mystery, **which is Christ in you**, the hope of glory." — Colossians 1:26–27*

From that day to now, the Holy Spirit, God, has made his residency inside of any believer of Jesus who asks. You don't have to live a life as a believer alone. You can try, but as Evan Roberts had said, you will lose a lot along the way. And, you don't have to share the gospel alone. You have the privilege and command from Jesus to do it in partnership with the Holy Spirit.

THE GREAT CO-MISSION

On September 16, 1964, Billy Graham hosted a public service announcement on the radio from Omaha, Nebraska. His announcement was clear. He would be preaching on national television in the United States as the voting for a new president was weeks away. Midway through the sixteen-minute announcement, Billy Graham proclaimed,

> *"The Christian is not to sit idly by and watch humanity go on without God, without hope and without the gospel. We are to step into the breach; we are to stand in the gap. And, we are to go and obey the command of our Lord Jesus Christ. The world is in desperate need. It needs the love of God. The world is confused; it needs the peace of God. 'Go,' said the great Commander and Chief. This word was spoken with a tremendous sense of urgency. It's an exciting, adventurous word. It is up to us to carry out the great commission to our generation."*[7]

Through the centuries, we have given the title "The Great Commission" as the command of Jesus to preach the gospel and make disciples. The king has commissioned us with a task. The Great Commission is not the Great Guilt Trip or the Great Option. Neither is it the Great Sacrifice. It's a great privilege. After all, "If the commission of an earthly king is an honor how can a commission by a heavenly king be considered a sacrifice?"[8]

This Great Commission is the earthly mission given to everyone from Jesus. But notice something. We are not to do it alone. It is also the Great Co-mission. We are to do it in partnership with God; with the Holy Spirit living in us and working through us.

These first believers knew how important it was to be filled with the Holy Spirit and waited to begin the Great Co-mission until they were filled. They prayed for ten days and then with the Holy Spirit, shared the gospel in one morning. Three thousand people became followers that day.[9] It was the model for the most important need in evangelism—working in partnership with the Holy Spirit.

The book of Acts is story after story of the early advancements of the gospel for the first thirty years after Pentecost. In many Bible translations, this book is titled the Acts of the Apostles. However, the better title should be the Acts of the Holy Spirit. The Holy Spirit is mentioned forty times in the first thirteen chapters—Jesus, is mentioned forty times, too. This is not a coincidence. It is the Holy Spirit who empowered those early believers to represent Jesus. And, it is only through the empowering and indwelling of the Holy Spirit in your life that you can share the gospel to those around you. You must have him.

BE FILLED

The most important decision you can make as a believer is partnering with the Holy Spirit. You must have him living inside of you! In Paul's letter to the Ephesians, he writes:

> *"Don't be drunk with wine, because that will ruin your life.*
> *Instead, be filled with the Holy Spirit." — Ephesians 5:18 (NLT)*

Notice that being filled with the Holy Spirit is not an option, it is a command. Paul was filled with the Holy Spirit after his conversion[10], and he knew it was impossible to try to be a believer without the infilling of the Holy Spirit. The Holy Spirit living inside a believer sets that individual apart from the rest of mankind. He takes ordinary people and makes them extraordinary for his kingdom's sake.

I've often heard believers make the excuse that they don't know how to share their faith or don't feel comfortable sharing their faith. Are you guilty of this? If so, I have exciting news! This is why you need God living in you. Jesus said that it was good for him to leave so that the Holy Spirit, the Comforter, will come and live in you.[11]

When you are filled with the Holy Spirit, he will speak through you when you don't know what to say, and he will comfort you when you feel uncomfortable. Again, you are not expected to believe in and share the good news alone!

The most important decision you can make as a believer is partnering with the Holy Spirit.

If you are not filled with the Holy Spirit, you can be at this very moment. It's simple. First, empty yourself of you. If you are full of yourself, there's no room for God to fill you with himself. Then, do what you did to become a follower of Jesus. Ask and receive.

> *"If you then, though you are evil, know how to give good*
> *gifts to your children, how much more will your Father*
> *in heaven give the Holy Spirit to those who ask him!"*
> — *Luke 11:13*

The Holy Spirit living in you is the best kept secret that is available to mankind. He equips you with all you need for life, godliness, and effectiveness for his kingdom. When he moves in, your life is never the same.

MORE THAN A SYMBOL

Throughout the New Testament, we read of ways the Holy Spirit works in the life of a believer. Oftentimes, these ways are spoken of as symbols of the Holy Spirit. Unfortunately, many believers mistake these symbols and the ways he works for who or what the Holy Spirit is. They confuse him with the way he works. Take the dove as an example.

One of the most classic symbols of the Holy Spirit is a dove. A church I once worked at had a huge wooden dove in the auditorium. One of the ladies in the church was convinced that the Holy Spirit actually *was* a dove. At times, I just wanted to shake her and say, "It's just symbolic to his working in our lives."

The metaphor of the Holy Spirit being like a dove is recorded at Jesus' baptism. Notice what scripture says: "The Holy Spirit descended from Heaven *like a dove* and landed on Jesus."[12] His work in the life of Jesus, and in our lives, is "like a dove."

Why a dove? Well, for one, the dove is the global emblem for peace. In biblical times, the symbol for the caesars was an eagle. A bird was represented as a king and the eagle represented the power through war and strength that was a characteristic of the leader of the Romans. When the Holy Spirit came upon Jesus, it was revealed to the people that Jesus was a king, whose kingdom would be characterized by peace, not war.

In our lives, we must be filled with the Holy Spirit, as he brings us peace in every storm. Try to share the gospel and just see if there isn't a storm that suddenly takes over your mind. You need the Holy Spirit living in you to bring you

> *If you are not filled with the Holy Spirit, you can be at this very moment.*

peace to continue with the Great Commission. Otherwise, excuses and fears will easily overwhelm you. Other symbols of the way the Holy Spirit works in our lives include oil, a finger, water, rain, wind, a guarantee, a seal, a river, wine, and a cloud.[13]

One of my favorite symbols of the Holy Spirit, when it comes to evangelizing, is fire. Remember those songs I would sing in that Pentecostal church? *Send the Fire* was a song I was hesitant to sing. I had no idea what was going to happen if I sang it. If the Holy Spirit really was fire, how would I survive if that fire landed on me?

Do you remember what John said to those he was baptizing in the Jordan river?

> *"I baptize you with water for repentance, but after me will come One more powerful than I, whose sandals I am not worthy to carry. He will baptize you with the Holy Spirit and with fire." — Matthew 3:11*

On the day of Pentecost, while those one hundred and twenty believers were praying, it says:

> *"Suddenly, there was a sound from heaven like the roaring of a mighty windstorm, and it filled the house where they were sitting. Then, what looked like flames or tongues of fire appeared and settled on each of them. And everyone present was filled with the Holy Spirit and began speaking in other languages, as the Holy Spirit gave them this ability." — Acts 2:2–4*

Notice a couple of things. The Holy Spirit was not fire, but rather came *like* fire. And, as he filled the believers, they were suddenly empowered to do something they couldn't have done before. The Holy Spirit enabled them to share the gospel to those outside the house that day.

It's not the bigness of words, but the fire that is behind it that matters.

Fire can represent many things: passion, purity, and power. Many followers of Jesus believe in him as their savior, but never walk in the power that is available to them. This should not be. In battle, would you "rather have a cannonball roll across the room or a rifle ball fired out of a gun? I know what I would choose. It's not the bigness of words, but the fire that is behind it that matters."[14]

Fire also represents movement. Most traditional motor vehicles move because of fire combustion in the engines. Without this combustion, a car won't move. So, the Holy Spirit moves us to be effective for his kingdom and speak on his behalf.

> *"But if I say, 'I will not mention his word or speak anymore in his name,' his word is in my heart like a fire, a fire shut up in my bones. I am weary of holding it in; indeed, I cannot." — Jeremiah 20:9*

Like a fire, the Holy Spirit wants to consume all of us with himself. This is what it means to be filled with him. He wants to have full control of our lives. For those early believers, speaking in tongues was necessary for them to communicate to the lost, but it also communicated to each other that the Holy Spirit had completely taken control. For the Bible says that "no human being can tame the tongue." (James 3:8)

MOTORBOATS AND SAILBOATS

There are two ways you can live your life as a believer—like a sailboat or a motorboat. Most live like a motorboat. They go where they want to go in life and choose their speed. Few believers live life like a sailboat—full of the Holy Spirit. When he blows, they move. They only go where and when he wants them to go. Their lives are completely controlled by the Holy Spirit.

This is how we all can and should live our lives.

When the Holy Spirit moves in, you must be ready for him to interrupt your plans. You must be ready for him to take you places you never expected. Just as wind enters a sailboat, it fills the sails and powers the boat, so the Holy Spirit will fill you and empower you for his purposes. You will have the power and authority to be his witnesses everywhere you go. When the Gospel Baton is carried by Holy Spirit-filled believers, the gospel quickly spreads.

Reinhard Bonnke, one of the most effective evangelists in world history, said of the moment he got the baton to preach in London on January 26, 1962:

> *"The gospel is like a baton in a relay race. That day I got the baton in my hands. The fire I had already within me. The fire is always fresh. The baton of the gospel is always old, and it is passed on. I now understood that on that day in London, the baton and the flame had met."*

The baton and flame had met.

The same happened to those first century believers. Full of the Holy Spirit, they took the gospel across the empire. Followers of Jesus began to appear all over Israel, Palestine, and Asia Minor.

Paul proclaimed Jesus across Macedonia, Spain, and Cyprus. Titus evangelized the island of Crete. Thaddaeus preached in Edessa, Mark in Alexandra, Peter in Bithynia, Thomas in India, and thousands of other unknown believers set out to make everyone a follower of King Jesus.

The Gospel Baton had been handed off. And, on that Pentecostal holiday, Paul declared, "The promise is for you and your children and for all who are far off— for all whom the Lord our God will call!" (Acts 2:39)

When the Holy Spirit moves in, you must be ready for him to interrupt your plans.

The global spread of the gospel had begun ... in partnership with God himself!

3

THE 100s–PRAYER
But ... I Can't Preach

"Don't go into your study to prepare a sermon—that's nonsense. Go into your study to God and get so fiery that your tongue is like a burning coal and you have got to speak." — C.T. Studd, nineteenth century British missionary to China

The Gospel Baton was handed off to a second century of believers full of prayer. This generation knew if they were intimate with God, they would not be intimidated by man.[1] And, no man would stop them from becoming witnesses not just in "Jerusalem, and in all of Judea and Samaria," but now with a mission to all the world. They carried the gospel eastward into Arabia and Persia; westward through Alexandria into North Africa; and northward into Armenia, Pontus, and eventually to modern-day France and Britain. They prayed and they preached.

Heroic stories of Christians laying their lives down because of their love for Jesus and his mission are plenty. Martyrdom was a common experience for Christians, but so was the power of the gospel. These believers would hold on to Christ and his message at all costs.

In roughly 155 A.D., an eighty-six-year-old man named Polycarp passionately shared the gospel throughout the city Smyrna, a port city in what is now Eastern Turkey. Polycarp was taught by John, one of the original twelve disciples of Jesus, and was ordained by John to be a bishop in Smyrna. Polycarp was a man of prayer and a preacher of the gospel.

The authorities arrested Polycarp for his faith and brought him to a crowded arena. His impeccable character and love for the people of Smyrna made them reluctant to feed him to the lions.

"Simply swear by Caesar," the governor begged.

"I am a Christian," Polycarp responded. "If you want to know what that is, set a day and listen."

The governor told Polycarp to recant his faith and his message or he would be thrown to the beasts.

"Bring on your beasts," said Polycarp.

"If you scorn the beasts, I'll have you burned," the governor replied.

"You try to frighten me with the fire that burns for an hour, and you forget the fire of hell that never goes out," Polycarp continued sharing the gospel to the governor and crowd.[2]

The governor had enough. The fire was lit, and Polycarp was given a final chance to stop preaching and recant. But, Polycarp had a gospel he wanted to preach. His final response came as a deep cry from his life of prayer.

"For eighty and six years I have served him, and he has done me no wrong. How then can I blaspheme my king and my savior?"

Polycarp was burned at the stake.

These second century believers saw firsthand how the gospel coupled with prayer was an unstoppable force.

KERUSSO

When, as a young Christian, I first heard the command of Jesus to "Go into all the world and preach the gospel,"[3] I immediately thought of my pastor or one of the famous preachers in the media and was gripped with fear. I couldn't preach. I hated public speaking. To me, preaching meant standing on a platform, microphone in hand, and giving a thirty-minute message out of the Bible. Does that image pop into your head when you hear "preach?" That's what it means, right? Wrong.

The word "preach" is a critical word for evangelism. This is one of my favorite words in the Greek language. When Jesus used it to describe how his kingdom and message would go around the whole world, his disciples would have immediately known what he meant.

Preach in the Greek is the word *kerusso*, which simply means to proclaim or announce a message. But, there's much more. You see, the specific message was given by a *kerux*. This wasn't just any message, and the *kerux* wasn't just any person.

The *kerux* was a critical person in a kingdom. He was the official spokesman for the king. He had the highest and most noble position in the kingdom because he was the only person who had access to the king twenty-four hours a day, seven days a week.

When the king wanted to make an announcement, declare a new law, give an order, or share news, he would tell the spokesman, the *kerux*, what he wanted to say, how he wanted it said, what his attitude was behind the message, and why the message was important. It was the *kerux's* responsibility to convey the sentiment, heart, and emotions of the king to the people.

Once the *kerux* knew exactly what was to be said and how the king wanted it to be delivered, he was ready to speak on behalf of the king. The *kerux* would leave the king's chamber, step out in front of the people and *kerusso* (preach) the message for all to hear. He represented the king to the people. As the king's spokesman, he had no right to speak his own mind, give his own personal commentary, or draw any attention to himself. It was all about the king and his message.[4] He would Go & Tell what the king wanted to declare.

Jesus gave the disciples, the first centuries of believers, and you and me, a command to "go into all the world and *kerusso* the gospel." You don't have to know how to deliver a sermon at a church service. This isn't what Jesus meant when he said to preach. He does expect us to be his spokesman in our everyday interactions with those around us. We have a message to preach, but how to preach it, when to preach it, the people we preach to all come from our personal time with the king.

We can never gain his heart for his people, or even for ourselves, if we don't spend time with him on a daily basis in prayer. We have to know him, ask him questions, and listen to him. He has to be our best friend, savior, and God. Then, through prayer, we are able to work together with God on his mission.

HEARING THE VOICE

Between 2000 and 2013, I was the football chaplain or assisting the chaplain for the professional football teams in Dallas, Texas. We had the honor to go into these locker rooms and share the gospel to the players, coaches, and staff. It was an incredible privilege.

On game days, for the teams where I was the head chaplain, I would stand on the sidelines during the game. When the crowd began shouting, the stadium could get incredibly loud. Since it was so loud, I would often have fun by standing beside a player and telling him all kinds of silly things. Since the player couldn't hear anything I was saying, he would look at me and smile thinking I was giving him a compliment.

One game, while I was standing on the sidelines, something remarkable happened. It was during a moment when everyone in the crowd was on their feet shouting. It seemed impossible to make out what anyone was saying over the noise. I was standing beside the head coach. He seemed bothered. The team was a few yards from the end zone, about forty yards from the coach, with their backs facing us. Suddenly, the coach yelled out, "Hey, Clint!"

Immediately, Clint, the quarterback, turned around and made eye contact with the coach. I could barely hear the coach even though I was beside him. The coach yelled out a new play, Clint nodded, changed the old play to the new play, and the team scored a touchdown.

The only way you will be able to hear the voice of our king and be effective in sharing the gospel is to spend time with him daily in prayer.

I stood there shocked.

Wow. Out of all the thousands of voices in the crowd, Clint somehow heard that coach's voice, and the team scored as a result. We won. But, more importantly, I won. I had learned a lesson about evangelism.

Clint heard the voice of the coach because he spent time with that coach every day in practice. Day after day; week after week; and year after year; they worked together. So, when the coach called his name, Clint's ears were tuned to the voice of the coach. He knew it was the coach's voice and not just another voice in the stadium.

Jesus said, "My sheep hear my voice, and I know them, and they follow me."[5] The only way you will be able to hear the voice of our king and be effective in sharing the gospel is to spend time with him daily in prayer. You can know the voice of God and win in your life calling. Otherwise, the voices of the media,

What happened in public was a direct result of what Jesus did in private. To put it simply, Jesus was a praying man.

our families, our friends, neighbors, co-workers, and the thousand others coming at us in all directions will keep us from hearing him.

WHAT DID JESUS DO?

Could you imagine what the disciples got to experience on a daily basis with Jesus? Everywhere Jesus went, he brought hope. His words had authority, his message had power, and his actions changed everyone. The blind gained sight. Lepers were healed. Demons fled. The dead were raised to life. The public life of Jesus left villages across Israel speechless.

But, the disciples noticed something in the three years they were with Jesus that the crowds never saw. Maybe even something you've read dozens of times but didn't pause to think of the depth of the scripture verses.

What happened in public was a direct result of what Jesus did in private. To put it simply, Jesus was a praying man.

Jesus prayed before daybreak, throughout the night, in secret, on a mountain, in the wilderness, before eating, in times of distress, among the people, at the grave of Lazarus, in Gethsemane, and even when he was dying on the cross.[6]

Jesus was a man of prayer. Even though he was the king, he put his royal robes to the side, took on the skin of man, and modeled to the first receivers of the Gospel Baton that prayer was the secret to an effective public life. Jesus would spend time with the Father in prayer, hear his voice, see his actions, and then would *kerusso* the good news.

> *"Truly, truly, I say to you, the Son can do nothing of Himself, unless it is something He sees the Father doing; for whatever the Father does, these things the Son also does in the same way. For the Father loves the Son and*

shows Him all things that He Himself is doing; and the
Father will show Him greater works than these, so that
you will be amazed." — John 5:19–20 (NASB)

It's no wonder that the only thing that the disciples asked Jesus to teach them was how to pray.[7] They could've asked how to be a better businessman, how to have a great marriage, how to make money, or what they could "invent." Nope. Their only request was that they wanted to know how to pray.

YOUR KINGDOM COME

In the locker rooms just before a team would run on the field, we would get on one knee and pray the Lord's Prayer. This was the simple outline Jesus gave his disciples when they asked to be taught how to pray. Tucked in the middle of this prayer are these words:

"Let your kingdom come, and your will be done, on earth
as it is in heaven." — Luke 11:2

Have you ever thought about how much of an honor it is to pray? Prayer is us spending time with the king. The pressures of life should not be the driving force to pray; but rather the pleasures of God's love. But when we pray, we have to remember that it is not us making a wish or forcing God to change his will. Instead, it is us conforming our will to God's will. We ask God to break our hearts with the things that break his

Prayer is not us seeking to control God or pull him to our will, it is us seeking God to control us.

heart. It's us allowing God to replace our selfish desires with his desire for all to be saved. It's his kingdom that we are asking to come to us.

Charles Spurgeon, a well-known evangelist in the 1800s, would often use an anchored boat to illustrate this point. He would say, "when you throw a boat anchor and catch hold of the shore and pull, do you pull the shore to yourself or do you pull yourself to the shore?" Of course, we pull ourselves to the shore. Likewise, prayer is not us seeking to control God or pull him to our will, it is us seeking God to control us.

Jesus told us to come follow him, but unfortunately so many people expect the same from Jesus. They tell Jesus to come follow them. The kingdom does not work that way. The life of a believer is not about us asking God to step into our world, but rather us stepping toward his. It is "let your kingdom come and your will be done."[8] Remember, we are the spokesman, not the king.

PRAY AND PREACH

You can't have one without the other. These are the two legs needed for effective evangelism. If you only do one, pray and not preach or preach and not pray, you will jump on one leg constantly going around in circles. You will be unbalanced.

At the end of the sixth century, Gregory the Great wrote a book called *Pastor Care*. In it, he stressed that a follower of Christ should not be so absorbed in helping others as to forget prayer, nor neglect our responsibilities as a believer because we spend too much time in prayer. "Our Lord continued in prayer on the mountain," Gregory wrote. "But wrought miracles in the cities; showing us that while aspiring to the highest, we should mingle in sympathy with the necessities of the infirm."

When Gregory died in 604 A.D., he had worn himself out with the preaching of God's Word and miracles in the city while not neglecting prayer on the mountain. His epitaph simply states, "God's Consul." He was a balanced believer, reaching many people with the Gospel of Jesus.[9]

Have you ever driven through the Swiss Alps? Around almost every corner are breathtaking views, majestic mountains, and old chalets. At the end of one of my favorite drives through the Swiss Alps, sits a small house up on the side of a mountain. The home belonged to Niklaus von der Flüe, better known as Brother Klaus, in the mid-1400s. Although Brother Klaus lived in solitude as a hermit, the setup of his house is a perfect example of how we are to live our lives.

His house has just two windows. One opens into the attached chapel, as a symbolic reminder for him to constantly be focused on the presence of God. The other faces outside, toward the people. Villagers would come to Brother Klaus' window asking him to tell them what God was saying to them. Brother Klaus would go between windows when counseling villagers. He knew that without the presence of God, there would be little use of the villagers coming to his window for advice. Like Brother Klaus's house, we should live our lives constantly going from one window to the other: in God's presence and to his people.

In Habakkuk, God has a dialogue with the prophet about what is to come. Afterwards, Habakkuk goes up to the watchtower in Jerusalem and sits on the wall. He is determined to sit and see what God will do. But that's not God's desire when he speaks to us. We are not to sit and see, but to Go & Tell.

God tells Habakkuk that he is achieving nothing by standing on the watchtower. He should go into the streets and write what God has said on the wall so that passersby could read it and a spokesman could run with it. Habakkuk should be warning the people, not sitting at a distance to see what God will do. When God speaks to us, oftentimes it's him telling us to tell others, not so we can wait around to see if it will happen.

PRAYER MOVES

Prayer moves mountains, but it also moves God. He speaks to us, we speak for him, and he moves the hearts of men. You were created to spend time with God and will never be as effective for him as you can be without prayer.

Prayer is like the tracks for a train. The train is powerful, but it does not move without the tracks. It can go for thousands of miles with a track but won't budge an inch without it. Similarly, God will wait to move until we spend time with him. Then, in our prayer time, God will build the tracks from heaven to earth so that we can effectively share the good news in words and deeds.

Do you remember the prophecy in Joel?

> *"I will pour out my Spirit on all people. Your sons and daughters will prophesy, your old men will dream dreams, your young men will see visions. Even on my servants, both men and women, I will pour out my Spirit in those days."*
> — Joel 2:28–29

This prophecy sat dormant for over five hundred years. Then, a hundred and twenty people gathered in a room and prayed for ten days.

They listened to God, stepped out to the crowd, *kerusso* to the people, and God moved.

> *"Then Peter stood up with the Eleven, raised his voice and addressed the crowd: "Fellow Jews and all of you who live in Jerusalem, let me explain this to you; listen carefully to what I say. These people are not drunk, as you suppose. It's only nine in the morning! No, this is what was spoken by the prophet Joel ..."* — Acts 2:14–16

Some of the most effective spiritual awakenings happened as a result of prayer.

The early church prayed continually and saw the good news spread exponentially around the empire. The second century believers were marked by their unwavering commitment to the gospel, birthed from their private time in prayer. The Great Awakening in the USA began with Jonathan Edwards' famous call to prayer. Charles Finney and D.L. Moody both attributed prayer to the many people getting saved.

In 1904, a young Welshman named Evan Roberts started praying for God to, "Bend the Church and save the world." The church people prayed. They preached. And, within two months, approximately seventy thousand people in Wales had professed Christ as their savior!

In 1995, a major revival swept through a church in Pensacola, Florida that would reach millions around the world. The Brownsville Revival was a direct result of the church praying. I had the honor of working at the church on their prayer team during the revival. I was reminded that a revival is not worked up, but rather prayed down. God speaks, his people tell, and heaven's population increases. It's clear that prayer was the reason for this great move of the Holy Spirit.

There are no shortcuts in evangelism. Prayer has to be a daily activity in your life for you to Go & Tell the good news.

BUT, I DON'T HAVE TIME TO PRAY

Frankly, we don't have time *not* to pray. Daniel knew this and thought it wiser to spend a night with a den of lions than a day without prayer. God can do more for us and speak more to us in one second, than we could strive to accomplish in a lifetime. We need to change our thinking that prayer is a waste of time and see that without prayer our work is a waste of time.

In order to be God's spokesman and to Go & Tell his good news, we must first take time to be with the king. I find it puzzling how many believers want to spend eternity with God in heaven but aren't willing to spend one minute with him on earth. This should not be. Instead, we should be like Martin Luther who said, "I have so much to do today that I must set apart more time than usual to pray."

Some time ago, I watched a live national television interview with Billy Graham on Fox.

The interviewer asked the ninety-two-year-old Billy Graham a pointed question, "If you were to do things over again, would you do anything different?"

Billy instantly responded with a simple, "Yes."

What could a man of such influence want to do differently?

He continued, "I would study more. I would pray more. I would travel less. Take fewer speaking engagements. I took too many of them in too many places around the world. If I had to do it over again, I would spend more time in meditation and prayer and just telling the Lord how much I love him and adore him and that I look forward to the time we are going to spend together for eternity."[10]

I find it puzzling how many believers want to spend eternity with God in heaven but aren't willing to spend one minute with him on earth.

Billy Graham. He would do one thing different. He would pray more.

God speaks to us. God equips us. And God sends us out full of his Word and Spirit from our time of prayer with him. This is why Satan trembles when he sees the weakest saint on his or her knees. A prayerless Christian is a powerless

Christian. Make prayer essential in your life and you'll be surprised how God uses you to preach his gospel.

THE GOSPEL SPREADS

Prayer is powerful. It's how we know how to preach the gospel. Billy Graham knew this. And so did the early Church. In the second century, the gospel made its way around the empire with improbable speed.

By the end of the second century, Christians could be found in all the provinces of the Roman Empire as well as in Mesopotamia. This seems to be an accurate assessment in light of this statement by Tertullian, a second-century theologian and early church father, to the pagans: "We have filled every place belonging to you: cities, islands, castles, towns, assemblies, your very camp, your tribes, companies, palace, senate, forum! We leave you your temples only!"

Tertullian may have exaggerated somewhat, but it does seem clear that the church penetrated every part of Roman society by 200 A.D.[11]

Having watched and heard the testimonies of the first century of believers, the second century continued to make prayer critical for the gospel to advance around the world.

And it did.

4

THE 200s–COSMOS
But … I'm Not a Preacher

"The Great Commission to go into all the world is not only geographical, but must include every field, profession, discipline, sport, etc." — *Rick Joyner*

As the Gospel Baton was passed to the third century of believers, it arrived full of momentum and power. Christianity was no longer a minor Jewish sect. It was fast emerging as the dominant rival to the old ways of the Roman Empire. People had taken the words of Jesus to Go & Tell the gospel seriously. These believers dearly loved Jesus and were moved by a burning conviction that God had invaded time to redeem mankind. The world needed to hear this amazing news.

Christians had infiltrated every realm of society with the gospel. There was Tertullian the lawyer, Origen the teacher, and Martina the student. For these three known Christians, there were countless unknown Christians who shared the gospel in their world no matter the cost. For most, obeying Jesus' command to Go & Tell would result in a death sentence. But, they knew that if their savior was killed for his message, they would be willing to give up their lives for it as well. In his writings, Tertullian would remind believers over the next two thousand years to remember what these Christians did; that, "the blood of the martyrs was the seed of the church."

Even though martyrdom continued, the spread of the gospel did not slow. It was during this time that one of the greatest persecutions of

Christians happened under Roman Emperors Severus, Decius, Valerian, Aurelian, and Diocletian. Decius even commanded all citizens of the empire to sacrifice to Roman gods or be killed. But, Christians knew they had a great king to follow and many would not give in to the fear of death. The gospel had to be preached.

There was Pammachius and his family who were beheaded because of their faith. Trypho and Respicius were dragged down the street, had nails put in their feet, torn with iron hooks, and then beheaded.

Quintin, in 287 A.D., went to the region of Picardy in France to share the good news in villages. As a result, he was arrested and condemned to die. The authorities tied ropes to his arms and legs, and he was stretched with pulleys until his joints dislocated. Then he was beaten with a wire, had boiling oil and tar poured on his naked body, and fire applied to his armpits and side. He was then put into prison where he died.

All because he wanted the good news to go to all the world.

An elderly Christian, Metrus, was beaten with clubs, pricked with needles, and stoned to death for telling the gospel of Christ.

Seventy-year-old Appolonia, who wouldn't stop telling others the good news, was tied to a pole and set on fire. She begged to be released, which the mob did thinking she was going to renounce her faith in Christ. To their amazement, however, she hurled herself back into the flames and died.

Saturninus, Secundulus, and Satur were made to run between two rows of men who whipped them until they died. These stories of this century of Christians are limitless. They were not paid staff members at a church, but were full-time evangelists to their friends, neighbors, and coworkers. They had a message to tell, and everyone around them would know.

There was Perpetua. The twenty-two-year-old mother of an infant baby, would not stop telling people about Jesus. Around 203 A.D., she was taken captive along with her pregnant friend, Felicity. When Felicity and Perpetua told authorities they would not stop their devotion to Christ, they, along with several other believers, were brought into a crowded arena of spectators. The men were to be eaten by leopards and the women gouged by bulls; all for the enjoyment of the crowds.

Felicitas was gouged first. Perpetua ran to her side and held her. The bulls didn't attempt to gouge them again. So, gladiators entered to finish them off. Felicitas was killed quickly. But, the young inexperienced gladiator assigned to kill Perpetua trembled violently and could only stab her weakly several times. Seeing how afraid he was, Perpetua held his sword blade and guided it to a vital area in her body. The crowd couldn't help but notice that these Christians were truly convinced in the message they shared. The gospel was talked about by all in the empire.[1]

Such was the example of this fearless, determined century of believers. Those in government, education, arts, and entertainment couldn't escape from hearing about the life of Jesus. They knew that this was their moment to run with the gospel. Families lost loved ones, businesses lost leaders, and the church lost teachers. But the gospel gained even greater momentum.

By 250 A.D., there were more than thirty thousand Christians in Rome alone. Tertullian would write that if the Christians all left the Roman provinces, the empire would be nearly empty. These believers knew that their message had to be told. For God so loved the world that he came. And, they were determined to go to their world too![2]

ETHNOS ...

Have you ever noticed that the Great Commission in Matthew is a bit different than Mark? Check it out. Before Jesus ascended back to heaven, he assigned two general areas where his disciples were to preach.

These are the last words of Jesus in Matthew and Mark:

> *"Therefore go **and make disciples of all nations**, baptizing them in the name of the Father and of the Son and of the Holy Spirit, and teaching them to obey everything I have commanded you. And surely I am with you always, to the very end of the age." — Matthew 28:19*

> *"Jesus said to them, "**Go into all the world** and preach the gospel to all creation." — Mark 16:15*

Both of these texts are critically important for us to know. Since the early believers in the Roman Empire spoke Greek, they clearly understood what Jesus was saying. And, as a result, almost won the entire empire over to him. If believers understood these two passages and acted on them, there could be the greatest revival our world has ever experienced!

Let's look at them again.

In Matthew 28:19 Jesus tells his disciples to, "Go and make disciples of all _nations_ ..." The Greek word for nations is _ethnos_. _Ethnos_ is where we derive the English word ethnicity or ethnic group. _Ethnos_ is essentially a tribe, a nation, and/or a people group.

This is where we get the idea to go overseas or across continents to do missions work. Our mission is to tell others about Jesus. And, we need to disciple the new converts; which is the next necessary step after someone becomes a believer.

There are countless people in tribes and nations around the world right now who have never heard the gospel. We are commanded to Go & Tell them about Jesus! Over the years, I've gone to tribal areas in Africa, drug cartel regions of Mexico, former communist villages in Russia, and the remote atolls of the Marshall Islands with the gospel message.

Unfortunately, most believers think this is all there is to evangelism.

They are often unaware that the mandate from Christ doesn't just include going overseas and telling people about the cross but also seeing the cross and going over to your neighbors, friends, and coworkers.

... AND COSMOS

Look again at Mark 16:15. There's a much more personal directive in this scripture verse about where to go. Here, Jesus tells his disciples to, "Go into all the _world_ and preach the gospel to all creation."

Before understanding the Greek, I would hear this text and imagine a globe; a Google Earth-view of our planet. I would correlate this verse as an additional verse to going to the _ethnos_ mentioned in Matthew. But, it's much more personal. You've got to see this!

The Greek word for _world_ in this scripture text is not _ethnos_ but _kosmos_. In English, we have simply changed the Greek spelling from kosmos to cosmos. A cosmos is anything of order. We call our universe the cosmos because of its order.

The universe isn't the only system of order. There's a political system, a corporate system, a fashion system, an entertainment system, a business system, an order of friends, an order of sports, of banking, of government, and the list goes on. Each of these different systems are their own cosmos.

Right this very moment, God has strategically placed you in more than one cosmos. You are one of his chosen representatives to bring his good news within each cosmos. Your family, your job, your neighborhood, your hobby, and your grocery store are your world to go to!

Therefore, "Go into all the cosmos and preach the gospel to all people."

YOUR MISSION FIELD

So, where is your mission field? It may be to a nation or tribe outside of your ethic group. God did that for me when he had me move my family to Europe from the USA. But, most likely, it is right in front of you.

Right this very moment, God has strategically placed you in more than one cosmos.

Above the exit doors of a church I was visiting was written, "You are now entering your mission field." As I left out those doors that day, I was reminded of my calling.

At the time, I was assisting the chaplain of the Dallas Cowboys and was also the head chaplain of multiple arena football teams in Dallas. God had not put me behind the scenes with these teams to get autographs, photos, or to ask for money. I wasn't there to take, but to bring life to the athletes, coaches, staff, and employees of the team. And, that is what I was determined to do.

Every time I would arrive at the stadium or practice facilities, I would walk the halls knowing that the world of professional football was my cosmos. I shared the good news with everyone. It didn't matter if you were the star player or the janitor. As long as I was in that cosmos, I was determined to share Jesus.

Let me remind you again. We are all full-time evangelists. You don't have to be employed at a church to be viewed by God as his worker. He's already hired you. You are his workman. He's counting on you.

Some of the most effective deliverers of the gospel that I know are not full-time evangelists on the mission field. I know a couple businessmen who share Jesus to every employee in their company and have seen many of them give their lives to Christ. I know some athletes who have shared the gospel to every team they were on. And, there are friends of mine who are determined to see their entire extended cosmos of family reached with the gospel. Your cosmos is your mission field.

I love the story of the influence an Englishman had on his cosmos in the eighteenth century.

In 1780, Robert Raikes, an owner of a publishing company, wanted to take the Gospel Baton to his home of Gloucester, England. Knowing that his cosmos was the business world and his neighborhood, Raikes was determined to use publishing to advance the kingdom. He started printing advertisements of a new program he was launching at his neighbor's house for boys in the neighborhood.

As the years change, so might your cosmos. But the mandate remains the same.

He started the program on Sunday mornings since the boys worked the other six days of the week. Raikes used his printing machines, employees, and materials to make a curriculum for those who came. And, they came! They would eventually call these gatherings Sunday School.

By 1788, there were more than three hundred thousand boys and girls attending one of his Sunday Schools. Within forty years, twenty five percent of the children in Great Britain attended to hear the gospel. By 1910, there were more than five and a half million children who came to Sunday School each week. Why? Because one businessman knew it was his moment to run with the gospel by sharing it to those in his cosmos.

So, what cosmos or cosmoses are you in? If you don't know where to start, think of the seven mountains of influence.

In 1975, Bill Bright, founder of Campus Crusade and Loren Cunningham, founder of Youth With a Mission (YWAM), developed a cosmos-driven mandate: Bring godly change to a nation by reaching its seven mountains of societal influence.

They concluded that in order to truly transform any nation with the Gospel of Jesus Christ, these seven worlds of society must be reached. The seven mountains are: religion, family, education, government, media, arts and entertainment, and business.

Take a moment and ask the Holy Spirit to reveal one of these mountains that he's placed you on.

As the years change, so might your cosmos. But the mandate remains the same. You are God's chosen representative in all the worlds he's placed you in. You have been strategically given that job, your family, placed in your neighborhood, and given that hobby because God believes in you to preach the gospel to them! He's counting on you.

God can save the world by himself but he chooses not to do it alone. He wants to do it together with you!

PLAY TO WIN

What could the story of your life be if you would determine to bring the gospel to everyone in your world?

When I was working with one of those sports teams, a coach made a profound statement at halftime. He said, "Team, we are playing not to lose. Let's play to win!"

Many believers live their lives "playing not to lose." They live cautious, secretive Christian lives. They don't want anyone in their cosmos to know they are a Christian, lest they might offend someone, be perceived negatively, or misrepresent Jesus. They are playing not to lose.

But, that's not the life God has for you. We are to shout from the rooftops what has been whispered in our ears. We are to live life loudly for Jesus. We should be running to win!

Remember those early believers? They weren't faced with offending anyone, but rather death. However, they knew they had a gospel to preach. Tertullian wrote to the emperors, "The more often we are mown down by you, the more in number we grow."

They were in the relay race, and they had the baton. They ran to win.

And so should we.

While we can't bring everybody to the Savior, we should bring the Savior to all. To make it your desire to reach those in your cosmos is the spiritual purpose God has for your life. And, as Robert Murray M'Cheyne, a writer, poet, and pastor in Scotland in the early 1800s would say, "O how sweet to work all day for God, and then to lie down at night under his smiles."

He has created you to win at life and has given you the playbook. Go into every cosmos and to every nation and bring them the gospel.

The believers in the third century took the words of Jesus seriously. One bishop in

What could the story of your life be if you would determine to bring the gospel to everyone in your world?

Constantinople remarked, "If in this city you ask anyone for change, he will discuss with you whether God the Son is begotten or unbegotten. If you ask about the quality of bread, you will receive the answer that, 'God the Father is greater, God the Son is less.' If you suggest that a bath is desirable, you will be told that 'there was nothing before God the Son was created.'"[3] Every conversation in Constantinople revolved around Jesus and biblical questions. Almost all of Constantinople was saved by the end of the century.

Why? Because, whether by life or by death, believers took the gospel to every cosmos and ethnic group they knew. They ran with the Gospel Baton and handed it off to the next century with even more momentum and hope than they had received it.

5

THE 300s–SUPERNATURAL
But … My Faith Isn't Big Enough

"Miracles are not contrary to nature, but only contrary to what we know about nature." — *Saint Augustine*

By the fourth century, all the apostles and early believers were long gone, but the power of the gospel continued on. Like with the early Church, miracles played an important role in advancing the good news. The gospel was quickly spreading across the Middle East, and in 301 A.D., a miracle led to an entire nation, a thousand miles away from Jerusalem, to declare itself the first Christian country.

Bartholomew and Thaddeus, two of the original twelve disciples, took the gospel to Armenia between 40 and 60 A.D. According to Eusebius, a church historian (265–340 A.D.), King Abgar V ruled the Armenian empire during the time of Christ and had requested Jesus to come heal him from leprosy. Although the meeting with Jesus did not happen, shortly after Jesus' ascension, Bartholomew and Thaddeus made the trek north. They brought the gospel to King Abgar who was miraculously healed. For the next two hundred and fifty years, the region remained committed to Zoroastrianism, but the gospel and its miraculous power had taken root in the country.

In 301 A.D., Tiridates III, known as the evil king of Armenia, fell sick. During his illness, he dreamed that Gregory, a Christian he had tortured and then imprisoned for thirteen years because of his faith in Christ, was the only one who could help him. After his dream, Tiridates III summoned Gregory, who boldly shared the gospel and declared healing over the king. Immediately, King Tiridates III was healed and converted to Christianity.

The king was so changed by the experience that he declared Christianity the official religion of Armenia; making Armenia the first official Christian nation. Armenians quickly turned from Zoroastrianism to Christianity when they heard the gospel and experienced the miracles associated with it. King Tiridates III worked passionately to spread Christianity throughout Armenia until his death in 330 A.D. For the rest of the fourth century, Armenia became more and more devoted to Christ.

Armenia would stand on its new faith in Christ. One hundred and fifty years later, the king of Persia, Yazdegerd II (438–457 A.D.), decided to do away with Christianity in Armenia. The more he tried to make Armenians abandon their faith, with bribes, blackmail, and persecution, the more passionately Armenians remained faithful to Jesus. This passionate faith is exemplified in this excerpt of a letter from Armenian nobles to King Yazdegerd II:

> *"From this faith no one can shake us, neither angels nor men, neither sword nor fire, nor water, nor any or all other horrid tortures. All our goods and possessions are in your hands, our bodies are before you; dispose of them as you will. If you leave us to our belief, we will, here on earth, choose no other master in your place and in heaven no other God in place of Jesus Christ, for there is no other God. But should you require anything beyond this great testimony, here we are. Our bodies are in your hands; do with them as you please. Tortures from you, submission from us. The sword is yours; the neck is ours. We are no better than our forefathers who, for the sake of this faith, surrendered their goods, their possessions and their bodies. Were we even immortal, it would become us to die for the love of Christ; for He Himself was immortal and so loved us that He took death on Himself, that we, by His death, might be freed from eternal death. And since He did not spare His immortality, we, who became mortal of our own free*

will, will die for His love willingly, so that He may make us participators in His immortality. We shall die as mortals that He may accept our deaths as that of immortals.

Do not, therefore, interrogate us further concerning all this, because our bond to faith is not with men to be deceived like children, but with God to Whom we are indissolubly bound, and from Whom nothing can detach or separate us, neither now, nor later, nor forever, nor forever and ever."[1]

An entire nation converted to Christianity all because one man shared the gospel with signs and wonders following it. To this day, Armenia is still a Christian country.

A MIRACLE IN A RUSSIAN SOUVENIR SHOP

Signs, wonders, and miracles are a sure way to get people's attention and open the door for the gospel. It worked for Jesus, for the apostles, for the early church, for Armenia, and will do the same for you—if you would step out of your comfort zone and pray for people.

Have you ever been to Russia? It's one of my favorite places to preach the gospel. In 2018, I was invited to preach at church conferences in three different cities in Russia. On the last day, I was with my friend, Jason, in Saint Petersburg. We were in a souvenir shop looking for matryoshka dolls for our wives when Jason asked the cashier, Dimitri, if we could pray for his back.

A look of surprise came over Dimitri's face, "How do you know something is wrong with my back?"

We explained that we were followers of Jesus and he speaks to us. We invited him to sit on a chair while we prayed for him, and a skeptical Dimitri complied. He explained to us that his back pain was so severe that he hadn't been able to bend over and touch his toes in many years and many of his activities had become limited due to the chronic pain. So, we laid hands on Dimitri and started to declare healing on his back.

As we were praying, Dimitri suddenly looked at us and asked, "What is this heat? Why is my back so warm?"

Jason explained, "That's God healing you."

People need to see the gospel as much as they need to hear it.

When we finished praying, Dimitri stood up, bent over, and touched his toes! He was overcome and shouting words of exclamation and surprise that aren't fit to print.

"Blank, blank, blank, I can't believe this!" I haven't been able to touch my toes in YEARS! This is a miracle! This can't really be happening!" he shouted. "Are you guys part of the David Blaine magic show?!"

We explained that no, this isn't magic. It's Jesus.

Dimitri called his coworkers and his store manager in to meet with us. The store manager even changed the sign on the door to "closed" while we met.

It's worth noting at this point that what we were doing in this shop was illegal in Russia. Evangelism, or any "religious extremism" is outlawed if our intention was conversion of the individual, which it was. If we had been caught, we would've been thrown in a Russian jail. At this time, you couldn't even visit the country for ministry work without a religious invitation from the Russian government. Even then, any preaching you do must be inside a church. These were the laws and consequences when we were in Saint Petersburg and at the time of this book's writing. But we knew God had a plan for those employees to hear about Jesus that cold winter day in Saint Petersburg.

With six of the souvenir store employees circled around us, we shared the gospel. The store manager told us about his shoulder pain and asked if we would pray for him, too. We did. And he, too, was healed! The store manager even responded to the invitation to accept Jesus as his savior. Dimitri and the other employees weren't ready to fully follow Jesus at that time, but a seed was planted. (More about seeds in Chapter Eleven.)

For several months after this encounter, knowing that discipleship should always follow evangelism, I met with him on a continual basis over social media. I discovered that I knew a pastor, whom I had met at our One Hope Warsaw, Poland[2] event a few years earlier, who was from the manager's hometown. I arranged an introduction and passed the discipleship on to that pastor.

Jason and I were a little worried as we left the shop, considering what we had done was against the law, and neither of us liked the idea of sitting in a Russian prison. But God did a miracle that day, the gospel went forth, seeds were planted, and one man's eternity was changed.

Oh, and the wives were happy to receive their matryoshka dolls.

IN WORD, DEED, AND SIGN

When Jesus was training his disciples on how to replicate his ministry, he gave them the blueprint.

> *"When Jesus had called the Twelve together, he gave them power and authority to drive out all demons and to cure diseases, and he sent them out to proclaim the kingdom of God and to heal the sick." — Luke 9:1–2*

Jesus made it clear that his disciples were to preach the gospel and work miracles. He was setting the precedent that the proclaiming of the good news was in word, deed, and sign. People need to see the gospel as much as they need to hear it. The disciples went alone, without Jesus, to villages doing exactly what Jesus had commanded. The gospel was proclaimed, and miracles followed.

This formula continues throughout the New Testament. When a crippled beggar stops Peter and John and asks them for money, Peter looks at the man and says, "We have no silver or gold, but what we do have we give to you, in the name of Jesus, walk."[3] Instantly, the man's feet and ankles became strong. The people were filled with amazement and wonder at what happened. Peter, with the crowd's attention, boldly proclaimed the good news of the victory of Jesus and roughly five thousand men were saved that day.[4] Aeneas, bedridden for eight years, was healed when Peter prayed for him,[5] and Tabitha was raised from the dead.[6]

Stephen, Judas's replacement, preached the gospel with "great wonders and miraculous signs."[7] Philip was miraculously transported to Azotus after preaching to an Ethiopian.[8] As a matter of fact, all the apostles "performed many miraculous signs and wonders among the people."[9]

Paul, who was converted after Jesus' ascension, continued the pattern given to Jesus' disciples. He reminded the Corinthians "my message and my preaching were not with wise and persuasive words, but with a demonstration of the Spirit's power."[10] And, to the Romans he said he would "not venture to speak of anything except what Christ has accomplished through me in leading the Gentiles to obey God by what

I have said and done—by the power of signs and miracles, through the power of the spirit."[11] In Lystra, Paul prayed for a man born crippled and he was miraculously healed.[12] In Philippi, he cast a demon out of a slave girl who made her masters money by fortune telling.[13] When Paul was preaching, a young man fell out of a window and was killed. Paul prayed for him, and he was raised back to life again.[14]

Miracles, signs, and wonders were completely normal in the early church when the gospel message was preached. Sharing the gospel is vital, but it must be backed by the way we live and by signs and wonders from God. We share the gospel in word, deed, and sign; two are for the eyes and one is for the ears. If such a balance made for effective communication throughout the New Testament times, it surely must do so in our social media age.

Those in the Bible didn't assume that people were waiting to hear the gospel, but they did assume that they were waiting to see it. The deeds were human proof that the message they were proclaiming was true.

DO YOU HAVE A $3 BILL?

Fifteen hundred years after Christ, John Calvin began teaching an idea called cessationism. This was a fancy term meaning that the signs, wonders, and miracles of the early Church ceased after the apostles died or that they faded away over the first three centuries of the Church. But, that's not what Christians in the first few centuries wrote.

Justin Martyr (100–165 A.D.) wrote, "For the prophetic gifts remain with us, even to the present time." Origen (184–253 A.D.) claimed to have been an eyewitness of many exorcisms, healings, and prophecies. Augustine (354–430 A.D.) noted the miracles he saw were not that spectacular, but he still saw miracles in his days.

Irenaeus (130–202 A.D.) said, "Those who are in truth his disciples, receiving grace from him, do in his name perform [miracles], so as to promote the welfare of other men, according to the gift which each one has received from him. For some do certainly and truly drive out devils, so that those who have thus been cleansed from evil spirits frequently both believe [in Christ], and join themselves to the Church. Others have foreknowledge of things to come: they see visions and utter prophetic expressions. Others, still, heal the sick by laying their hands upon them, and they are made whole. Yea, moreover, as I have said, the dead even have been raised up, and remained among us for many years ... The name of our Lord Jesus Christ even now confers benefits [upon men], and cures thoroughly and effectively all who anywhere believe in him."

Unfortunately, many people don't believe in the supernatural today because they have seen fake miracles or received false prophetic words. Just as miracles open the door for the gospel, these false prophets and pseudo-healers close people's hearts to the good news. This, too, has been happening since the beginning of the church.

In 156 A.D., Montanus and his two prophetess friends, Prisca and Maximilla, went around Asia Minor prophesying the second coming of Jesus. In contrast to prophets in biblical stories, these three "prophets" spoke in a state of ecstasy as though their personalities were suspended while the Holy Spirit spoke through them. These three believed they were the harps across which the Holy Spirit swept to play a new song. Through their passion to prophesy, they stepped over what God may have been saying to the lost and made up false prophecies. Their super-spirituality went too far and closed many people off to the gospel.[15]

The same has happened throughout Church history and still happens today. Have you seen this before? People passionate to prove God's healing power, might subconsciously fake a miracle or make up words to "prove" they have the ability to speak in tongues. And, like Montanus, it's not uncommon to find people declaring a prophetic word that God supposedly told them, only for that prophecy to not happen.

Let me share with you something I've learned. These false miracles should not discourage you that supernatural gifts have ceased, but rather it could encourage you in the opposite.

When paying cash in Europe, the United States, or China you will never receive a €3, $3, or ¥3 banknote. Why? Because there is no such banknote in any of these currencies. Counterfeits and fakes only happen when there is a real version. If the real thing didn't exist, there wouldn't be counterfeits. Counterfeit miracles are a sure sign that there *are* real ones. As the old saying goes, "Where there's smoke, there's fire."

The gospel has and is still accompanied with signs, wonders, and miracles. And, is available for all who believe.

MIRACLES ARE NOT JUST FOR THE APOSTLES

After Jesus sends out the twelve disciples in Luke 9, we then read in Luke 10 that he sends out another seventy-two people. Jesus tells them the same thing as he told the disciples, "Heal the sick who are there and tell them, 'The kingdom of God has come near to you.'"[16] Besides this one chapter in Luke, we don't read of these seventy-two people again. These were ordinary followers of Christ, like you and me.

These seventy-two returned to Jesus full of joy. They obeyed what Jesus had commanded them to do, and saw the miraculous signs and wonders follow their declaration of the gospel. They exclaimed, "Lord, even the demons submit to us in your name."[17]

Jesus replied, "'I saw Satan fall like lightning from heaven. I have given you authority to trample on snakes and scorpions and to overcome all the power of the enemy; nothing will harm you. However, do not rejoice that the spirits submit to you, but rejoice that your names are written in heaven.' At that time Jesus, full of joy through the Holy Spirit, said, 'I praise you, Father, Lord of heaven and earth, because you have hidden these things from the wise and learned, and revealed them to little children. Yes, Father, for this is what you were pleased to do.'"[18]

It pleased Jesus that these ordinary believers would follow his command in sharing the gospel and working miracles. Jesus is still overjoyed when we, his children, share the gospel in both word and deed. This is expected of followers of Christ.

DON'T STOP BELIEVING

When I first became a believer, I devoured the Word of God. I couldn't get enough of it. I wanted to read the Bible every waking moment. On one occasion, I read Mark 16:17 where Jesus said, "These signs will follow them who believe. In My name they will cast out demons; they will speak with new tongues; they will take up serpents; and if they drink anything deadly, it will by no means hurt them; they will lay hands on the sick, and they will recover."

A few days later, I was at the state fair in Florida where I saw a woman in a wheelchair. My heart broke for her. I knew I was a believer, and I knew what Jesus had said. I knew he meant it. After all, if he didn't mean what he said, then why didn't he say what he meant?

I hurried to the lady.

"Ma'am, my Jesus can heal you. Can I pray for you?"

She cordially agreed.

For ten minutes, I prayed for this lady over and over again. I would ask her how she felt and if she could get out of the wheelchair. Nothing happened. Eventually, I thanked her for her willingness and

> When Jesus is calling you to walk in the supernatural, all you have to do is step out in obedience and leave the results to God.

apologized that God didn't heal her. I walked away feeling completely deflated.

However, I didn't give up. I've always lived with the principle that when scripture doesn't line up to my experience, it's always important to default to the fact that scripture is right and I'm the one learning. Miracles follow those who believe. If Jesus didn't mean what he said, then why didn't he say what he meant? But he meant it. So I kept praying for the sick.

Now, years later, we've seen countless people in our ministry healed. Just this week (as I'm writing this), I received a letter from a lady in Latvia. With her letter, she sent a picture of her child. She told me, "Thanks for praying for my infertility issue. After you prayed for me the following month, my husband and I conceived a child. It's a miracle. Thank you."

I noticed something about this text in Mark. Because of the tense used with the Greek word for "believe" in this passage in Mark, it would better be translated as saying, "And these signs will follow those that are constantly believing ..." In other words, these signs don't particularly follow someone immediately after they become a believer in Christ. More precisely, these signs follow those who are constantly believing for signs, wonders, and miracles. If you want signs and wonders to follow you, you must be constantly believing for them to happen!

Have faith, step out of your comfort zone, and begin believing for the supernatural to be part of your life as you proclaim the good news.

BUT I HAVE LITTLE FAITH

It's not the size of faith that you have, but rather whom your faith is in that matters. After all, this gospel message is not about you. It's about Jesus.

Katheryn Kuhlman, a great faith preacher in the 1900s was once asked how she had such great faith to see all the people healed in her gatherings. Her response was perfect, "I am not a woman with great faith; I am a woman with a little faith in the great God!"

You don't need incredible faith to see the miraculous in your life. You already have enough faith to begin. Do you remember when Peter took that brave step of faith out of the boat and began walking on water to Jesus? As Peter is walking towards Jesus, he becomes frightened by the waves and begins to sink. Why would Jesus be so harsh with Peter by rebuking him for his "little faith" when Peter was trying. It just doesn't seem like it was in Jesus' character to be so rude. But, maybe we've read the story wrong.

I believe Jesus' rebuke wasn't about criticizing Peter, but rather complimenting him. He was essentially saying, "with little faith you can walk on water, imagine what would happen if you believed even more in me!" This life-changing dialogue would prove to be a pivotal point in Peter's life as miraculous signs and wonders would follow him the rest of his life. But, it all started with that one step out of the boat onto the water.

Like Peter, when Jesus is calling you to walk in the supernatural, all you have to do is step out in obedience and leave the results to God. It's your business to obey, it's his business to act. God has a way of commanding us to do things in which we can't control the results.

The very first commandment to Adam was to be "fruitful and multiply." Did you know that it is impossible for you to multiply? We think we can multiply, but the reality is, we can't. There is a simple act that a man and a woman play in the process. But, after that, it's up to God for there to be conception and for a baby to grow in the womb. There's an act of faith and then a miracle eventually takes place.

So it is with any other miracle. You act in faith, and God brings the results. You can do nothing apart from God.

WHAT IF NOTHING HAPPENS?

What if nothing happens when you try to get pregnant? Again, there's a physical responsibility that we play in a pregnancy and a supernatural response needed from God in any miracle. We do our part, and trust that God knows what he's doing on his end to make it happen or not.

I often find it more difficult to have faith in believing God is sovereign over those needing a miracle than praying for them. As I left that lady in the wheelchair at the Florida State Fair, I was discouraged. I went home that night asking God why he didn't heal that woman. After all, I felt that if she had jumped out of the wheelchair, there's no telling how many people would have rejoiced and openly accepted the gospel. I was reminded that day that healing is not up to me, but God.

In an interview, Kathryn Kuhlman was quoted saying, "I cannot heal a single person. God does the healing. Whom he heals and whom he chooses not to heal is his business."

Can I underscore the obvious? I've learned over the years that God is much bigger than I am. And, his ways of working with man and building his kingdom sometimes are contrary to what I think is best. We've all wondered why God doesn't heal everyone we pray for. But, let's be honest. Our little finite minds can't always comprend our infinite God. All we can do is pray for the sick to be healed, for God's kingdom to come on earth as in heaven, and trust the outcome to God.

Kuhlman wrapped up her interview by saying, "I've never written a book on the how and why of divine healing—even though I've been besieged with requests to do so—simply because I don't know the how and the why. You see, just about the time the book is about to be published, the Holy Spirit would do something absolutely contrary to what I said. I'm still learning the mysterious way in which God moves. I'll tell you one thing—I'm sure God has a sense of humor!"

So, relax.

As much as we want to see a miraculous sign with every person we encounter, for whatever reason, it may not always happen as desired. Still, trust God for it, and don't let a lack of healing for one person hold you back from praying for healing on the next person. Just remember that God does not expect you to heal anyone. All he wants you to do is trust his word, pray for the sick, and leave the healing to him. You do your part and let God do his.

SO WHAT DO I DO?

Being used in the miraculous is much easier than you may think. Your part is quite simple. The simplicity is found in how the ordinary seventy-two believers returned to Jesus after preaching the gospel, healing the sick, raising the dead, casting out devils, and cleansing the lepers. They were full of astonishment and stories. Remember their response? "They exclaimed, 'Lord, even the demons submit to us in your name.'"[19]

… in your name.

Again, it's not about how great your faith is, how hard you beg, how tightly you squeeze your eyes together when praying, or how elegant your prayers are. You don't have to beg God or do some kind of spiritual ritual to operate in the miraculous. All you have to do is speak to the situation to change, "in the name of Jesus." Then, leave the results to Jesus, knowing in faith that your great God takes it from there.

I was speaking at a large conference in Switzerland in 2020. When the service was over, a lady approached Tanja and me and asked for prayer for healing. She said that she had recently visited a witchcraft store where, afterwards, she had pain in her back.

If it wasn't obvious that she was not in need of healing from her story, it became obvious by what happened next.

When we said the name of Jesus, her eyes rolled back in her head and she began shaking.

"You don't need healing; you're demon possessed!" I exclaimed.

My wife, Tanja, looked at me with that, "Well, here we go" look. So, we began casting out demons from this lady.

With her eyes rolling and body shaking, I said, "Demons, I command you in the name of Jesus to leave this woman!"

She fell back on the stage as a demon left her. After a couple of seconds, she looked me in the eyes and began shaking again.

Again, I said, "Demons, I command you all to leave in the name of King Jesus!" Again, she fell back on the stage as more demons left her. This went on five more times.

After the fifth time, she slowly opened her eyes and smiled. Her look was priceless. She thanked Tanja and me as she gave us a hug. She had been delivered. A miracle had taken place. And, we, like those seventy-two, returned home that night rejoicing in what God had done.

I was reminded that what we have to do is simple.

In the name of Jesus, we speak healing to sick bodies.

In the name of Jesus, we tell demons to leave those possessed.

In the name of Jesus, we cleanse and loose those bound by pornography, drug addiction, and suicide.

In the name of Jesus, we speak life to those who are dead.

In the name of Jesus, we do the speaking, God does the miracles, and the gospel can be freely declared to the lost. Over the centuries, the Church has known this truth, and the gospel rapidly spread from Jerusalem, to Armenia, and to the ends of the earth.

6

THE 400s–VICTORS, NOT VICTIMS
But ... I Was Wronged

"You intended to harm me, but God intended it for good to accomplish what is now being done, the saving of many lives." — Genesis 50:20

At the turn of the fifth century, Patrick, a sixteen-year-old from what is modern-day Scotland, suffered a great injustice. While playing by the sea, Patrick was captured by Irish pirates and sold into slavery. While enslaved, Patrick turned to the Christian faith of his parents and began seeking God earnestly.

Six years later, Patrick escaped his slave owners.

Traveling on foot for more than two hundred miles, he made it to the coast, boarded a ship carrying dogs, and was immediately employed as a dog tender. Eventually, Patrick made his way back to his home in Britain. Patrick easily could have seen himself as a victim of great injustice, disliked the Irish people, and lived out his life in obscurity in his hometown. But that's not what he did. He knew who he was in Christ.

Instead of becoming bitter, with the Gospel Baton in hand, Patrick decided he would return to Ireland to share the good news of Jesus. He even had a life-changing dream where he saw Irish children begging him to bring the gospel to them saying, "We beseech you to come and walk among us once more." And, he did.

Patrick returned to Ireland in 432 A.D., not as a slave, but rather with the free message of salvation. Patrick's years as a slave in Ireland built him into a man of prayer and courage and gave him insight into the Irish culture and people.

This helped him preach throughout Ireland for 30 years until his death in 460 A.D. Ireland would never be the same. Almost everyone in Ireland had converted to Christianity during this time. He was later sainted, and by the end of his life, Saint Patrick had established more than 200 churches and baptized more than a hundred thousand people.[1]

God turned Patrick's tragedy into victory, and an entire nation was reached with the gospel.

GOD CAN TURN IT FOR GOOD

Life isn't fair. Can I get an amen? Bad things happen to good people. It's not *if* an injustice will happen to you, it's what you will do with it that matters. Have you heard the famous verse, "What the enemy intended for the bad, God turned it around for the good"? Do you know where that comes from? Take a look …

> When Joseph's brothers saw that their father was dead, they said, "What if Joseph holds a grudge against us and pays us back for all the wrongs we did to him?" So they sent word to Joseph, saying, "Your father left these instructions before he died: 'This is what you are to say to Joseph: I ask you to forgive your brothers the sins and the wrongs they committed in treating you so badly.' Now please forgive the sins of the servants of the God of your father." When their message came to him, Joseph wept.
>
> His brothers then came and threw themselves down before him. "We are your slaves," they said.
>
> But Joseph said to them, "Don't be afraid. Am I in the place of God? **You intended to harm me, but God intended it for good to accomplish what is now being done, the saving of many lives.** So then, don't be afraid. I will provide for you and your children." And he reassured them and spoke kindly to them." — Genesis 50:15–21 (emphasis added)

This was a verse from the life of Joseph. Do you remember Joseph's story? His family was supposed to be the model of obedience to God before the world. God gave him a dream that he shared with his family. Instead of rejoicing over the dream with Joseph, his jealous brothers plotted to kill him. They threw him in a pit where presumably he would be left to die.

However, at the same time, slave traders happened to pass by, and they sold their seventeen-year-old brother to the traders. Like Saint Patrick, Joseph found himself as a teenage slave in a foreign country. And, like Saint Patrick, Joseph remembered his identity, his dream, and his God. For the next twenty years, he didn't allow the injustices done to him to define who he was. Joseph living out his life through his identity in God led to "the saving of many lives."

You, too, can live a life that leads many to Christ, no matter what wrongs you've suffered. Life is not what someone else did to you, it's what God did for you! It's that simple.

WHO YOU ARE

When you became a follower of Christ, your whole identity changed. You are someone important. Not because of anything you have done, but because of who Jesus is and what he has done for you. The Bible declares that you have been bought, not with "perishable things such as silver or gold ... but with the precious blood of Jesus."[2] You are, as Paul wrote in 2 Corinthians 5:17, "a new creation: the old has gone, the new has come."

Salvation is not about good deeds as many other religions force upon their followers. It's about being adopted as a son or a daughter of the king. Nothing you can do would make him love you any more than he loves you at this very moment.

When Jesus was baptized, he came out of the water and his Heavenly Father said, "This is my Son, whom I love, with him I am well pleased."[3] This happened before Jesus had performed any miracles, preached any sermons, or had done any humanitarian works. He was loved because of whom

Nothing you can do would make him love you any more than he loves you at this very moment.

he belonged to. And, so are you! When you have died to your old selfish ways and have turned to the saving faith in Jesus, your Heavenly Father gives you a new identity. He says, "That's my child, and I'm proud of you!"

And there's more. You aren't just a child of the king, the Bible says you are …
… chosen (Ephesians 1:4)
… forgiven (1 John 2:12)
… beautiful (Psalm 45:11)
… whole (Colossians 2:10)
… a masterpiece (Ephesians 2:10)
… victorious (1 Corinthians 15:57)
… the Temple of God (1 Corinthians 3:16–17)
And,
You are loved. (John 3:16)
You are his! (Isaiah 43:1)
We have been given this new identity for a purpose. Peter, whose identity was dramatically changed when Christ gave him a new name, boldly declared:

> *"But you are a chosen people, a royal priesthood, a holy nation, God's special possession, that you may declare the praises of him who called you out of darkness into his wonderful light." — 1 Peter 2:9*

We have a new identity so that we can Go & Tell others about Jesus!

YOU ARE NOT A VICTIM. YOU ARE A VICTOR!

One of the biggest hurdles for us who are carrying the Gospel Baton is not in understanding who God is, but rather who we are.

Over the years, I've seen countless Christians not fulfill their God-given destinies because of a past tragedy. This could have been something that happened to them while attending church, as a child by a family member, the environment they grew up in, or even something

Persecutions and injustices may be the very platform God uses to bring many to Christ.

that happened within their lineage centuries before they were even born. They have a victim mindset due to this past injustice. I'm not saying that what happened wasn't bad, but I am saying that it's important that it doesn't define your life and destiny.

If anything, like Patrick and Joseph, the persecutions and injustices may be the very platform God uses to bring many to Christ.

Satan and his angels work overtime in the cruel business of identity theft of Christians. The Bible says that Satan is the accuser of the brethren. Before he tried to steal your identity from you, he tried to steal your identity from God. Revelation gives us a glimpse of this identity theft attempt:

> *"Then I heard a loud voice in heaven say: 'Now have come the salvation and the power and the kingdom of our God, and the authority of his Messiah. For the accuser of our brothers and sisters,* **who accuses them before our God** day and night, *has been hurled down."* — *Revelation 12:10*

Night and day, Satan makes negative accusations about believers to God. Eventually, God booted the devil out of heaven. Now Satan comes to us, constantly accusing us and trying to steal our identities. He knows that he will lose in the end and that believers are and forever will be victorious in Christ.

In 1 Peter 5:8, Peter tells us that Satan, "goes around like a roaring lion looking for who he can devour." Notice that he is a *roaring* lion. That's all he is, a bunch of noise, trying to intimidate you. He may be roaring, but he has no teeth. He can't do anything to you but try to gum you to death. The only weapon Satan has is his voice. His lies. All other power he may have had was lost when Jesus died on the cross. Check it out:

> *"When you were dead in your sins and in the uncircumcision of your flesh, God made you alive with Christ. He forgave us all our sins, having canceled the charge of our legal indebtedness, which stood against us and condemned us; he has taken it away, nailing it to the cross. And* **having disarmed the powers and authorities,** *he made a public spectacle of them, triumphing over them by the cross."* — *Colossians 2:13–15*

As an expat living in Europe, I've seen many soccer games. When a player makes a goal, he slides on his knees, throws his arms out, and screams. Like soccer, this simple illustration is one of the many things that happened on the cross. Jesus, with his arms outstretched, let out a big shout.

At that moment, not only did he take away the sins of the world, giving all humanity an opportunity for a new identity, but he also took away all the weapons of the enemy. This was a crucial part of Jesus' victory. Satan became powerless. Now, all he can do is constantly accuse you, hoping you will buy into his lies and give up your identity in Christ. When he comes at you with his accusations trying to steal your identity, fight back with scripture verses about who you are in Christ. And, when the enemy reminds you of your past, remind him of his future! You are on the winning side of eternity, not him. Jesus, the king, is coming back.

Be alert. Be diligent. Be aware of the enemy's schemes on your life and identity. And, as Paul tells the Corinthians, forgive any injustice against you, "in order that Satan might not outwit us. For we are not unaware of his schemes."[4]

SAVE MANY OR DEFILE MANY, IT'S YOUR CHOICE

Shortly after the Civil War in the USA in the 1860s, Robert E. Lee, the Commander of the Confederate States Army, visited a lady in Kentucky. In frustration, the woman lamented a battered tree outside of her home. Before the war, it had been a beautiful Magnolia. But the Union Army had shot it up, taking its beauty. Looking out at the barren tree, she asked Lee, "What do you think about that?"

Robert E. Lee looked at her and simply said, "Cut it down and forget about it."

Are you struggling with something that happened to you in your past? If so, I recommend gathering courage and start chopping it out of your heart. Let it go. This is the best advice I can think of for getting over a past injustice so that it won't define you or hold bitterness in your heart. Don't simply look past it; cut it out of your heart entirely. Hebrews urges us like this:

> "See to it that no one falls short of the grace of God and that no bitter root grows up to cause trouble and defile many." — Hebrews 12:15

We are commanded to uproot any bitterness and to be good stewards of our identity. The phrase "see to it" comes from the Greek word *episkopos*. This is a compound of the two Greek words *epi* and *skopos*. *Epi* means "over" and *skopos* means "to look." *Episkopos* is the word used in 1 Timothy 3:1 for the word "bishop."

Hebrews is telling us to be the bishops, or overseers, of our hearts and to not allow negative circumstances from the past to define who we are today. This is imperative because a misguided identity has the potential to defile many people even beyond ourselves. But when we see ourselves the way God sees, we get to watch him work through us, saving others, just like he did with Joseph and Saint Patrick.

TALK LIKE GOD SEES

If you're having a difficult time walking in the identity of a son or daughter of the king, I encourage you to begin proclaiming who you are as a believer. You can use the verses above or find dozens of others with a simple Bible verse search on the internet.

There have been times in my own life where I began to find my identity in things other than in who I am in Christ. One of my strategies to get refocused is to write out scripture verses on sticky notes and put them in visible places throughout my house, car, and office. I put these verses on my mirrors in the bathroom, the refrigerator door, my car's steering wheel, and my office desk. As you declare these verses daily over your life, your identity in Christ will be strengthened, and your passion for others to hear the gospel will grow.

Patrick spoke life over himself, too. He knew that he was the temple of God. Each day, he would arise declaring God's word over him. The Prayer of Saint Patrick:

> "...I arise today
> Through God's strength to pilot me;
> God's might to uphold me,
> God's wisdom to guide me,
> God's eye to look before me,
> God's ear to hear me,
> God's word to speak for me,

God's hand to guard me,
God's way to lie before me,
God's shield to protect me,
God's hosts to save me
From snares of the devil,
From temptations of vices,
From everyone who desires me ill,
Afar and near,
Alone or in a multitude.
I summon today all these powers between me and evil,
Against every cruel merciless power that opposes my body and soul,
Against incantations of false prophets,
Against black laws of pagandom,
Against false laws of heretics,
Against craft of idolatry,
Against spells of women and smiths and wizards,
Against every knowledge that corrupts man's body and soul.
Christ shield me today
Against poison, against burning,
Against drowning, against wounding,
So that reward may come to me in abundance.
Christ with me, Christ before me, Christ behind me,
Christ in me, Christ beneath me, Christ above me,
Christ on my right, Christ on my left,
Christ when I lie down, Christ when I sit down,
Christ in the heart of every man who thinks of me,
Christ in the mouth of every man who speaks of me,
Christ in the eye that sees me,
Christ in the ear that hears me.
I arise today..."[5]

With a declaration like that, there's no wonder he had the boldness to share the gospel with the very people who had enslaved him. Declare the life of God's Word over yourself daily. You will be amazed at how it will also transform you to courageously share the good news of Jesus everywhere you go!

CHEER UP!

Oftentimes you'll hear people talking about how great their lives are as a follower of Christ. They almost seem to imply that nothing bad can happen to you once you become a believer. Unfortunately, that is simply not true. But, one thing you can be sure of is that God will work all things together for good.[6]

Just before Jesus was arrested and crucified for doing no wrong, as if to prove my point exactly, he told his disciples, "In this world you will have trouble. But be of good cheer! I have overcome the world." (John 16:33)

During WWII, a Romanian Jewish believer named Richard Wurmbrand saw an opportunity to share the gospel with the German occupiers. Wurmbrand knew that by doing this he would be risking his life and freedom, but that didn't stop him. He knew that his true identity was not in his race or the time he lived, but rather in whose he was. And, it was his passion to tell as many people about the King who had saved him. Wurmbrand shared the gospel in bomb shelters and while rescuing Jewish children out of the ghettos. He was repeatedly arrested and beaten. Once, he was nearly executed.

When the war was over, Romania pledged allegiance to Communism. That didn't stop him from evangelizing. Between 1945–1947, Richard gave away over a million books of the gospel to Russian troops. He also smuggled the Bible into Russia himself. He was arrested, beaten, and faced unimaginable hardships. But, to Richard, the gospel had to be preached. He never allowed his hardships to define him.

Instead, like Jesus commanded, he kept his joy. Later in life, Richard laughed at the situation, "It was strictly forbidden to preach to other prisoners," he said. "It was understood that whoever was caught doing this received a severe beating. A number of us decided to pay the price for the privilege of preaching, so we accepted their [the communists'] terms. It was a deal; we preached and they beat us. We were happy preaching. They were happy beating us, so everyone was happy."

Wurmbrand went on to create Voice of the Martyrs, an organization devoted to bringing awareness to the untold millions of believers killed for their faith or those who keep sharing the gospel in spite of the many wrongs done to them.[7]

As a matter of fact, unknown millions of believers over the past two thousand years have been imprisoned, tortured, and even martyred because they passionately shared the good news of Jesus. As Revelation says, "they loved not their lives even unto death." We may not know their names, but they knew who they were in Christ.

No matter what happens to us, we have a reason to rejoice.

And, as a result, they shared the gospel and it continued to increase in popularity around the globe throughout the centuries.

No matter what happens to us, we have a reason to rejoice. Our identity is not found in our trials, but rather in the fact that our names are written in heaven. We have the ultimate victory.

7

THE 500s–CREATED TO CREATE
But ... I'm Not Creative

"If sinners be damned, at least let them leap to hell over our dead bodies. And if they perish, let them perish with our arms wrapped around their knees." — Charles H. Spurgeon

The Gospel Baton was passed on to sixth century believers, and the human race was about to face an unseen enemy that would lethally affect the entire world.

The century got off to a quick start for the advancement of the gospel. In 510 A.D., the Celtic missionary movement began in Ireland as zealous believers left the familiarity of their homeland to take the gospel to unreached villages across northern and central Europe. This movement would last for the next four hundred years.

But in 541 A.D., the world faced a test of resilience. Thousands of people in the Sasanian Empire, modern-day Turkey and Saudi Arabia, suddenly fell ill with fevers, vomiting, and swollen lymph nodes. Death was imminent. The first bubonic plague (aka the Black Death) had begun. By the spring of 542 A.D, this infectious disease, caused by bites from infected fleas, arrived in the metropolis port city of Constantinople.

From there, the plague spread from port to port throughout the Mediterranean and eventually around the world. More than twenty five million people died of the plague in the following fifty years and another twenty five million died in the seventh century. Close to a quarter of the world's population at the time was gone.

The tragedy of the sudden outbreak of the plague was especially felt throughout Europe and the Middle East. Empires crumbled, economies were decimated, political powers and militaries were crippled, and millions of jobs were lost. Organized Christianity was also dramatically affected. Church doors were shuttered, corporate worship was silenced, and the Gospel of Jesus appeared to be on the brink of ending.

However, not everyone would stay silent in the midst of great sorrow and loss. Those Celtic missionaries, the Berbers of North Africa, and the heavily persecuted eastern believers took it upon themselves to see that the Gospel Baton wasn't dropped in their generation. These groups of nameless, faceless Christians spontaneously took the missionary tasks upon themselves. They saw the advancement of the gospel as not only a task for religious leaders, but a call for everyone who claimed to be a follower of Jesus. Though the reality of death was very real, they refused to be silent or still. After all, the world needed good news. It was these ordinary followers of Jesus, not the hierarchies of the Greek or Latin churches, that set out to spread the gospel.

They saw the advancement of the gospel as not only a task for religious leaders, but a call for everyone who claimed to be a follower of Jesus.

Due to the lack of public gatherings, these believers came up with *creative* ways of sharing the gospel. They took it upon themselves to learn the language and cultures of the cities they visited. At a time when transcontinental travel was expensive and difficult, this was a bold and creative strategy. They adapted their methods and innovated ways to reach as many people in each city as possible. Their creativity rapidly advanced the gospel message with extraordinary success.

Creativity has been a powerful tool in advancing the gospel throughout the centuries.

CREATED TO CREATE

Has anyone ever told you that you aren't creative? Well, let me debunk that lie. You are very creative! The very first sentence of the Bible gives us a clear picture of one of the amazing qualities of God and us, "In the beginning, God *created* the heavens and the earth." God is a creator; a God of great creativity!

I can recall countless nights at the Brownsville Revival in Pensacola when the worship leader, Lindell Cooley, would sing *Creation Calls*:

> *"How could I say there is no God*
> *When all around creation calls*
> *A singing bird, a mighty tree*
> *The vast expanse of open sea*
>
> *I love to stand at ocean's shore*
> *And feel the thundering breakers roar*
> *To walk through golden fields of grain*
> *Beneath endless blue horizon's frame*
> *I believe, I believe, I believe"*

The amazing creativity of God is beyond our comprehension. He could have made a boring environment to sustain life here on Earth. Instead, he created majestic mountains, roaring oceans teeming with sea life, rainforests populated with tropical plants and spectacular animals, and galaxies hanging overhead to be a canopy for his world.

Twenty-six verses later, in Genesis 1, God tells the story of how he made us:

> *"Then God said, "Let us make mankind in our image, in our likeness, so that they may rule over the fish in the sea and the birds in the sky, over the livestock and all the wild animals, and over all the creatures that move along the ground." So God created mankind in his own image, in the image of God he created them; male and female he created them." — Genesis 1:26–27*

So, what does that have to do with you being creative? Let me remind you. We were made in the image of God; created by a creative creator. Part of your DNA (and mine) includes creativity. Simply put, we were created to create. And with that mandate, coupled with the topic of evangelism, he has given us unique creative thoughts for the advancement of his kingdom. Creativity is one of the greatest tools in evangelism.

BE A VOICE

In 2016, Tanja and I answered the call of God and moved to Switzerland to be missionary evangelists in Europe. Our mandate was to help bring unity to churches, passion for Jesus to lukewarm believers, and hope to the lost through the gospel message with the ministry he named Ignite Europe.

After getting settled in our new home in Zürich, I was itching to evangelize, but I wasn't sure what to do or where to start. I had watched a video on social media of a well-known evangelist telling people about Jesus on the streets in Dallas, TX. I thought since it worked for him, it could work for me. After all, Jesus did say in Luke 14:23 to "go out to the roads and country lanes and compel them to come in, so that my house will be full."

I headed out to the city-center full of passion to see the lost come to Jesus. I went to one of the main train stations, spotted my first target, and made my approach. He was standing on the train platform quietly waiting for his train to arrive. I had seven minutes before it came, so there was plenty of time to share the gospel. I stealthily walked up beside him and positioned myself for a conversation. This gentleman was probably in his mid-forties, dressed in a nice suit, and obviously a businessman.

"Entschuldigen, Sprechen Sie Englisch?" I asked.

"Yes, I do speak English."

"Great. Well, I was standing over there and God put you on my heart. I wanted to tell you that Jesus loves you. Have you ever heard the gospel?"

Startled, the man gave me a curious look.

"Sir," I continued. "Jesus died on the cross for your sins and he loves you very much."

Puzzled, the man looked me straight in the eyes, "Son, what is wrong with you?"

Nothing, I thought to myself.

Cautiously, the man scooted away from me and focused his attention the other way.

Now what, I asked myself as I stood there, embarrassed, for the next seven minutes waiting on the train.

I went straight home and told Tanja to pack the bags because we were moving back to America. Trust me, you probably would have done the same.

But we stayed in Switzerland. And, two weeks later, I decided to try again.

I stood in line to buy an annual train pass. I had decided to share the gospel with whomever was working the desk at the train station. I was ready! The train attendant was probably in his fifties and clearly Swiss. When the time came for him to take my photo for my train pass, I knew it was the moment. Instead of going straight into the gospel message, I took another approach I had seen on videos. I went first for healing. After all, if he got healed, he would surely be open to hear the gospel.

"Entschuldigen, Sprechen Sie Englisch?" I asked.

"Yes, I do speak English."

"Great! I serve an amazing God who can heal you. Is there anything you need healing for in your body?" I asked.

"No."

"No? We all have something that can be healed. Are you sure?" I responded.

"Nope."

"Nothing? How about your knees?" I randomly inquired. After all, knees do tend to wear out over time.

The man lifted each leg, moved both knees, and simply said, "Nope."

"For real? Are you serious? Look, pretend like I'm God and you can ask me to be healed for anything and you would get it, what would that be?"

The guy looked at me like I was crazy.

"No, no, no. I'm not God. I'm using it as an illustration to help you. Ugh … never mind."

By this time, he was really looking at me like I was strange. And, I didn't blame him. I was desperate to see him touched by God so I could share the gospel to him. After all, that's why I moved to Europe.

"OK. What about your finances or family, is there a need you have? I want to pray for you," I tried again.

"Nope."

"Ummmmm, so there's nothing you would want a miracle for?"

"Nope. And, I need to get back to work." He said and quickly walked away.

I stood there completely defeated. It was deja vu all over again. I prayed under my breath, "God, living in Switzerland is a complete waste of time. Why am I here?"

*Don't be an
echo; be a voice.*

Then, the Holy Spirit spoke, "Don't be an echo; be a voice."

That's when everything changed.

When we see someone who is successful, it's understandable to want to emulate that person. We often think we need to copy their methods to achieve success too. But, that's really not the case. Most of the time that success is a result of being original.

Originals stand out, not the copies.

Outside the Louvre in Paris there are countless copies of the *Mona Lisa* for sale for a dollar. There are prints on shirts, magnets, mugs, and posters. But inside the Louvre, thousands of tourists from around the world wait in line for hours to catch a glimpse of the original *Mona Lisa* by Leonardo da Vinci. And the original isn't worth a dollar, but over eight hundred million dollars.

You are called to be an original, to have your own voice. God has a unique purpose and calling specifically for you.

You weren't created to copy someone else and simply be an echo of someone else's life. No! God has wired creative ideas into you to use in sharing the gospel. You have a voice. And, that voice will only reach its maximum volume when it's expressed through *your* unique gifts and abilities. Otherwise, you will be a cheap echo of someone else, constantly wondering why you look like that successful person but get little to no results.

I knew I had to do something differently if I was going to make an impact in Zürich. I knew it would be something creative. The question was, what would it be?

LUNCH OR LISTEN?

Again, it's important to remember that we are creative by design. But, at the same time, our creativity for kingdom purposes must be birthed by God. Usually, this comes through prayer or after a time of prayer. Through prayer, God connects with our creativity and speaks direction about how our creativity can be used for his purposes. We must have this direction from God. Otherwise, as Psalm 127:1 says, "Unless the LORD builds the house, its builders labor in vain."

Imagine with me that you own a nice house. Your best friend, an amateur carpenter, comes over one day with his toolbox and a blueprint.

Without any notice, he begins hammering boards to the back of your house. Puzzled, you run outside and ask him what in the world is he doing. In all sincerity, he pats you on the shoulder and with a huge grin, says, "You're my best friend. I know we never talked about this, but I decided I would build a game room on the back of your house." How would you respond?

Through prayer, God connects with our creativity and speaks direction about how our creativity can be used for his purposes.

Of course, you probably would respond with appreciation for the thought. But, you'd probably quickly remind him that you never asked him to do this. You would want to know exactly what blueprints he drew up and what it would look like first. You would have to decide if he is competent to do it and if it is what you want. After all, it is your house!

Now, imagine the same friend comes to your house for lunch. You sit around the table, enjoying each other's company. Near the end of the conversation, you are impressed that he has really developed into a great carpenter as obvious from the many testimonies he tells you about. He pats you on the shoulder and with a huge grin, says, "You're my best friend. It is my absolute dream to add on to your house. I want to do it for free and build it exactly the way you want." Now what is your response?

There's a good chance you would say, "Wonderful!" And, over a few weeks you two would draw out a plan of what this new addition to your house would look like. You would set up a schedule, decide who else to get involved in the project, and what materials to use. Then, you would help your friend, and together you would build your house.

This is how it should be in the kingdom. Unfortunately, I've seen many people begin to build onto God's kingdom with their own desires and not God's plan, even though their intentions were good. We must first sit around the table and enjoy our fellowship with Jesus. We must spend time in prayer with God. During our time of fellowship, we will understand what he wants us to do. And, more importantly, he will do it with us.

Do you remember the story in Luke 10? Martha invited Jesus and his disciples to her home. In her zeal, she focused all her attention on the preparations needed for her guests. Who knows exactly what those preparations were, but let's just say it was making lunch. Food would be a good guess since there were thirteen men at her home. In the meantime, her sister, Mary, was hanging out with the guys clinging to every word Jesus said.

Exasperated, Martha marched over to Jesus and asked if he was aware that Mary wasn't helping with the preparations. Jesus told Martha there was only one thing she needed to do. And, that one thing was what Mary was doing—spending time with him.

Out of our creative hearts, our love for Jesus, and our desire to serve God, I often wonder if we make lunches that Jesus hasn't ordered. If we are building on to his kingdom when he first wants us to spend time with him. When we give him that time, sit in his presence, and listen to his plans, he will use our creativity to build his kingdom on earth.

THE SEED PROJECT

After months of trying to share the gospel in less-than-successful ways, I finally decided to go the route of Mary. I decided that the greatest mission field in the world was not Zürich, but the heart of God. I spent many days just reading the Bible, worshipping, and telling God how much I love him. I told him I was ready if he had something unique for us to do. In the meantime, I just kept telling people about Jesus and being faithful with what I knew. Then, he spoke!

I woke up one morning with God speaking to my spirit. There was no audible voice, but I sensed that clear inner direction from the Holy Spirit.

I felt the Lord say, "Use a flower to share the gospel in Zürich."

"Really?" I thought. "There's gotta be a better way. And, a flower? I don't want to be known as a flower evangelist. I'm from Texas!"

Despite my reservations, I'm thankful I obeyed.

In just a few minutes, creativity took hold and along with the Holy Spirit's leading, an evangelistic strategy unfolded for Ignite Europe: The Seed Project. We bought nice flowers and put them in porcelain vases with a card. The basic message in the card was: as a seed went into the ground, died, and rose to become this beautiful flower, so Jesus came to the Earth, died, and rose again so you could have eternal life. We put a website address on the card where readers could read the full gospel message and contact us with questions or to let us know if they decided to follow Christ.

We placed a flower on the doorstep of all homes in our small town outside of Zürich, more than two hundred and fifty. We simply placed the flowers on the doorstep and left. However, sometimes God created divine appointments where we encountered someone at the door who would ask us what we were doing and why. It gave us an open invitation to personally share the gospel and pray for many people.

When we finished giving away the flowers, we were shocked at the results. For every one flower we gave away, we had three people in our neighborhood read the gospel on our website! Neighbors responded on the website saying they had begun to follow Christ or that they needed prayer for something. We know that God had given us the creative idea, and this was one way he wanted us to build onto his kingdom in Zürich.

Since that time, we've given away thousands of flowers here in Switzerland, and the gospel has been proclaimed.

THROUGH THE AGES

Creativity has played a huge role in advancing the Gospel Baton through the ages. Jesus modeled the way by preaching his good news outside of the synagogue, the expected way of communicating theological truths in the first century. His famous Sermon on the Mount was delivered on a hillside near Galilee. Matthew 5:1 says that when he saw the crowds, he went up a mountainside and sat down, and began to teach them. Luke 6:17 mentions that Jesus went to a "level place" and began teaching them.

Creativity has played a huge role in advancing the Gospel Baton through the ages.

If you ever get the chance to visit this spot in Israel, you will quickly realize just how creative Jesus was being in delivering his message. He strategically used the hill as a natural amphitheater so that his message could reach a much larger audience than just his disciples. The sound of Jesus' voice would be caught upwards by the amphitheater-shape of the mountain. The crowds grew throughout the day, as they often would, and spread up the hills. Yet, no matter where people sat on the mountainside, they could clearly hear what Jesus was saying. "When Jesus had finished saying these things, the crowds were amazed at his teaching, because he taught …".[1]

Jesus used this creative acoustic strategy not only on mountains, but also on a boat near a shore to crowds on land.[2] This creativity allowed the gospel to spread beyond the synagogues and the private gatherings of his disciples to large crowds of more than 5,000 people.

In the Renaissance period, due to the high level of illiteracy and lack of biblical knowledge, stained-glass windows became a part of new churches that were built. These windows were designed with ornate images inspired by Bible stories so that the gospel could be read with pictures instead of words.

The eighteenth century, German composer Johann Sebastian Bach would solidify himself as a powerful evangelist, not with words but with music. After pouring over Martin Luther's three-volume translation of the Bible, he came up with the creative idea of sharing this good news through his music. His 1727 composition *The Passion of St. Matthew* planted the gospel in the hearts of millions who have heard it. More than a hundred years after Bach's death, the radical atheist Friedrich Nietzsche admitted upon hearing it that, "One who has completely forgotten Christianity truly hears it here as gospel."

Before the invention of the microphone, Charles Spurgeon, the famous Baptist preacher of England, thought of a creative way to spread the gospel to the lost. He would preach outside on windy days, with his back facing the wind, so his voice could travel up to half a mile and be heard by many who would never step into a church.

In modern times, creativity is just as effective and needed.

The In-N-Out Burger food chain in America prints scripture verses on the bottom of their cups and their boxes for fries. Anyone who eats at their restaurant is presented with the gospel with every meal. Anonymous businessmen put scripture verses on billboards near busy intersections and highways. And, due to the increasing dependence on cell phones, Life Church out of Tulsa, Oklahoma created a Bible app for smartphones that has been downloaded over half a billion times!

And during the COVID-19 pandemic, like those sixth century believers faced, countless churches and ministries came up with creative ideas to advance the gospel and disciple believers. Online services and training programs sprung up around the world. Churches hosted drive-in services to keep the government regulations of social distancing while still offering live services.

Creativity has always played a key role in evangelism. And there are creative ideas in you that God wants to use for the advancement of his kingdom.

The ordinary Christians who fearlessly proclaimed Christ during the perilous sixth century are rarely spoken about in Church History and are generally unknown. Their names, stories, and testimonies were almost completely destroyed by the Mongols seven hundred years later. But, the impact of their creativity would be felt for centuries to come. The plague slowly came to an end, but the advancement of the Gospel Baton was successfully passed on to another century.

8

THE 600s–THE POWER OF YOUR TESTIMONY
But ... My Story is Boring

"We are the Bibles the world is reading; we are the creeds the world is needing; we are the sermons the world is heeding." — Billy Graham

The seventh century brought a glimmer of hope for a fresh start for much of the world. The plague of the previous century tore a path of destruction through every city it entered. Even the great city of Rome was in agony. People had seen enough of carts piled high with corpses of friends. Many people had gone insane. A mass exodus of people had left the once great empire that now sat as a desert in central Italy. The seventh century marked a time of healing from the plague and the increase of the gospel spreading throughout Europe through the testimonies of countless believers like Kilian.

In 687 A.D., Kilian (Killien or Kiffien), an Irishman, set out to evangelize the Eastern Franks in the capital of Würzburg, Germany. He experienced early success as he eagerly and relentlessly shared his testimony and presented the truths in the Bible to everyone around. Large numbers of people left paganism to follow Christ and would soon begin sharing their own testimonies. His message reached the ears of the nobles of the country. Even the governor, Duke Gozbert, committed his life to Christ and Kilian baptized him.

Kilian met with difficulty as well, though. He refused to retract his message when faced with the ire of the Duke's wife—who was unhappy with her husband's conversion—and was subsequently martyred. It was later recorded that due to Kilian's passion for sharing his testimony, the vast majority of Würtzburg was converted to Christianity within two years. The testimony of believers has always been a strategic way of sharing the gospel throughout the centuries.

WELL, WELL, WELL

> *"Now Jesus had to go through Samaria. So he came to a town in Samaria called Sychar, near the plot of ground Jacob had given to his son Joseph. Jacob's well was there, and Jesus, tired as he was from the journey, sat down by the well. It was about noon.*
>
> *When a Samaritan woman came to draw water, Jesus said to her, "Will you give me a drink?"* — John 4:1–8

John tells us a story of a Samaritan woman whose personal testimony, like Kilian's, pointed many in her hometown to Christ and made her one of the first evangelists in church history. The meeting between the woman and Jesus at Jacob's well in Sychar, Samaria is told in John 4:1–42. Before her encounter with Christ she was a bad woman, with a bad past, from a bad lineage. Like most people you will have an opportunity to share the gospel with, she was not anticipating hearing the good news, but rather going about her everyday life. Her story is the perfect example of the power of a testimony.

Have you ever paused and wondered who this Samaritan woman was and why her story made it into the Bible? So, who was she?

First, she was a bad woman. Her interest that day was most likely not to "fetch a pail of water." It is more likely she was looking for a romantic, sexual encounter. We know this because she came to the well alone, in the middle of the day. This was out of the ordinary for a good Samaritan woman. Women would usually travel as a group to the local wells because they liked the company of other women and they would need help with loading the jugs of water on their heads to carry home. Oh, and let's not forget, this woman had a pretty wild past being married to five different men and was currently "with" a man who wasn't her husband.

Secondly, she wasn't a religious woman. She was from Samaria. Although Samaritans claimed descent from the tribe of Ephraim and Manasseh, they weren't looking for a messiah like most Jews, but rather a teacher like Moses. Samaritans were typically stuck between a Roman worldview and a Jewish one. History helps us understand the confusion this Samaritan lady probably dealt with.

> *The testimony of believers has always been a strategic way of sharing the gospel throughout the centuries.*

Herod the Great rebuilt Samaria after Augustus Caesar ended the Roman civil war and brought peace to the empire after the Battle of Actium mentioned in Chapter One. On the western edge of the city, Herod built an impressive temple with a fourteen-foot altar and statue in honor of Caesar.

After Caesar died, the Roman Senate gave him the title of "Divus Augustus" and shortly afterwards, "savior of the world." The temple to Augustus was only ten miles from Jacob's Well. This lady would have known about the temple and would have been torn between the faith of the Jews (a coming savior) and the proclamations of the Romans (Caesar is the savior). She would've been familiar with the idea of a world savior, but not sure if it was a coming Jewish messiah or a Roman leader like Caesar.

Needless to say, this woman at the well needed an encounter with Christ. And, that's exactly what happened. She came to the well looking for a man, but she left with a Messiah.[1] She left her jug of water and immediately went back to her town with a new story: her testimony. And, as a result, Samaria would never be the same.

> *"Many of the Samaritans from that town believed in Jesus because of the woman's **testimony**, 'He told me everything I ever did.' So when the Samaritans came to Jesus, they urged him to stay with them, and Jesus stayed two days. And because of his words many more became believers."*
> — John 4:39–41

THE ABCs OF A TESTIMONY

Most of us want to share the gospel with our testimony, but we simply don't know where to start. If you could learn to share your testimony in a few minutes, you could affect the eternal destinies of many people—like those Samaritans who heard the testimony of a woman at the well or the people of Würzburg who heard Kilian's testimony.

There are three main points to your testimony. I like to call them the ABCs of a testimony. You can use these simple steps to quickly share your testimony with anyone in just two or three minutes.

A. Beginning: This is a quick description, just a minute or two, of what your life was like before you came to Christ. This can be what you thought about God before coming to him. It can be how you were searching for meaning and purpose in life through drugs, sex, insecurities, etc. It's not necessary to go into great detail here. Just hit the highlights. What is important, though, is that it is honest. This is your testimony, not your testi-phony.

B. Middle: This is your conversion experience; your encounter with Christ (like the woman at the well). It, too, should be a minute or two long. It's important to share the gospel here as this is, essentially, where sharing the gospel occurs.

C. End: This is how you talk about how your life has changed since your conversion. The lady at the well immediately went back and told her community about Jesus. And we see that afterward she was not living in immorality but rather in the immortal, genuine Savior of the World. Remember to be joyful, current, and avoid religious jargon.

Your testimony of becoming a follower of Jesus is a story that must be told, whether you became a disciple of Jesus at four years old or you were rescued from a satanic cult at the age of forty. Every testimony of a life rescued by the blood of Jesus is equally as powerful as all the others. After all, the most important part of a testimony is the fact that the story is not about you. It's all about Jesus and his redeeming power. He is the main storyline and character in every testimony.

Every testimony of a life rescued by the blood of Jesus is equally as powerful as all the others.

PREPARE FOR DIVINE ENCOUNTERS

When was the last time you had a divine encounter? Do you know what I'm talking about? When I was a student at the Brownsville Revival School of Ministry in Pensacola, Florida, one of my teachers was Larry Tomczak. His class was easily one of my favorites. They were never boring. Larry was an animated teacher, passionate about us being healthy both in spirit and in body. I remember many days where we had to start the class off with jumping jacks. After our exercises, Larry would share an inspiring story of him sharing his testimony. I was always encouraged and stirred inside. Most of the time, his stories would be about everyday encounters while he was at a bank, eating at a restaurant, or pumping gas.

Larry had printed his testimony on small pamphlets that fit in his back pocket. When he met a stranger, many times, he would share the gospel through his testimony and then give them one of these small pamphlets. Larry called these meetings divine appointments. He had told his testimony tens of thousands of times, including to Hollywood celebrities, sports icons, and high-ranking politicians. Larry challenged us to work on our own testimonies. He said we would be surprised how God would bring us divine appointments to share his gospel if we would prepare ourselves by working on effectively sharing our testimony.

I took him up on the challenge. I wrote out a two-minute speech of how Jesus had changed my life. Although my testimony doesn't include getting delivered from years of drug addiction or being miraculously healed, it was still powerful. Jesus had saved me! Again, the story is about Jesus, not us. I prayed over my two-minute testimony and said, "God, if you can use Larry, you can use me."

That next day, I was at John F. Kennedy International Airport in NYC headed to Africa for a short-term mission trip.

I looked at my friend and said, "I'm prepared to share my testimony and message of Jesus as Larry had encouraged us to do. I'm believing for a divine appointment."

Before I could finish my sentence, someone on our team exclaimed, "Look who that is!"

Just as I looked over, Kareem Abdul-Jabbar walked by me. Kareem was a Hall of Fame basketball player and all-time leading scorer in the

NBA. As a sports fan, I knew exactly who Kareem was. Born, Ferdinand Alcindor Jr., he changed his name in 1968 to Kareem Abdul-Jabbar after converting to Islam. I knew he was not a follower of Christ and needed to hear the gospel.

"This is my moment. It's a divine appointment God has set up for me with share the gospel to Kareem!" I jumped out of my seat and took off. I had to run to catch up to Kareem's seven-foot-two-inch strides. I came up beside him.

"Excuse me, Mr. Kareem!" I excitedly said as I looked up into his eyes. "I have great news for you today." For the next two minutes, as we walked down that terminal, I shared the ABCs of my testimony being specific to share the gospel in the process.

As we arrived at his gate, he looked down at me and said, "Thank you, young man. I appreciate it." He scanned his ticket, went through his gate, and boarded the plane.

My heart was pounding. I did it. I shared the gospel through my testimony. Although I didn't have a dramatic conversion story from Kareem hearing the gospel at that time, one thing I do know, I sowed a seed. Who knows where Kareem was going, what was on his heart at that time, or where he was in his pursuit of knowing the one true God? Either way, he had plenty of time to contemplate the words I had shared with him. I walked back to my gate feeling like I had just conquered the world. I had learned a lesson: God is ready to use us when we have readied ourselves for his service.

That day, I made a declaration to God. If he would set up more divine appointments with celebrities, friends, strangers at the grocery store, anyone, ANYWHERE, I would be prepared and faithful to share his gospel with them. Little did I know, a year later I would be serving the chaplain of the Dallas Cowboys every week at the team's chapel services reaching hundreds of professional athletes over the next ten years.

Norm Miller, the founder of Interstate Batteries, not only believes in the power of a testimony, but he even started a non-profit organization called I AM SECOND to get testimonies to the lost. On the website, iamsecond. com, hundreds of celebrities share the ABCs of their testimonies in an interview style. The website was heavily promoted on many billboards throughout Dallas, Texas, and tens of thousands curiously went to the site, heard the stories, and gave their lives to Christ.

There are countless examples of people whose testimonies have led people to Christ. Celebrities such as Bono, Dolly Parton, Sadie Robertson, and Tim Tebow make it a point to share the gospel through their testimonies. I'm sure that for every one celebrity there are ten thousand unknown Christians around the world who shared the gospel through their testimonies, too.

A ONE-TWO PUNCH KNOCKOUT

As a lifelong sports fan, I've always loved the old one-two punch in boxing. This one-two punch is a strong combination of two punches. It is usually a left-handed punch to the ribs followed by a right-hand cross punch to the opponent's face. It puts a twist on the 'turn the other cheek' command by Jesus. The results are almost always a knockout of an opponent. Game over. Other sports now use this term when they have two superstars on one team that makes that team unstoppable.

Revelation 12 talks about a one-two knockout punch that sends the devil to the ground. It always results in a life that wins and the kingdom of heaven advancing. It has past, present, and future implications. In verses seven through twelve, there's a past war that broke out in heaven that resulted in the devil being hurled to the earth with his angels.

> *"Then war broke out in heaven. Michael and his angels fought against the dragon, and the dragon and his angels fought back. But he was not strong enough, and they lost their place in heaven. The great dragon was hurled down—that ancient serpent called the devil, or Satan, who leads the whole world astray. He was hurled to the earth, and his angels with him."* — *Revelation 12:7–9*

Satan, the devil, is now on the earth accusing believers day and night. This is currently happening.

It's Jesus who is the center of it all.

As a believer, this includes you as one who is constantly condemned by the devil or his angels (we call demons):

> *"Then I heard a loud voice in heaven say: 'Now have come the salvation and the power and the kingdom of our God, and the authority of his Messiah. For the accuser of our brothers and sisters, who accuses them before our God day and night, has been hurled down.'"* — *Revelation 12:10*

But, there's a prophetic insight that God gives us of a future event. As all this is going on, there's a one-two knockout punch that all believers will use to defeat the devil and gain eternal life in the end:

> *"They triumphed over him **by the blood of the Lamb <u>and</u> by the word of their testimony**; they did not love their lives so much as to shrink from death."* — *Revelation 12:10*

The blood of the Lamb and the word of our testimony are the two game-changing, winning moves that will eventually bring eternal triumph. Both the blood and the Word of God that we use in our testimony must be proclaimed; even if it costs us our lives. It is important to remember, though, that our testimony is not the gospel. It's what we use to deliver the gospel. It's Jesus who is the center of it all.

Do you use these two powerfully effective tools when sharing the gospel? The woman at the well used them and shared her testimony all over Samaria. Kilian did too. He shared the gospel through his testimony and was even martyred because of it. Countless believers in the seventh century and beyond have used their testimonies to share the good news that came from the blood of Jesus. And, in the end, we will meet the many people who heard the gospel through our testimonies.

In the meantime, the century came to an end and the Gospel Baton was passed on to the next generation.

9

THE 700s–A TIME FOR ACTION
But … I Will Just Pray

"Yesterday is gone. Tomorrow has not yet come. We have only today. Let us begin." — *Mother Teresa*

In 700 A.D., the Gospel Baton was firmly placed into the hands of men and women of action.

Europe was rapidly becoming evangelized, but paganism and idol worship still had a stronghold in places like Germany. Tacitus, a Roman historian, wrote that the Germans during this time were notoriously heavy drinkers and gamblers who loved telling tales of their tribal heroes and gods. Sacred forests were venerated to these gods. Any disciple of Jesus wanting to evangelize these regions would have to take action in both word and deed.

In 723 A.D., a group of believers led by Boniface did just that. They wanted to share the gospel with the tribal people in Germany near the sacred forest of Thor, named for the god of thunder. Pagans gathered in this forest to worship at a shrine built around a massive tree called Thor's Oak.

Boniface and his men confidently marched into Thor's forest proclaiming that Jesus was the one true God. To prove this gospel was true and powerful, Boniface did the unthinkable. With a large number of pagans looking on, Boniface took an axe to Thor's Oak. And just as he leveled the first strike to the tree, an unexpected breath of wind from heaven blew and toppled the tree. The oak crashed to the ground, splintering its crown of branches, and exploded into four identical pieces. The pagans marveled, heard the message of Jesus who hung on a different tree, and were converted. Boniface took the wood from Thor's Oak and built a church with it.[1]

His bold action brought salvation to many of the pagans.

Stories like Boniface and Thor's Oak would take place throughout this century. And although we still remember Thor's Day in our Thursday, most of the pagan gods were completely erased and the gospel was written on the hearts of more and more unbelievers. The Gospel Baton was in good hands with these faithful men and women of action.

YOU HAVE TO GO

The Brownsville Revival School of Ministry was a small, startup Bible school in Pensacola, Florida in the late '90s. The school was filled with students and staff who were passionate for the gospel to go around the world. We shared the gospel in public places across Pensacola every weekend. We were a school of action for the gospel. Well, most of us were.

During my three years at the school, I had many wonderful and memorable roommates. Chris definitely stands out.[2] He became my roommate near the end of my second year at the school and immediately impressed me. Day after day, Chris would spend hours praying in his room. Sometimes the rest of us in the house would laugh as he prayed because we assumed Chris must have thought God was deaf. Chris would literally shout his requests to God.

But there was one prayer that we heard most. Hour after hour, day after day, week after week, Chris cried out for Jesus to "save Pensacola." He prayed this in the morning, when he got home from school, late at night when we all were trying to sleep, and even while we were out evangelizing in the city. Near the end of the semester, Chris was distraught and asked me why God was not answering his prayers. He complained that in all his praying, he hadn't led anyone to Christ and had not, personally, seen anyone converted.

"Chris, God is saving people all across Pensacola!" I exclaimed.

"Then why doesn't God use me? Why haven't I experienced it?"

"You have to go," I told him. "You can't just pray all day and expect God to move. You have to pair your prayers with action."

Chris got it. He prayed. He went. And, God used him to bring the gospel to many people across Pensacola.

GOD GOES WITH GOERS

The late Reinhard Bonnke, whose evangelistic ministry preached the gospel to over a hundred million people, often said, "God goes with goers. He doesn't sit with sitters, sleep with sleepers, or talk with talkers. No! He goes with goers."

Yes, we are supposed to pray, as we saw in Chapter Three. But there is more to evangelism than just praying. If all we do is pray, we will be like Chris. Always crying out for the salvation of others, but never seeing the answer to our prayers. Often, I find it easier to pray for a person to be saved than to actually tell that person about Christ. Have you experienced this too?

God can save the world on his own, but amazingly, he has decided to partner with us.

God can save the world on his own, but amazingly, he has decided to partner with us. Many times, God will wait to bring salvation to an individual until someone takes action and shares the gospel with that individual. Often, God moves once a word is spoken. This has been a pattern since the beginning of time.

> *"Now the earth was formless and empty, darkness was over the surface of the deep, and the Spirit of God was hovering over the waters. And God said, "Let there be light," and there was light." — Genesis 1:2–3*

The Hebrew term translated "hovering" refers to an eagle who hovers with loving care over the nest of its young (see Deuteronomy 32:11). Who knows how long the Holy Spirit lovingly hovered over the unformed world? Perhaps it was a day? A decade? Maybe it was a million millennia? I don't know. But what is clear is that the Earth was formed only after a word was spoken. There's a spiritual insight we can learn from this story: God moves when a word is spoken. He did then, and he still does. We must speak the word and then watch God work the miracle of salvation.

Bonnke noted that effective evangelism is like walking. It takes two legs to walk. One leg steps, then the other. So, the gospel takes two legs. One leg is prayer, the other leg is preaching. We must use both. Otherwise, we just hop around in a circle, getting nowhere. As we pray, our prayer leg gets stronger. As we preach, our preaching leg gets

As you faithfully pray and preach, your walk becomes a jog, and before you know it, you will be running with the Gospel Baton full of power, anointing, and fruit.

stronger. The stronger our legs are, the more effective we will be. We pray. We preach. We walk.

As you faithfully pray and preach, your walk becomes a jog, and before you know it, you will be running with the Gospel Baton full of power, anointing, and fruit. My friend Chris learned this lesson, and so can you.

SMALL STEPS ARE GIANT LEAPS

Do you remember what Neil Armstrong said when he made that first step on the moon? He proclaimed what would become one of history's most famous one-liners. Say it with me, "That's one small step for man, one giant leap for mankind." And, it was. Space history was forever changed.

A first step is often the hardest step you will ever take. In my mid-twenties, I got a gym membership for Christmas. It was a present to myself. I was eager to get back in shape as I hadn't worked out at a gym in years. On January 1, I jumped in my car and set out to the gym. As I got closer, I began questioning if I really wanted to go. I mean, it was a holiday. Oh, and, I didn't have any kind of exercise plan. And, and, and … Excuses for not wanting to work out flooded my mind. I pulled up to the 24-Hour Fitness really unsure if this was a good idea.

What if everyone was in perfect shape, and I could barely lift any weights?

What if I looked stupid or didn't know how to use one of their machines?

What if, what if, what if … I sat in my car in the parking lot staring at the gym for ten minutes. People came and went. But, I could barely move.

Finally, I turned my car back on, pulled away, and left. I never took that first step into the gym. It was too hard.

I find that many people are this way with evangelism. They have great intentions, but the closer the time gets to actually telling their unsaved friend about Christ, they begin to talk themselves out of it. "What if they think I'm crazy?" … "What if I can't answer their questions?" … "What if I say something wrong?" … What if, what if, what if. And, before they know it, they are walking away from a conversation without ever sharing the gospel. They have successfully proven a business theory called

Paralysis Through Analysis. We over analyze something so much that we paralyze ourselves from ever taking that first step.

And isn't it that way with just about anything? Writing a book, asking someone on a date, overcoming a fear of drowning or heights, starting a business, or learning a new language. All these things require that first step. So it is with God using you to share the good news with those around you and for history to be changed forever.

As a dad, I've watched as my children begin the process of walking. It's not graceful. A first step often includes faceplants, bruised butts, and a lot of video retakes before that first step is taken. Then, confidence builds. Before long, videos are full of sprints, jumps, and flips, and lots of laughter and joy from my kids and me! But all that joy hinges on that first, small step. Small steps lead to great achievements for the gospel as well.

WAKE UP AND GO!

> *Small steps lead to great achievements for the gospel as well.*

Today is the day of salvation. Today is the day for those you have been praying about for years to hear the gospel. Now is the time. You can do it. It's time to act. Invite that friend that you've been praying about to lunch and share the gospel sometime during your conversation. Share the gospel with the cashier scanning your groceries. Water your grass at the same time as your neighbor so you can strategically slip in the gospel message.

Proverbs 13:4 says "a dreamer craves and gets nothing, but the desires of the diligent are fully satisfied."

There's a time to dream and a time to act. Have you been dreaming about your family member, friend, neighbor, or co-worker coming to Christ? Have you been praying but not preaching? It's time to move from words and into action. You are just one step, one conversation away from watching the gospel message radically transform those around you.

I wonder what it was like for Boniface and his crew. Their passion for evangelism to the tribal people was a dream, a desire. They could have sat around and strategized about how to bring the gospel to the forest of Thor. They could have prayed for the people in the forest all day like my old roommate, Chris.

> *You are just one step, one conversation away from watching the gospel message radically transform those around you.*

They could have wished that Germany would be saved. But they did something about it. They were diligent and put actions to their plans and took a step toward the tree.

With each step into the forest, boldness and strength grew. With every person they shared the gospel with, their fear of people was changed to faith. One by one, the message spread through the forest. When they approached Thor's Oak, knowing it stood in the way of others hearing the gospel, they audaciously took action. The tree fell, and the gospel message sprang up throughout Germany.

Hundreds of years later, an apologist named Ignatius would proclaim, "Pray as though everything depends on God alone, but act as though everything depends on you if someone would be saved."

10

THE 800s–LOVE

But … You Don't Know My Family and Friends

"The world does not understand theology or dogma, but it understands love and sympathy." — D.L. Moody

In Greece, a high ranking official in the Byzantine army and his Slavic wife gave birth to sons in 824 and 826 A.D. Methodius, and his younger brother, Cyril, were typical brothers. They played together, laughed together, and had their share of fights and arguments. Their parents wanted the best for them and created a home dedicated to education and success.

The brothers would become young men and go on to study at the Imperial School of Constantinople. Cyril would become a professor of philosophy at the school while Methodius would become a governor. Not much more is known about their upbringing but somewhere along the way, they would both become followers of Jesus.

Although their family was focused on careers instead of spiritual callings, the brothers would not allow their upbringing to stop them from sharing the good news to their family and friends. Surely, many of their family members would be puzzled about why these educated brothers were more interested in talking about Christ instead of politics or philosophy.

Their love for their Slavic (Eastern Europe) lineage grew. The brothers quit their professions to work together as missionaries in their homeland. They wanted everyone in the Slavic region to hear and read this gospel message. Since Slavic had no written language at the time, Cyril invented the Slavic alphabet and then, with his brother Methodius, he proceeded to translate the scriptures into the Slavic language.[1]

Also, due to the peculiarity of the Slavic language and customs of the people, Cyril and Methodius affectionately called them "Rus." The people of the area felt so loved by the lives and message of these brothers that they started to call themselves Rusiny (children of Rus) and their land Rusyn—now called Russia.[2] The brothers also came up with the idea to have these new believers sing love songs to God in their Slavic language. Up until this time, worship would only be sung in either Latin or Greek. [3]

The love these brothers had for each other and those living in Rusyn allowed the gospel to quickly take root in the hearts of all who heard. These brothers exemplified the outcome of a gospel that flows from love for everyone, family included. By 864 A.D., the Rusyn people joyfully proclaimed themselves to be followers of Christ. Today, these two brothers are still known as the "Apostles of the Slavs."

The genuine love shown by these brothers, and others in the ninth century, rapidly propelled the Gospel Baton forward.

THE GO(NG)SPEL

What goes through your mind when you are with your friends in a busy city and hear a guy shouting scripture verses on the corner? Do you hear the gospel, or do you turn a deaf ear to what he is saying? Do you find yourself more receptive to his message or more repulsed by it?

My wife and I stood in the courtyard of the Grossmunster in Zürich, Switzerland one cold evening. Our hearts broke. There in the middle of this beautiful, twelve-hundred-year-old church courtyard stood a middle-aged man. He shouted at the top of his voice scriptural warnings of the consequences of sin and the reality of a hell without Christ. Everything he said was biblically accurate. This brought great joy to our hearts. The sadness came not from what he said, but rather how he said it and the response of the people. There seemed to be no love from this man.

He was shouting at every stranger walking by as if he'd known them for years and they just inflicted the worst pain on him. Each passerby would roll their eyes, say some choice words, and keep going. We watched as hundreds walked past this man, not one listening to a full sentence of anything he had said.

Occasionally, he would look at my wife and me and even shout at us. I just smiled and listened. After about ten minutes, he put his Bible in his briefcase and started to walk away. I stopped him to commend him for his bravery, but even in my compliments he just kept shouting. Finally, after two or three minutes of me trying to convince him that I was a believer he looked me in the eye, said thanks, and walked off. We never saw him again.

Take out love, and the entire Bible crumbles to the ground.

Paul's words to the Corinthians echoed in our hearts that evening, "If I speak in the tongues of men or of angels, but do not have love, I am only a resounding gong or a clanging cymbal."[4]

The entire message of the Bible is built on love.

> *"For God so loved the world ..." (John 3:16)*

> *"... God is love" (1 John 4:8)*

> *"... the greatest of these is love." (1 Corinthians 13:13)*

> *"Love covers over a multitude of sins." (Proverbs 10:12; 1 Peter 4:8)*

There are six hundred and thirteen commandments in the Old Testament. A teacher of the law tried to trap Jesus by asking him which of all these commandments was the greatest. Surprised to hear Jesus responding, everyone gathered around to hear what Jesus would say.

> *Jesus replied: "'Love the Lord your God with all your heart and with all your soul and with all your mind.' This is the first and greatest commandment. And the second is like it: 'Love your neighbor as yourself.' All the Law and the Prophets hang on these two commandments."*
> *— Matthew 22:37–40*

Love.

All the scriptures hang on love. The Greek word for hang in this verse is *kremannymi*. It is the word that is used when someone hangs a picture on a wall. In other words, love is the nail that keeps the entire picture up. Take out love, and the entire Bible crumbles to the ground.

If our gift of the gospel isn't wrapped in love, no one will be interested in receiving it. Instead, we will be like an annoying gong, shouting away in a courtyard, with no one listening.

LION AND A LAMB

It is no coincidence that the Greek word *kremannymi* mentioned above is also used by Peter in Acts 5:30 when he says, "The God of our ancestors raised Jesus from the dead—whom you killed by *kremannymi* him on a cross." As the adage goes, nails didn't hang Jesus on the cross, love did. Jesus exemplified the effectiveness of loving others while also sharing the truth with them.

I've had the honor of mentoring several young men, many of whom have a passion for evangelism. They love how Jesus is mentioned as the lion of the tribe of Judah. These young men often tell me how much they want to be a lion, like Jesus, roaring with the gospel everywhere they go. And, many of them do. It's great.

However, Jesus was also compared to a sheep—humble and full of love. Throughout the gospels, we read how Jesus was moved with compassion when he saw the crowds and then healed them.[5] It was his love for the sinner and the sick that propelled him to preach and heal. Likewise, our passion for sharing the gospel should be birthed out of our love for the sick and sinner.

Did you know that one of the main benefits that comes from being a believer is that you have the honor of representing Jesus to our lost world? Have you ever noticed the root word of represent? Look again. The root word is present. When the "re" is added it means we do it again. Represent means to re-present. What is it that we are re-presenting; that we are showing again to the world? We re-present to our world the love and the message of Jesus to everyone, even those who are closest to us.

FAMILY MATTERS

Can I be vulnerable with you? I find it the hardest to love and share the gospel to those who know me the best. What about you? It's not that I have anything to hide or that I am ashamed of my beliefs. Rather it's more that they know both my ministry and my mistakes. And, when it comes to family, they've known me since I was young. Like Cyril and Methodius, we've lived together, vacationed together, fought together, and forgiven together.

Something powerful happens when we can look past all the insecurities and experiences of our past with our family and still love them

Something powerful happens when we can look past all the insecurities and experiences of our past with our family and still love them unconditionally.

unconditionally. We have to remember that those we call our brother or sister, our mother or father, grandma, grandpa, aunt, and uncle are all still our brothers and sisters in Christ. Every one of them holds an equal place in the eyes of God. We are all created equal.

When we see and love our family and those closest to us the way God does, like Cyril and Methodius, the gospel quickly advances.

One of the most influential believers in Church history is Peter. He was one of the original twelve disciples. He witnessed most of Jesus' miracles and teachings. He walked on water. He found the temple tax in the mouth of a fish. He was told that on his testimony of Christ, the Church would be built. We can go on and on. But, what we often forget is how he became a follower of Christ.

Peter's brother, Andrew, happened to hear Jesus speak one day. The first thing Andrew did was to find his brother and tell him, "We have found the Messiah!" Andrew proclaimed to his brother Peter, known as Simon at the time.

Andrew brought his brother to Jesus. And when Jesus saw him, he said, "Simon son of John, you will be called Peter."[6]

It was Andrew, Peter's brother, who led him to Jesus.

The rest is history.

There's a story about a man who approached Mother Teresa and asked, "Mother, I want to do something great for God, but I don't know what. Should I start a school, be a missionary in a foreign land, or build up a charitable agency?"

He had great aspirations for God.

You were strategically born into your family and your circle of friends for a purpose.

Mother Teresa looked at him precisely and kindly responded, "What you need to do is make sure that no one in your family goes unloved."

I want to remind you that you were strategically born into your family and your circle of friends for a purpose. You are to be light in that cosmos. Your family and friends need to know that they are loved. And, many are silently paying attention to your life.

YOU ARE BEING WATCHED

In the Italian village of Assisi in the thirteenth century was a believer named Francis. He had made it his life mission to imitate Christ and share the gospel in love. He would often say, "It is no use walking anywhere to preach unless our walking is our preaching." This quote has evolved over the years to what is often quoted as, "Preach the gospel at all times. When necessary, use words."

Do you like to be secretly watched? Probably not. Who does? But, guess what? As a believer, there's a great chance that unbelievers are watching you to see if your words match your lifestyle. If they don't, there's a good chance they won't listen to your message. If your words match your life, you may be surprised of how fruitful your life can be for the advancement of the gospel.

When Tanja and I moved to Switzerland, we made it our goal to share the gospel to everyone in our apartment building. There were no believers living near us, and although we shared the gospel, it seemed like no one was interested. Little did we know, we were being watched. Months later, two of the families found themselves in some stressful times.

Can you guess what happened? Yes, you're right. They came to Tanja and me asking for help. Once again, we were able to share the gospel and pray for them. Years later, they are still asking us Bible questions and for prayer.

The actions we walk out and the way we love, preach a powerful message to those around us. When you live a life of love, many times

The actions we walk out and the way we love, preach a powerful message to those around us.

people will see the fruit that hangs on your tree and pick it. Sometimes, they will go out of their way to ask what is different about you instead of you having to go to them. Even Jesus, before he began preaching, lived such an influential life in front of his siblings that years later they, too, would re-present him and his words.

JAMES

James was the younger brother of Jesus. After Jesus ascended into heaven, James would author a letter that would make its way into the New Testament. Whether James wrote the book or had a scribe write down his words into Greek is unknown. But what is remarkable is how similar James sounds like his older brother, Jesus.

Take the famous message of Jesus called The Sermon on the Mount. Of the one hundred and eight verses in the book of James, thirty of those verses sound very familiar to Jesus' sermon.

> *Every good and perfect gift is from above, coming down from the Father of the heavenly lights, who does not change like shifting shadows. — James 1:17*

> *If you, then, though you are evil, know how to give good gifts to your children, how much more will your Father in heaven give good gifts to those who ask him! — Matthew 7:11*

> *"Do not merely listen to the word, and so deceive yourselves. Do what it says." — James 1:22*

> *"But everyone who hears these words of mine and does not put them into practice is like a foolish man who built his house on sand." — Matthew 7:26*

> *Has not God chosen those who are poor in the eyes of the world to be rich in faith and to inherit the kingdom he promised those who love him? — James 2:5*

> *"Blessed are the poor in spirit, for theirs is the kingdom of heaven." — Matthew 5:3*

Jesus had made a lasting impression on James. Long before Jesus was crisscrossing Israel proclaiming the gospel to the multitudes, he was in a carpenter shop with his brothers loving them and living the life in front of them first. The impact he made on his younger brother in those unknown years played such a role that James would repeat them years later in his own letter.

You are being watched. Are you living a life of love?

WE ALL NEED TO BE LOVED

Love is a universal language, and we all speak it. But oftentimes, our actions speak louder than words. As a believer, there are many practical ways to *be love* to those around you. We have to remind ourselves that we are the body of Christ. We have …

As a believer, there are many practical ways to be love to those around you.

Eyes—Be alert to what is going on around you. Life isn't about you. There are many people sending nonverbal messages that they desperately need help. Ask the Holy Spirit to give you eyes to see and ears to hear what God wants you to do for others.

Ears—Sometimes the greatest way to show love is just to listen to others. God gave us two ears and one mouth. Maybe he is trying to remind us to listen twice as much as we speak.

A Mouth—There is power of life in the tongue. Timely words are like "golden apples served on a silver platter."[7] Look for ways to encourage others. Ask others if you can pray for them. Not all may be healed, but all will feel loved.

Arms—When the Holy Spirit "fell" on the believers in Acts 10:44, the Greek word used is *epipiptō*. This word evokes an image of young children in the embrace of a loving parent. The Holy Spirit hugs us with such a weight of love that we fall to the ground. Just giving someone a hug is a powerful way to share love without saying a word.

Hands—Our giving is another way to show love. This can be an act of service, a financial gift, or a helping hand.

Feet—Going out of your way for a family member, a neighbor, or colleague is a great amplifier of love. People tend to live very self-centered lives. Stepping out of your comfort zone and lifestyle to step into someone's mess can open their heart to hear the gospel.

As the body of Christ, we are to be love. Love is what brightens our face, puts a hop in our step, and makes the difference in our actions. If we ever lose our love, our appearance to unbelievers looks sick and our gospel is repulsive.

THE PAINTING

Have you ever read *The Message* translation of the Bible? Eugene Peterson translated this version of the Bible with the purpose of using contemporary slang from the USA instead of the more neutral International English language. The rich love of God and his people are felt in a deeply impactful way throughout the scripture verses. However, you may be surprised by the most unlikely person who left an impression on Peterson years earlier.

Eugene Peterson tells the story of the time he was a theology student in New York City and employed by a Presbyterian Church to work with a group of young people. The church janitor was a German man named Willi Ossa.

Unfortunately, while living in Germany during WWII years earlier, Ossa experienced the sad reality of many believers in Germany who capitulated to the hate promoted by Adolf Hitler. Even Ossa's pastor during that time had exchanged the love for people and the gospel to become a fervent Nazi. This had negatively influenced Ossa's view of the church and the gospel. Although Ossa was the janitor, he was also a very outspoken skeptic of the global church. Yet, he and Peterson had become friends. Ossa could not help but notice the love that Peterson had towards him.

Ossa also happened to be an artist.

One day, Ossa asked Peterson if he could paint his portrait. There was one catch. Peterson would not be allowed to see the portrait until the work was finished. They agreed and the painting began.

Week after week, they would set a time to continue with the painting. One day, Ossa's wife came into the room and shrieked when she saw the painting. She emphatically shouted that Peterson looked sick. Ossa had painted Peterson with a gaunt face, lifeless eyes and no expression. In a rapid exchange with his wife, Ossa explained why, "He's not sick now, but that's the way he will look when the compassion is gone, when the mercy gets squeezed out of him."

Peterson never forgot that message. And, he never got rid of the painting. He realized how important the love of God in and through his life was to those around him, especially to skeptical unbelievers.[8]

Take a moment today and look in the mirror. Imagine yourself, like Ossa did with Peterson, without love. You would look incredibly lifeless and empty. Love gives you a healthy visual of what a genuine life of a believer should look like. Lose love and your appearance is repulsive and your message goes unheard.

Centuries of believers have understood this obvious principle including those in the ninth century. Cyril and Methodius loved the Rusyn people and their land, Russia. The alphabet they created has since been renamed Cyrillic, in memory of Cyril, and is still the alphabet of Russia, Ukraine, Bulgaria, and Serbia. That love propelled them and the gospel continued its rapid expansion around the world.

The Gospel Baton continued on through the ninth century as unreached lands heard the gospel and experienced the love of Christ exemplified by his people.

11

THE 900s–SEEDS
But ... I'm a Nobody

"We won't be judged by the number of souls saved, but by the number of seeds sown." — Reinhard Bonnke

In 943 A.D., an introverted dad and mom in Parma, Italy raised their son to be a follower of Jesus. After working the fields each day, they would give Jesus thanks for their seasonal harvest and protecting them from the many dangers they were exposed to. At night, they acted out stories from the Bible as their child lay in bed. They made it a point to remind their son that without Jesus, they were lost for all eternity.

The parents didn't see much change in their son. As a teenager, he married a girl in their village, had kids, and became a locksmith. Even though there was no outward passion for Christ from their child, his parents continued sharing the gospel with him. The parents not only shared the gospel with their son, but also their neighbors and those in the local market. Like most believers in the Medieval Church, they never considered their faith a private thing.

Night after night, over many years, they wondered if the life they lived and the message they planted in their child and neighbors was making any eternal difference. The parents died with this question in their hearts. Little did they know, the gospel had taken root in many people, including their son. As a matter of fact, he not only became a devout follower of Christ, but he would copy his parents' example of faithfully sharing the gospel with his children and grandchildren. So did many in their village.

Who were these parents? We will never know.

Who was this child? That, too, is a mystery.

And, who were those neighbors who became followers of Jesus? Only God knows.

They joined the countless disciples of Christ. They are part of the nameless, faceless followers of Jesus who have carried the Gospel Baton through the ages. They were not famous, had no full-time ministry, and were not esteemed by many people.

But it was, and still is, nameless people like these in the tenth century who have advanced the gospel the most through the ages. Historians call this time in history as the last century of the Dark Ages. But there was nothing dark about these Christians who let their light shine and planted seeds that would produce an eternal harvest throughout the following centuries.

ONE HOPE BOLZANO

God needs willing and faithful people to advance his kingdom.

That is what I believe you are, and it's the reason you are reading this book. I've learned that faithfulness goes much further in advancing the gospel than almost anything. Let me encourage you with a story of how God used my willingness to sow the gospel in the hearts of some refugees.

In December of 2017, Tanja and I sensed God was asking if we would be willing to share the gospel in a town in Italy. We were! We decided to host an evangelistic outreach in Bolzano, Italy through our ministry, Ignite Europe. We blitzed the famous Christmas market in the city center with thousands of fliers inviting everyone to the free event. One Hope Bolzano was hosted in a ballroom inside the four-star Parkhotel Laurin beside the Christmas market with free food and drinks. Our team believed for many Italians to be saved. That's not what happened.

When the event began, the ballroom was packed with Muslim refugees from Syria who were fleeing ISIS. One of our fliers made its way to the refugee camp, and enticed by the offer of free food and drinks, they came.

As I stood in front of these refugees that evening, I boldly declared Jesus as the king. I quoted Acts 17:26–27 and noted that God had strategically placed every person in that room so they might know Jesus.

(More on this in the next chapter.) When the call for salvation was made, several of the refugees in the room raised their hands declaring Jesus as their savior.

Once the event was over, we had gotten word that our children may be in danger. We noticed that one of the Muslim refugees had been streaming the event live on his social platforms. No one was sure of his motives, and we knew we needed to be wise and leave immediately. After a few photos, we quickly grabbed our two toddlers and our equipment, and our team left. We felt like Christian Navy SEALS flying into enemy territory, preaching the gospel, and getting out before we got into a dangerous situation.

> *That is what we are expected to do: be willing and faithful servants to share the gospel wherever we are called.*

I've often wondered what happened to those refugees. How many of them are still following Christ? What did they talk about that night when they went back to their camp? Where are they now?

Those refugees will probably never know who I was. And I may never know if their eternal destinies were changed that night. But I do know that the gospel was planted in their hearts. And that is what we are expected to do: be willing and faithful servants to share the gospel wherever we are called. We are called to be spiritual farmers!

WE ARE FARMERS

Think of a farmer, a field, and a seed. Before there can be a harvest, a farmer must first plant a seed. The seed takes root, is nourished by the sun and water for a period of time, and then its fruit is harvested.

As followers of Christ, we are farmers. The fields are the hearts of individuals. The seed is the gospel. When the gospel is shared with someone, it is like a farmer who sows a seed in the ground. Then over a period of time—whether seconds or years—other people come along and water the seeds by pouring the love of God and Scripture on that individual. Finally, when the harvest is ready, the individual comes to Christ.

Paul reminds the church in Corinthians of this truth:

When the gospel is shared with someone, it is like a farmer who sows a seed in the ground.

"I planted the seed, Apollos watered it, but God has been making it grow. So neither the one who plants nor the one who waters is anything, but only God, who makes things grow. The one who plants and the one who waters have one purpose, and they will each be rewarded according to their own labor. For we are co-workers in God's service; you are God's field, God's building." — 1 Corinthians 3:6–9

Just as a farmer can't miraculously make a harvest, we can't miraculously save anyone. However, every Christian must sow and water the gospel seed and be prepared to reap a ripe harvest.

Have you ever thought of yourself as a spiritual farmer? It's never too late to begin. There are people who need the gospel sown in their hearts, others who need it repeated, and still others ready to give their allegiance to King Jesus. Let me explain more.

Jesus had just finished his discourse with the woman at the well when he looked at his disciples and said this:

> *"Don't you have a saying, 'It's still four months until harvest?' I tell you, open your eyes and look at the fields! They are ripe for harvest." — John 4:35*

We often hear this verse quoted with the application that every person is ready for salvation. I wish this were true. However, living in a farming community in Switzerland, I've learned that there's a lot that goes into a ripe harvest.

There are months of sowing, watering, and tending to the fields before a harvest is typically ready. The same goes in the spiritual. Jesus was in Samaria when he told his disciples that the fields, those not following Christ, were ready to be harvested (saved). But, he reminded the disciples a few sentences later that it was only because others had already sown and watered before they arrived.

"For here the saying holds true, 'One sows and another reaps.' I sent you to reap that for which you did not labor. Others have labored, and you have entered into their labor." — John 4:37–38 (ESV)

After Jesus told the disciples that the Samaria harvest is ready, he sent out the twelve to other villages to share the gospel. But, unlike Samaria, he tells them this time:

"If anyone will not welcome you or listen to your words, leave that home or town and shake the dust off your feet."
— Matthew 10:14

Unfortunately, not everyone is ready to become a follower of Christ. And, not everyone will care about what you have to say. Many people will reject you just like they did Jesus and the disciples. I'm sure you know what I mean. Just like many of those refugees did to me in Bolzano.

Keep running with the Gospel Baton. Keep sowing the seeds of the gospel! There are more than three billion people who have never heard the good news of Jesus. We have much sowing and watering to do. However, be encouraged. Most of the time, you never know the power of the seed you've sown.

SEEDS

I had a friend who was a personal assistant to Reinhard Bonnke, an evangelist who saw more than fifty million people saved during his lifetime. My friend told me that Bonnke would say, "We won't be judged by the number of souls saved, but by the number of seeds sown."

The same goes for you. It goes for me. Our purpose as spiritual farmers is to sow the gospel everywhere we go. Making it grow is God's job, not ours. We just sow, water, and stay ready to harvest when the time is ripe. Jesus said,

"This is what the kingdom of God is like. A man scatters seed on the ground. Night and day, whether he sleeps or gets up, the seed sprouts and grows, though he does not know how. All by itself the soil produces grain—first the

stalk, then the head, then the full kernel in the head. As soon as the grain is ripe, he puts the sickle to it, because the harvest has come." — Mark 4:26–29

The encouraging thing is that every seed sown has the potential, not only for that one individual we sow into but possibly for countless people who are still to come.

As the old saying goes, "You can count the apples on the tree, but who can count the apples in a seed?" One seed could lead to a great harvest. Consider the results of one man's actions in the 1800s.

On April 21, 1855, a lowly Sunday school teacher named Edward Kimball attempted to sow the gospel message to one of his students who was also a shoe salesman. This student would often fall asleep during his lessons, seemingly uninterested in learning about Christ. One day, Kimball, undeterred, set out to reach the student at work.

Kimball's heart was pounding as he entered the store where the young man worked. Kimball would write about the occasion in his diary:

"I put my hand on his shoulder, and as I leaned over, I placed my foot upon a shoebox. I asked him to come to Christ."

Kimball left thinking that he had botched the job. His presentation of the gospel had felt halting. Even though he had sown the gospel, he was downcast as there seemed to be no interest. The young man, on the other hand, perceived it differently. He left work that day as a new man. He believed his teacher's words and became a believer. That young shoe salesman was D. L. Moody. Moody would eventually become the most prominent evangelist in America in the late 1800s.

As the old saying goes, "You can count the apples on the tree, but who can count the apples in a seed?"

Moody spoke at Lake Forest College in the late 1870s, and J. Wilber Chapman, a student at the school, attended the lecture and met with Moody after the service. Moody sowed the gospel in the heart of Chapman, who afterwards became a follower of Christ.

J. Wilber Chapman started working for Moody. He hired Chicago Cubs baseball player Billy Sunday as his assistant and mentored him. Billy Sunday would eventually become a great evangelist, attracting large crowds of his own. Sunday was determined to reach the people in his cosmos and launched the Charlotte Businessmen's Club.

In 1934, the Charlotte Businessmen's Club hosted a series of evangelistic campaigns in Charlotte, North Carolina. They invited a man named Mordecai Hamm to preach the messages. At one of those meetings, a young man gave his life to Jesus. That man was Billy Graham.[1]

Reverend Billy Graham preached on TV, and a young man named John Weber gave his life to Jesus listening to Graham's message. John Weber became the chaplain for the Dallas Cowboys and took a young college graduate under his wing to mentor him in his faith. Twenty-two years later, that college student would write a book on evangelism that would be read by … YOU.

I was that college student.

You are reading this book as a direct result of a seed sown by a Sunday school teacher into a shoe salesman April 21, 1855.

We don't know who sowed the seed in the heart of Edward Kimball, the Sunday school teacher. His or her name goes unknown through history, but it's not unknown in heaven. Faithfulness in sowing the gospel seeds can lead to a harvest through the centuries that is much bigger than your lifetime.

JUST BE FAITHFUL

No one in the Bible ever set out to be great. They attempted to be faithful to God's word, and for some, earthly greatness was the result.

Our mandate by God is to be faithful in sowing and watering his gospel to those around us. Whether God chooses to make you known or unknown on this earth is his business. Our goal should never be to set out to be superstars. After all, there's only one star, and that is Jesus. We should strive for faithfulness.

We often celebrate the person who leads someone to Jesus. But we tend to forget that, most likely, there are countless unknown Christians who have sown and watered the gospel seeds in that individual long before the salvation moment. A hundred years before there was a Reinhard Bonnke reaping a massive harvest in Africa, there was a David Livingston who lived most of his life on the mission field of Africa as a missionary explorer. He contributed to leading one person to Christ in his ten-plus years in Africa, although Livingstone himself even disputed if there was even one.

But, the seeds were sown. And, if we know about David Livingstone, can you imagine how many other believers we don't know about? Believers who labored for the cause of Christ over the hundred years in Africa before the great harvest that Bonnke reaped? Each seed sown and each person watering played a part in the harvest. And, all share in the eternal reward.

As a believer, you are not called to "save" anyone. You can't cause anyone to believe in Jesus and become part of his kingdom. All you are called to do is to be faithful with sowing the seed of the gospel, and God does the saving. Sometimes you sow the gospel and reap a harvest immediately. Other times, you may be the one sowing the message, others may come along and water the seed, while still someone else gets the privilege of seeing the harvest.

Many times, sowing the gospel message is not glamorous. And, even at times it can be hard work. When Jesus compared the gospel to farming, he understood the ramifications of what he was saying. Aside from the difficult manual labor, oftentimes farms weren't even located where the farmer lived. Farmers would walk six-to-eight miles to get to their farm to sow their fields. It took commitment and work.

But, keep going. Press on, Christian. You are on a winning team.

WE ARE THE CHAMPIONS

Sharing the gospel is like playing on a championship sports team. Yes, there may be some players who are more known than other players on the team. Some play an important position on the field without ever scoring a point or being recognized. Still, others are coaches, trainers, and chaplains who are completely unknown outside the team. But, when the game is won, everyone on the team is given a championship ring. So, it will be for us all when King Jesus returns. We are all going to celebrate his victory together and he will reward us for our labor.

When Jesus talked about the ripe harvest to his disciples in Samaria, he immediately reminded them that all will be rewarded equally, whether you plant a seed, water the seed, or reap the harvest. *The Message* says it like this:

> *"Now the Sower is arm in arm with the Harvester, triumphant." — John 4:36*

The NIV translates John 4:36 as, "The sower and reaper rejoice together."

One person coaches the athlete, one player passes the ball, and another scores the goal. All three are champions.

One person plants the seeds, others water the seed, and one reaps the harvest, but all rejoice together, triumphant in the end! We need to celebrate the team, not just one individual.

YOUR PART IS CRITICAL …

A fast-growing church I visited in Norway has a great way of applying this lesson. The church has their members label all the unbelievers in their cosmos on a scale of 3, 2, 1, and 0. A 3 is someone who has never heard the gospel; a 2 is one who has heard it but isn't interested, a 1 is a person who is interested but not yet a follower of Christ, and a 0 is someone who has just been converted and is ready to be discipled.

The staff told me they attribute their church's growth to the fact that they celebrate the planting and watering of the gospel as much as they celebrate when someone was harvested, i.e., gave his or her life to Christ.

Glamorizing the "reaper" as the only effective evangelist is a destructive approach to the advancement of the kingdom. Everyone's role, including yours, is important for evangelism. It reminds me of the farm across from my first house in Switzerland.

I spent many days watching out our living room window, mesmerized at the techniques of the farmers, the mechanics of the equipment they used, and the crops that rewarded the hard work.

As the months and years passed, I noticed a trend. Every year, this farm grew pumpkins. The annual cycle was the same. One day in spring, ten to fifteen farmers planted pumpkin seeds on the tilled soil. Then, over the next three months, countless farmers would tend the farm. They watered the soil, pulled weeds from among the growing vines, and shewed away animals intent on stealing the fruit.

Finally, in the fall, after months of waiting, the pumpkins were ready for harvest. A farmer arrived with his tractor, and within hours, all the pumpkins were picked, loaded onto a truck, and hauled down the road to a local outdoor market and restaurant. The tractor-driving farmer beamed with pride as he entered the market grounds with the load of pumpkins. Hundreds of people cheered and clapped with excitement for the harvest. For several days, tens of thousands of people would celebrate this pumpkin harvest, the largest in all of Switzerland. The occasion was joyous, and I was reminded that, as a believer, we are all called to farming as well.

When we see large crusades with thousands of people getting saved or a YouTube video of a street evangelist leading everyone who passes by to Jesus, it can make us feel like we are nothing. These evangelists are praised, have many followers, and seem to be the experts in evangelism.

The reality is far from this. Remember, long before that famous evangelist reaps the harvest, countless other unknown evangelists have most likely already sown and watered the gospel in the heart of the new convert. That famous evangelist just happens to be the one God chooses to reap the harvest. These are not experts; they're each just one of the players on the team.

Everyone's role is important.

... AND URGENT

Tomorrow isn't promised to anyone. Everyone needs to hear the good news of Jesus, immediately.

That's where you come in.

It's our job to let people know that they have a choice to make when it comes to their eternal destination. That choice must be made before it's too late, because there truly is an eternal heaven or eternal hell awaiting everyone.

Many people flippantly respond to their lack of evangelism with, "so what?" or "who cares?" It's easy to get caught up in the busy-ness of our day-to-day lives and forget that eternity is a serious matter that must be urgently communicated to everyone. You and I may be the only ones who sow the good news of Jesus in the hearts of our friends and families.

We see this urgency as a key theme of Christ and his ministry. Throughout the Gospel of Mark, the Greek word *eutheos* is used more than forty times. It means *immediately*. Notice how often this word is used in the first chapter of Mark alone:

- And *eutheos* coming up out of the water, Jesus saw the heavens opened, and the Spirit like a dove descending upon Him (v. 10)
- And *eutheos* the Spirit drove Jesus into the wilderness (v. 12)
- And when Jesus had gone a little further, He saw James the son of Zebedee, and John his brother, who also were in the ship mending their nets, And eutheos Jesus called them (vv. 19, 20)
- And they went into Capernaum; and *eutheos* on the sabbath day Jesus entered into the synagogue, and taught (v. 21)
- And *eutheos* when they were come out of the synagogue, they entered into the house of Simon (v. 29)
- And Jesus came and took her by the hand, and lifted her up, and *eutheos* the fever left her (v. 31)

Jesus was on a mission. *Eutheos* shows us the urgency of Jesus' mission. So, our mission of sowing seeds must be urgent as well.

MAKE THE WORLD UNWORTHY OF YOU

When we get to heaven, we may be surprised at who is there, and at who is considered greatest in his kingdom. Those we consider superstars in the church today may not be as esteemed as we would think in heaven. It's important not to measure outward success as the world does to the eternal success that results in faithfulness to God.

Hebrews gives us a glimpse of what a truly successful person looks like in the eyes of God. It's all summed up by living a life of faith in God. Sowing the gospel seeds is part of that faithfulness. The eleventh chapter of Hebrews has been nicknamed the "Hall of Faith." Great Old Testament men and women are mentioned throughout the chapter. There's Noah, Abraham, Isaac, Jacob, and Moses to name a few. Then, the writer says this:

> *"And what more shall I say? I do not have time to tell about Gideon, Barak, Samson and Jephthah, about David and Samuel and the prophets...about those who faced jeers and flogging, and even chains and imprisonment. They were put to death by stoning; they were sawed in two; they were killed by the sword. They went about in sheepskins*

and goatskins, destitute, persecuted and mistreated...They wondered in deserts and mountains, living in caves and in holes in the ground." — *Hebrews 11:32–38*

All because of their faith in God and fulfilling his purpose through them on Earth. To the average person, these people would not be too esteemed. We only know a dozen names out of the hundreds of thousands of people the writer is alluding to. On Earth, most of these believers would be considered "nobodies." But, that is not how God views them. He says of these nameless and faceless believers: "the world was not worthy of them."[2]

For the past two thousand years, the Church, like the faithful saints of the Old Testament, has been built by a predominately nameless, faceless people. They are Sunday school teachers, parents who teach their children the Bible, mentors, God-fearing businessmen, babysitters, and classmates, all who may never be famous in this lifetime. But, God says of them, and he says of those who are faithful: "The world may say you are a nobody, but to me, you are more valuable than anything the world has to offer."

That can be you, my friend. And it can be me, too.

12

THE 1000s–LOCATION

But … You Don't Know Where I Live

"Some wish to live within the sound of a church or chapel bell. I want to run a rescue shop within a yard of hell." — CT Studd

As the new millennium arrived, the Church had been firmly established. The gospel was making its way around the world. In Europe, the Middle East, and Africa, the Church was growing in power and majesty. To remind the people in each city of the majesty of God, architects tried to attain the utmost height possible for each new church they built.

Cathedrals such as The Strasbourg Cathedral, which began construction in 1015, reached staggering heights equivalent to a skyscraper forty stories high. The gothic architects used flying buttresses to eliminate massive walls and slender pillars in place of bulky ones used in centuries past. Even the statues of the saints and angels were given elongated arms, necks, and legs. The church was seemingly soaring upward, and the builders and the church leaders wanted to make sure everyone knew. But not everyone lived in a town that was seeming to soar with God's blessing on earth.

Many of the nameless, faceless generation of believers mentioned in the previous chapter faced great persecution because of their faith and for sharing the gospel. In this century, there were times of peace followed by times of great unrest throughout Europe and around the world.

In England near the end of the century, William I, the first Norman King of England, died and passed on his reign to his son William Rufus. Rufus didn't respect spiritual things as his father did, and he persecuted believers.

One of these believers was a sixty-year-old Italian living in Kent, England, named Anselm. Anselm would eventually become one of the greatest scholars of the Bible, giving the Church some of the finest writings of the purpose of Christ over the past two thousand years. Anselm is nicknamed "The Second Augustine" because of his understanding of Scripture.

King William Rufus thought he could use Anselm's influence as a way to promote his agenda. Not willing to be negatively impacted by William, even though William made him Archbishop of Canterbury, Anselm would not stop shining the pure light of the gospel everywhere we went.

As a result, on two different occasions, Anselm was forced into exile and lived in foreign territories. This didn't stop him from following Christ and sharing the gospel. Anselm would not miss his chance to be part of this great plan of redemption through the ages. He, like countless others, knew that God was strategically in control of his life and that no matter where he was living, it was God's plan for his life and for those around him.

CONSTRUCTION WORKERS AND GOD'S WORK

When I was nineteen, I worked for my dad's construction company in Dallas, Texas. Although I loved to joke with my coworkers—I even let them nickname me chango (the Spanish word for monkey)—my heart was for them all to have a relationship with Christ like I did. I knew that without Christ, our eternities are hopeless. I had found God and wanted others too as well. This truth compelled me to continuously talk about salvation and sing worship songs while working.

One day, I was adding a new wall onto an office addition. As I was working, I was singing a song about repentance and following God. Above me, I heard a raspy voice, "Hey, preacher boy." At the top of a twelve-foot ladder stood an air-conditioning technician wearing work boots, a hard hat on backwards, torn blue jeans, and dust from head to toe.

"Son, you tryin' to tell me that if I don't repent of them sins of mine, I'm gonna go to hell in a handbasket?"

Before I even thought about what to say, I responded confidently, "Sir, you won't even get a handbasket!"

With that, I briefly shared the gospel. The man shook his head and went back to work as I stood shocked by what I said. I knew it was the truth, but he didn't work for our company. I couldn't throw the "my dad's the boss" card to this guy. I bobbed my head a few times, took a deep breath, grabbed some screws, and got back to work singing *Thou Oh Lord Are a Shield Around Me.*

Fast forward five years. I had graduated with a bachelor's degree in biblical studies and was serving on staff at a church in Waterloo, Iowa, eight hundred miles from Dallas. I rarely preached to the main Sunday morning crowd, but one particular week was my opportunity. Nothing was out of the ordinary. I shared the message and stood at the front of the auditorium after the service in case anyone wanted to talk. A gentleman and his wife approached me. I assumed that they wanted me to pray for them. He was dressed like a mechanic who had just clocked out for the day.

Little did I know what was about to happen.

"My wife and I were passing by this church this morning when our tire blew out. We're from out of town and can't really go anywhere until tomorrow, so we decided we'd just come in to the service. Anyways, I've got something to ask you. Son ... do I know you?" the middle-aged gentleman asked.

"Um, I don't know. Do you?" I asked, joking around.

"Did you happen to live in Dallas at one time?" he asked.

"Yes," I replied, wondering how this guy knew me.

"Did you happen to work construction?" he continued.

"Um, yes sir," I answered, now getting curious about where this was going.

"And did you happen to once tell an air-conditioning guy that he was going to hell without a handbasket if he didn't repent of his sins?"

My thoughts raced as the flashbacks poured into my mind ... *Oh, NO! ... What do I do now? ... Do I run? ... How did he find me? ... He's hunted me down ... I'm dead.*

"Um, yes sir. I believe I did," was all I could manage as I stood there like a deer in headlights.

The grin he gave me is ingrained in my mind. "That was me," he replied. "After you told me that, I really looked at my life and realized that I did need God. I always wanted to tell you, but I didn't know who you were or where to find you. Anyways, thank you for leading me to Christ!"

We shook hands, gave each other a man hug, and he was gone as quickly as he had arrived. I was in disbelief over the whole ordeal for a week. I mean, what were the chances? Out of the billions of people on the planet and more than eight million miles of roads, how was it that this one guy, eight hundred miles from home, had a blowout in front of this exact church, on the exact day I was preaching? And on top of that, instead of hiring a tow truck and getting a hotel room, he decided to come to church. And, he remembered me from one day working together five years earlier. And, and, and …

Is it possible that God placed me in that man's life, at that certain moment in time, for that specific reason because God had a plan? Did God set that man up?

If it was that way for him, what about me? What about you? What about all of mankind?

Is it possible that our entire lives are set up by an amazing God for a specific purpose? And, if so, what is that purpose? Could it be that every day God is bringing construction-worker moments in each of our lives without us even noticing in order for us to share the gospel to them?

Is it possible that our entire lives are set up by an amazing God for a specific purpose?

Or was this just a coincidence?

YOUR LIFE IS STRATEGICALLY PLANNED

Did you know that God strategically positioned you in world history and in your geographic location so you might know him? Not in a predestined way where you have no say in the direction of your life, but rather in a providential way where God is continually setting you up for a divine purpose.

In Acts 17, Paul gives one of the most significant speeches in the entire New Testament. His revelation of Jesus Christ as the fulfillment of the "unknown god" to the Grecians echoed through the philosophical minds of those gathered on the top of Mars Hill in Athens. For two-thirds of the speech, Paul proclaims the greatness of God. But then he shifts and says something important about everyone who has or will ever live.

"From one man, God made every nation of men. And, he determined the times set for them and the exact place where they will live. God did this so that man will seek him and perhaps reach out and find him although he is not far from each one of us." — Acts 17:26–27

God has determined when everyone would be alive and where everyone would live.

Albert Einstein once said, "God does not play dice." Nothing is a coincidence. It's not by chance that you live where you do at this time in history.

Did you know the word coincidence doesn't exist in Hebrew, the language of the Old Testament? You won't find this word or thought anywhere in the Old Testament. And the word coincidence is only used once in the Greek New Testament—by Jesus. In the parable of the Good Samaritan in Luke 10:31, Jesus says, "And by coincidence a certain priest was going down that way, and having seen him, he passed over on the opposite side."

> *God strategically positioned you in world history and in your geographic location so you might know him.*

Upon first glance, it seems that Jesus clearly is saying that things can happen by chance. However, the word used here is the Greek word *synkyrian*. This word is a combination of the Greek words *sun*, meaning "together with," and *kurious*, meaning "supreme authority." In this parable, Jesus isn't saying that the priest passed by coincidence, but that his passing by occurred "together by God's arrangement of circumstances."

You were strategically born during this time in world history and currently live where you do for a purpose. God alone can save the world, but he chooses not to do it alone. God wants you to find him. And, he wants to use you to point others to Christ.

BUT YOU DON'T KNOW MY CIRCUMSTANCE

Location is never an excuse not to share the gospel. God sees you and knows your circumstance, even if it doesn't seem like a desirable time or ideal place to live. It could be much worse.

Have you read the second chapter of Revelation recently? If not, let me remind you of one of the churches Jesus mentions. Imagine living in Pergamum in the first century.

This northernmost city of all the seven churches mentioned in Revelation was given a dreadful title by Jesus. Although it was a wealthy, cultural city just 16 miles from the Aegean Sea in what is modern-day Turkey, we read this dreadful fact where Jesus says:

> "I know where you live—where Satan has his throne. Yet you remain true to my name. You did not renounce your faith in me, not even in the days of Antipas, my faithful witness, who was put to death in your city—where Satan lives." — Revelation 2:13

These early believers lived in the city where "Satan has his throne." Whoa. And, they remained pure to Jesus and his gospel even at the expense of their lives. Many of them, like Antipas who is mentioned by Jesus in this verse, were martyred because of their faith. It may not have looked like an ideal place and time to share their faith, but they did. They did not renounce their faith, but shared the gospel. And their testimony of remaining true to God's word lives on throughout eternity in the Bible.

Their situation wasn't an isolated case.

What about believers in communist countries or followers of Jesus in places ripped apart by war? What about being a Christian during the reign of Nero in Rome or a Jew in Europe during WWII? This must have been a mistake God made, right? Surely these individuals' life situations are not planned by God, right? Not according to Corrie ten Boom who miraculously survived the Nazi concentration camps and lived to talk about it.

Corrie spoke to audiences for forty years after being freed and described the horrible things she witnessed and went through. It sounded as though Satan had moved his throne from Pergamum to Berlin in the 1940s. During her speeches, Corrie would look down and work on a piece of needlepoint. At the end of her speech, she revealed the needlepoint.

She would show the backside, revealing a confused mess of colors and threads. She'd often remark, "This is how we see our lives." Then she would flip the needlepoint over to reveal a beautiful design on the front. She would conclude by saying, "This is how God views your life, and someday we will have the privilege of viewing it from his point of view."

Corrie ten Boom did not let her circumstance keep her from talking about God's love and saving others.

And neither should we.

We have no excuse for not sharing the gospel right where we are. Sure, we all live in different regions of the world where believers are celebrated while in other places they are tortured. But, be encouraged. God knows exactly where you live. And, it's all for a purpose.

> *We have no excuse for not sharing the gospel right where we are.*

YOU ARE GOD'S CHOSEN

Remember the story of Queen Esther? Because of her beauty, she was selected to be the Jewish wife of the Persian King Xerxes. Through a series of events, King Xerxes was tricked into proclaiming the complete annihilation of the Jews in the empire. Mordecai, Queen Esther's cousin, wept bitterly at the edict that was about to be passed down upon his people. But, he knew something about Esther that you need to know about yourself!

Mordecai knew that Esther was not alive at that time and living where she was for no reason. He believed that she was born to save the Jews from a sure death. Mordecai wrote these words in a letter to Esther:

> *"For if you remain silent at this time, relief and deliverance for the Jews will arise from another place, but you and your father's family will perish. And who knows but that you have come to your royal position for such a time as this?"* — Esther 4:14

Mordecai had faith the Jews would be saved. He encouraged Esther to speak up. He knew that where she lived and at that time in history was no coincidence. Esther believed, met with the king, and ultimately saved the Jews from death.

You must know today that, like Esther, you are royalty. You have come into the Kingdom of God for such a time as this. Remember what the Apostle Peter says about you?

> *"You are a chosen people, a royal priesthood, a holy nation,*
> *God's special possession, that you may declare the praises*
> *of him who called you out of darkness into his wonderful*
> *light." — 1 Peter 2:9*

You are God's chosen ambassador to represent him to your neighbors, co-workers, and relatives. When God was thinking about who he wanted to declare his gospel to those in your city at this time in world history, he chose … YOU!

He didn't choose any of the apostles, any of the well-known Christian leaders of centuries past, or some great theologian. No! It's you that God knew was the perfect person to Go & Tell his good news to this generation.

THIS IS YOUR MOMENT

Don't be like some Christians who dream of a better life in a different location or even a different era. They complain that they don't live in an ideal situation. They focus on the dark circumstances around them instead of realizing their God-ordained opportunity.

> *"You are the light of the world. A town built on a hill cannot*
> *be hidden. Neither do people light a lamp and put it under*
> *a bowl. Instead they put it on its stand, and it gives light*
> *to everyone in the house. In the same way, let your light*
> *shine before others, that they may see your good deeds and*
> *glorify your Father in heaven." — Matthew 5:14–16*

Be the light to those around you. Don't waste time cursing the darkness. Instead, start lighting some candles.

Be the light to those around you. Don't waste time cursing the darkness. Instead, start lighting some candles. Boldly tell everyone in your cosmos about Jesus. God has strategically positioned you as his representative.

One of the saddest verses in the Bible is found in Jeremiah 46:17: "Pharaoh king of Egypt is only a loud noise; he has missed his opportunity."

The amazing influence, fame, wealth, and resources were all at Pharaoh's disposal. From an earthly standpoint, he was poised for greatness. But, instead, he was just a loud noise who missed his opportunity.

How much greater is your opportunity from a spiritual standpoint? You have the message, you have the Holy Spirit, and you have been positioned for success. Don't let what was said about Pharaoh be said about you!

In the late 1700s, German author Johann Wolfgang von Goethe wrote, "Hell begins the day God grants you the vision to see all that you could have done, should have done, and would have done, but did not do."

NO ONE IS TOO LOST

When I was a youth pastor, many of our students were passionate about sharing Jesus everywhere they went. I was so proud of them. One day, a high school student was walking his pit bull past the church when one of the students stopped and asked if he would come to youth group that night. He did. And, so did his pit bull.

To say he was an unbeliever is an understatement. Let's just say his character and life were not in alignment with a follower of Christ. If there were a way to measure one's degree of distance from God, he would be on the furthest end of the scale. But, to his credit, he came to church … with his pit bull. They would arrive when service began, would stand at the back throughout the whole service, and immediately leave when it was over.

We all would share the gospel with him during the greeting times in the service, even though, with no facial expression, he would say, "I'm atheist, leave me alone. I am not interested."

That's about all the conversation we could get out of this student. The weeks turned into months. The routine stayed the same. And so did our persistent love and witness to him.

One day, he arrived with no pit bull. Midway through the service, I opened the stage for testimonies. Slowly from the back of the room, this student came forward. With everyone on the edge of their seats he said, "I'm now a follower of Jesus. Thanks for loving me and telling me the good news of Jesus."

We had a party that night in youth group and the celebration surely carried on in heaven![1] He was back with his pit bull the rest of the year until he graduated.

I learned that no one is too lost to be reached. No matter what the outward appearance looks like, sow the gospel and watch what God can do.

What friend, acquaintance, relative, or coworker of yours seems too distant from God? Are they so far from God that they cannot be reached? Think again!

Half the New Testament was written by Paul. But, before his name was changed to Paul, his name was Saul. Paul tells Timothy that before he met Jesus, as written about in Acts, he was a, "blasphemer, a persecutor and a violent man."[2] Paul hated God and followers of Christ.

He was a blasphemer. This isn't just talking about one who speaks negatively towards God; which Paul did. But it is used to mean nasty, shameful, and ugly speech with the intention to humiliate someone else. A persecutor. Persecutor in this verse is the Greek word, *dioko*. It is the very word used to depict a hunter. Paul aggressively pursued believers to capture or kill them like a relentless hunter tracking the scent of an animal. And, a violent man.

In a second, God turned Saul to Paul. In a night, God turned an atheist student into a believer. And, any day, God can turn anyone you have labeled "too lost" to a devout follower of Christ.

Ecclesiastes 9:4 says, "Anyone who is among the living has hope —even a live dog is better off than a dead lion!"

What is the indicator to know whether or not someone still has hope in being saved? If they are alive, there's hope. The gospel can reach to the lowest valley and pull out anyone. Who knows if God has placed them in your life because he trusts that you will be the one to Go & Tell them about him!

SEEING EYES AND HEARING EARS

When it comes to sharing our faith, most of us are much like the Pharisees. No, not that we are hypocrites. But rather that we "have eyes but we don't see, and ears but we don't hear." Jesus told them that all they had to do was ask him and he would give them "eyes that see and ears that hear."[3] He then looks at his disciples and says, "But blessed are your eyes because they see, and your ears because they hear."[4]

We need seeing eyes and hearing ears.

Remember when Jesus told the disciples that the harvest was ripe? Before that, he says this:

> "I tell you, open your eyes and look at the fields! They are ripe for harvest." — John 4:35

Many of us walk through life blindly asking God to use us to share his gospel. When, in reality, we just need to open our eyes and look. Most likely, the answer is right in front of you.

When Abraham sent Hagar and Ishmael away, they wandered through the desert. After several days with no water, Hagar and Ishmael sat under a bush crying. Dehydration was setting in, and death was moments away. But, God opened Hagar's eyes and she saw a well of water. She got water, and the two lived. The water was right in front of them the whole time.

Take a moment and ask the Holy Spirit to give you eyes to see and ears to hear. We do need them to understand the things of God, but we also need them to see the lost around us and to hear their desperate cry for life. They are right in front of you as you read this book. And, you are the well with the water of life right in front of their dire situation.

There's a multitude that God has placed around you that, whether they know it or not, are desperate for you to share the gospel with them. You are alive today and living right where you are for a reason; to find God and to lead others to him.

This is your moment to run.

What will you do with it?

Esther knew it was her time, and many were saved.

Anselm knew it as his time, and he faithfully proclaimed the good news.

And, those in the High Middle Ages understood and the Gospel Baton continued to another century.

13

THE 1100s–DO GOOD
But … I Don't Know Where to Begin

"God divided the hand into fingers so that money could slip through." — Martin Luther

The Gospel Baton entered the height of the middle ages. The twelfth century was a time of social, political, and economic transformation. The first two universities were established in Paris and Oxford. The windmill was invented in England, paper began to be manufactured in Spain, and the magnetic compass was first used for navigation. Most importantly, faithful followers of Christ pointed people to the hope of the gospel no matter the consequences.

Men like Arnold, an abbot at Brescia, stood up for the truth of the gospel and were executed by fire as a result. Bernard of Clairvaux, during a time of war and sorrow, would make a decision as a young man to wholeheartedly follow Christ, which in turn would lead to many men and women who, too, would unswervingly follow Christ. And then there's Waldo.

In 1160, a wealthy unbeliever named Peter Waldo lived in Lyons, France. One day, Peter heard a French song of a wealthy youth who left his riches to follow Christ. Deeply moved by the song, Peter hired two priests to translate portions of the Bible for him to read. It didn't take long for the gospel of Jesus to radically impact Waldo, who became a devout follower of Christ. Peter saw himself as the foolish rich man who was busy laying up treasures on Earth, becoming truly poor, instead of

One of the easiest starting points is just using what you have to meet the needs of those around you.

being rich towards God. He knew he could not serve both God and money.

Although it is not wrong to have money as a believer, it is important that money doesn't have you. Peter used his money to impact the kingdom and advance the good news he had discovered. After setting some money aside for his wife and two daughters, Peter began giving his money away to help the poor and those in need.[1] Not only did his generosity impact people's physical lives, but it opened up their hearts to hear the gospel. It was not long before the masses were drawn to Peter. Many were not content with mere existence, but desired to really live as disciples of Christ and make a difference in their world for him. These new believers became known around Lyons as Waldensians due to the impact the gospel had on them through the life of Peter Waldo.

These Waldensians would Go & Tell the gospel beyond Lyons to Lombardy, Austria and Germany before spreading out around the world. Going out two-by-two, the Waldensians visited the marketplaces and everyone in their cosmos, preaching the gospel to the common people.

It's said that by the end of the century there was hardly a country that had not been reached with the gospel through the Waldenses. Waldo's leading principle was this: What Christ commanded must be done and his word must be supreme. Many historians consider Peter Waldo one of the four church "reformers before the Reformation."[2] His life and example of generosity launched an evangelistic movement that boosted the gospel around the world.

IF YOU'VE GOT CABBAGE, GIVE IT!

In 2019, our ministry was doing evangelistic outreaches in villages across southern Ukraine. We were asking God to give us favor in sharing his gospel in one of these small villages when he reminded us of a local gift from a farmer. A farm in the region had an abundance of cabbage and instead of trashing the leftovers, he gave our ministry one ton of cabbage. Literally, one full ton of cabbage.

An idea came to one of our staff evangelists to give three hundred kilograms of the cabbage to the local hospital. This gift allowed us to preach the gospel in the hospital where six people committed their lives to Christ while many others received prayer for healing.

I often hear believers say that they would love to share the gospel, but they don't know where to begin. I've found that one of the easiest starting points is just using what you have to meet the needs of those around you. The need may be food. It may be time. And, many times it may be money. Look what God has given you and then look to see who needs what you have.

Not only do these resources meet an immediate need but they can also open hearts to hear about the great giver, Jesus Christ.

JESUS THE PHILANTHROPIST

Peter, the one who spent the most time with Jesus, gives us a unique insight we often miss in the narrative of the four Gospels. In Acts 10, Peter has a conversation with a man named Cornelius and his friends. As he is talking about Jesus he reminds them how,

> *"God anointed Jesus of Nazareth with the Holy Spirit and power, and how he went around doing good and healing all who were under the power of the devil, because God was with him." — Acts 10:38*

I've often read this verse through the lens of Jesus's power in regards to the advancement of his gospel And, in one way, that's right. Jesus heals and he resurrects the spiritually dead. He did then. He does now. That's all part of the good news. I also like this verse because it reminds us that the Holy Spirit was with Jesus to perform the supernatural. As mentioned in Chapter Two, we also must have the Holy Spirit living in us if we want to be fruitful.

But, this isn't all Jesus did. Look at this verse again.

Peters tells Cornelius and his friends that Jesus also, "went about doing good." This is fascinating because the words, "doing good" are one word in Greek, *euergeteo*. In those days, an *euergeteo* was a philanthropist, one who financially supported charitable works, or a person who used his resources to meet the needs of others. Peter was revealing to us that one way Jesus was strategic in sharing the gospel was by being a great philanthropist.

To be more like Jesus doesn't mean we only walk in love and in the supernatural, it means we are givers.

To be more like Jesus doesn't mean we only walk in love and in the supernatural, it means we are givers. We make it a lifestyle to use the resources and finances available to us to advance his kingdom and bring physical relief to those in need. This may look like buying groceries for a neighbor who is going through a rough time, giving clothes to a charitable organization, or financially partnering with ministries and churches that use those resources to help those you may not physically be able to reach yourself.

When we were given a literal ton of cabbage by a local farmer in Ukraine, we couldn't wait to *euergeteo* with it. We knew it has always been in the nature of God to look after the wellbeing of his people on earth while also giving them hope for eternity. And, he uses us to do this.

We've all been the recipient of God's loving kindness in a tangible way. As a believer, you received the greatest gift in Jesus, when God "gave" him to us.³ And, you most likely also know what it is like to receive a physical blessing as well.

When Tanja and I began to feel the reality that God was calling us to Europe for ministry, we simply didn't have the funds to go. We knew we needed around fifty thousand dollars. We reminded the Lord that if he wanted us to go, he would need to use someone to meet the financial need to make it happen.

A couple weeks later, we were invited to dinner with some of our closest friends, who are family to us. We hadn't shared with them the financial need we had or the amount. But at dinner, they surprised us with two checks that totaled fifty-five thousand dollars! We were shocked. That is a lot of money.

After giving tithes on the money we had forty-nine thousand five hundred dollars left. Their *euergeteo* was the exact amount we needed to get to Switzerland.

We moved to Europe. And, many people in Europe have heard the gospel as a result.

SOCIAL WORKER OR GOSPEL DELIVERER?

Jesus used philanthropy to share his message; but he wasn't solely a philanthropist. Jesus did not come to the world to feed the hungry or give to the poor. No, he came to seek and to save that which was lost. When it came to giving a resource to an unbeliever, generosity was a tool Jesus used to reach their hearts and came as an overflow from the love he had for them. Helping an unbeliever is very important.

Richard Wurmbrand said, "Churches assert their wish to save men from a future hell. Then they should prove their love toward men by helping save the world from today's hell of illiteracy, hunger, misery, tyranny, exploitation, and war."

> *If we only give but never preach, we are sending people to hell on a full stomach and a mouth of clean water.*

But it is even more important that we share the gospel to those in need. Meeting physical needs is only a temporary relief. When the crowds came to Jesus, in love he fed them. But, he also preached to them.

As followers of Christ, we are to do the same. We give. But, we also preach. If we only give but never preach, we are sending people to hell on a full stomach and a mouth of clean water.

During one of my speaking engagements in Switzerland, I looked on the wall of the church in Geneva and saw a plaque dedicated to Henri Dunant. This was the church Dunant attended in the late 1800s. It was here where Dunant founded the Red Cross and the Young Men's Christian Association (YMCA). As much good as the Red Cross and the YMCA have done for humanity since they were founded, I couldn't help but think that when social movements stop preaching while doing their humanitarian projects they face the danger of losing the Church's mission altogether.

WHO'S YOUR KING?

Many people remind me of the banks in Switzerland. Not particularly because they are loaded with money but rather because when it comes to the topic of money, they are sealed shut. Money is a topic that you simply don't talk about. However, when it comes to evangelism, money is a topic that has to be discussed.

Jesus talked about money more than he spoke about faith and prayer, combined. Of the forty parables of Jesus in the four Gospels, he used money to teach spiritual truths in eleven of them. Jesus uses money as a tool to reveal our true priorities. People's budgets can often be considered as a theological document. It indicates who or what we worship.

Martin Luther said, "Every man needs two conversions. The first is his heart, the second is his wallet."

At the center of Christianity lies the premise that God created everything, and it all belongs to him. We are only stewards of his resources.

Martin Luther said, "Every man needs two conversions. The first is his heart, the second is his wallet."

It's not wrong to be rich, but it is wrong to think it is all for your pleasure only.

In English, we often use the word currency as a substitution for "money." Why? Maybe because it is supposed to flow like a current. Let it flow, and watch God use you to advance his kingdom in your cosmos.

WHERE'S WALDO?

Our greatest fear as a disciple of Christ should not be of failure, but in succeeding at things in life that have no eternal significance. Once Peter Waldo understood he was to steward the resources God had given him for eternal purposes and not just for his own pleasure, God was able to use him as a significant runner of the gospel in the middle ages.

Peter is no longer here. God is looking for Waldos to use today. When he looks at where you are, will he see a Waldo or just another person in the crowd more interested in increasing your bank account more than impacting as many people with the gospel as possible?

Can I ask you a tough question? Are you greedy or are you generous? Greed is a condition of the heart and not the value in a bank account. It is ok if you are wealthy as long as you are also a good steward and generous with what God has given you for the advancement of the gospel. I have many friends that are both financially well off and passionate followers of Jesus. They are wealthy because they are good stewards of the resources God has given them. But to have money and no generosity is a sad reality for many people.

Our greatest fear as a disciple of Christ should not be of failure, but in succeeding at things in life that have no eternal significance.

Do you remember what Simon Peter said to the crippled beggar at the temple gate in Acts 3? "I have no silver and gold but what I do have I give you. In the name of Jesus, rise and walk." I wonder why Peter had no money. Maybe he was just short on money that morning. Or, perhaps, he had no money at all because he was using what he had for the advancement of the kingdom.

Either way, I find something interesting. For many believers in first world countries, we can no longer say, "I have no money" but we also can't say, "rise up and walk." Is it possible that miracles and greed can't work together in a believer's life?

God wants us to be rich in what matters for eternity. He wants us to walk in the supernatural, representing Jesus on this earth. Oftentimes, we get our eyes off what matters most and focus on our earthly success. We store up our savings, but we forget the words of Jesus,

> *"You can never out-give God."*

> "Do not store up for yourselves treasures on earth, where moths and rust destroy, and where thieves break in and steal. But store up for yourselves treasures in heaven, where moths and rust do not destroy, and where thieves do not break in and steal. For where your treasure is, there your heart will be also." — Matthew 6:19–21 (ESV)

Whether you have money or no money is not the point. What matters is understanding that you can't take money with you to eternity. It is a resource to be used for the gospel.

You may not be able to take it with you, but you can send treasures ahead of you by being an *euergeteo* for the advancement of the gospel.

GOOD DEEDS

Jesus went around "doing good," and so should we. The resources he's given you can change a sinner to a saint. "Let your light shine before others so that they may see your good deeds and praise your Father in heaven." (Matthew 5:16)

What has God has given you to use for those in need around you? Perhaps the very resource you have may be the key to opening a hardened heart that has been closed to Jesus for many years.

Be a giver. As Billy Graham would often say, "You can never out-give God."

Paul tells the Corinthians that the God who, "gives seed to the sower and bread for food will also supply and increase your store of seed and will enlarge the harvest of your righteousness."[4] I've learned that as

I sow both financially and with resources into the lives of people and ministries, God often gives me more to sow. And, as a result, the harvest increases.

You've only got one chance at this thing called life. Learn the principle of giving now. It's an incredible starting place in sowing the gospel message to those around you.

You have what you have for a divine purpose. Give, and watch God's kingdom advance. Peter Waldo did, and the gospel moved on with great momentum into the thirteenth century.

14

THE 1200s-SIMPLICITY

But ... I Don't Know What to Say

"Educators take something simple and make it complicated. Communicators take something complicated and make it simple." — *John Maxwell*

The thirteenth century had begun. Marco Polo was exploring the world. William Wallace would lead Scotland. And the Mongol empire took root under its founder Genghis Khan. But it was the gospel message that continued to build momentum. Pious men and women, who dearly loved Christ and his word, brought the simplicity of the gospel as a counter to the confusion brought on by the culture, family pressures, and philosophers; no greater example than that of Thomas Aquinas.

Thomas Aquinas sat huddled on the cold prison cell of the family castle tower. Seventeen months had gone by since his parents had imprisoned him for his desire to follow Christ fulltime in the ministry as a Dominican monk. Yet, despite his family's attempts and persuasion, Thomas was unshakable in his resolve. He had a Christ to follow and the gospel to carry.

One night, his brothers arranged for an incredibly beautiful prostitute to visit Thomas in his cell, hoping that he would give in to temptation and change his mind. "With pains in my loins," Thomas would later write about the experience, he rejected her advances and chased her out of his cell with a burning log he took from the fireplace. By 1244, his family gave in and set him free to go to school to pursue his passion.[1]

Although the shy and lumbering Thomas would be nicknamed "the Dumb Ox" from his students, he was everything but dumb. His brilliant mind coupled with the simplicity of his approach to make the Bible comprehensible would lead a revolution in biblical thought and communication. He would help believers and nonbelievers distinguish between philosophy and theology, giving them simple labels like reason and revelation. He made sure that the average person could easily understand the gospel message and the truths found in the Scriptures. The writings of Thomas Aquinas would be a powerful influence on the church over the next eight hundred years serving as a tool to lead people to Christ.

Like Thomas, this century of believers understood that if their message was going to be heard over the philosophical movements of the day, they had to simplify the deep truths of God for all to understand.

They did, and the gospel continued to advance.

BRING IT!

It was early February in 2020. My team and I were feeding the poor in a park in Odessa, Ukraine. To say it was cold is an understatement. This park looked like the inside of a freezer. The trees, the grass, the benches, everything was frozen. Including me.

About fifty locals stood in line for their warm bowl of soup that we offered. The look on their faces when the warmth of the soup touched their frosted lips was priceless. But what came next was even better. My translator asked if the crowd would quickly gather around. The crowd was clearly ready to find warmth somewhere soon as the wind whistled through the park. But they obliged and gathered closely together in a circle.

My translator said a few words to them and then looked at me. "Bring the gospel. You've got two minutes before this crowd takes off because of the cold." I'm not usually good at speaking when I get put on the spot. But, not this time.

I shared the gospel, several of them repented of their sins, and we collected addresses for follow-up discipleship for the ones who were not homeless. All in a couple of minutes with a translator.

How? Because I was prepared. And, when you are called upon, you can be ready, too.

KISS

Have you ever heard of a marketing technique called KISS? When it comes to preaching the gospel, I've learned that utilizing this KISS principle is key. I first heard the KISS principle in a business development and communication class when I was working on my MBA. Let me give you the background.

This principle was started by the U.S. Navy in 1960 as a reminder when designing jet aircrafts. The engineer must remember to KISS, or "Keep It Simple, Stupid" with the final design. This means that a product must be designed to be repaired by an average mechanic in the field during combat conditions. Stupid refers to how stupid easy it is to fix the broken aircraft and not the intelligence of the designer or mechanic. It has to be simple.

So what does this have to do with sharing the gospel? You and I are in a spiritual war. Any time we are given the opportunity to share the gospel, we must remember, like those Navy engineers, to KISS. We have to keep our message simple for the average person to understand. The gospel should not be complicated.

Do you remember all the conversations of Jesus in the Bible? His messages were simple and clear, "Repent, for the kingdom of heaven is at hand"[2]; "From that time Jesus began to preach, saying, 'Repent, for the kingdom of heaven has come near'"[3]; "Jesus came into Galilee, proclaiming the gospel of God, and saying, 'The time is fulfilled, and the kingdom of God has come near; repent and believe in the gospel'"[4].

When Paul was closing his letter to the Colossians, guess what he asked them to pray for? You're right! Paul asked to be able to share a clear gospel presentation "which is how I ought to speak."[5]

The average person needs to clearly understand the gospel we are presenting to them. It's not the time for some deep theological discussion.

Did you know that the book of John is written to unbelievers, but the book of Romans is written to believers? What's interesting is that Romans tells us much about sin and the way to salvation. John, on the other hand, does not. It's simple and to the point. So should our gospel presentation to unbelievers.

Billy Sunday, one of the leading evangelists in the 1900s, saw tens of thousands of people come to faith through his preaching. He believed that was because he never burdened his audiences with theological

Preparation is the key to being ready to share the gospel.

lectures but tried to reduce Christianity to its lowest common denominator so the average person could understand the message.

Effective evangelists follow this one creed: Be simple.

Evangelist Reinhard Bonnke said of the many mass evangelistic messages he presented throughout Africa, "My sermons might never be homiletical masterpieces. They might never be printed in books and reproduced as examples of form and content. They were meant for the ear and the heart of the sinner, not for professors, or grade books, or classrooms. Before God, the only critic that counted was the man or woman who raised their hand and came forward to receive Jesus. All else counted as dung."[6]

PUT YOUR SHOES ON

In the Roman era, soldiers had to be ready for war at all times. An unprepared soldier was a dead soldier. One of the items that was important was their shoes. If the soldier had his shoes off, he did not expect to be attacked; wearing the shoes represented his readiness.

Remember Paul's letter to the Ephesians? He parallels a Roman soldier's armor with the Christian life. Look at what he says about the shoes: "Stand firm then ... with your feet fitted with the readiness that comes from the gospel of peace."[7] Paul told his disciple, Timothy, to "Preach the Word; be prepared in season and out of season."[8]

If Paul were alive today, he would tell us the same thing he told Timothy. Be ready at all times. We need to always live our lives with our gospel shoes on. You never know when the next opportunity to share the good news of Jesus will come. Expect it to be today at the store, at your office, around the dinner table, over social media, anywhere.

Evangelist Smith Wigglesworth often said, "I don't get ready; I stay ready." Are your shoes on? Are you ready to share the good news today?

NO MORE ANXIETY

When a soldier put his shoes on, it did not just mean he was at war, but rather that he was prepared for when, or if, it would suddenly come. Preparation is the key to being ready to share the gospel.

Does your heart feel like it's about to burst out of your chest when you are about to share the gospel with someone? Do dozens of excuses flood your mind why it is a bad idea?

When I was just starting out in ministry, I was always nervous to share my faith. My heart would pound, palms would sweat, and wildest excuses often held me back. When I was asked to speak at a church or an evangelistic event, I would nearly have a panic attack.

One evening, I asked evangelist Steve Hill of the Brownsville Revival if he ever got nervous when preaching. I was secretly hoping he would say yes to give me confidence. His response was the opposite. I was incredibly discouraged until he told me why. He said he didn't get nervous because he always came prepared.

Since that time, I've shared the gospel one-on-one and to large audiences. I've realized, like Steve told me, when I'm prepared, I'm not nervous. When I'm not prepared, I'm timid, afraid, and insecure. Preparation removes these obstacles. 1 Peter 3:15 says that we should be ready to give everyone an answer for the hope that we have.

Preparation includes prayer, partnership with the Holy Spirit, knowing the word, and being ready to clearly present the gospel.

BUT I DON'T KNOW HOW

One of the biggest excuses I hear from believers on why they don't evangelize is that they don't know what to say. I get it. I've been there myself. However, I've learned that you have to stay focused on the good news, and not allow the many conversational detours to distract you. Remember, as we saw in Chapter One, that the overall message of the good news is that Jesus has won! He is the king. This reality has three important pieces:

1. *Something happened.* Our world's ultimate king has come. Jesus' life, death, and resurrection won the battle over evil. Creation is being restored and the saving of man from evil or eternal destruction has begun.
2. *Something is happening as a result.* People are called to repent of evil, turn and follow Jesus.
3. *Something will happen in the future.* Jesus is coming again. And, with his return all of creation will be put right. Evil and those not

following Jesus will be put away forever. True followers of Jesus will live in eternal bliss both in this restored world and for all eternity. The final union of heaven on Earth will be established.

I've got exciting news for you. After spending time with the king and relying on the Holy Spirit to equip you, which is most important and a must, there's plenty of additional resources that are available to prepare you to share! There are tools to help simplify your thinking and bring clarity in what you are proclaiming. Over the years, I've used many of these.

Here are a few:

- The Romans Road: This is sort of a road map of salvation from selected verses out of Romans. The goal is to start showing the bad news as described in Romans, "all have sinned and fallen short of the glory of God" (3:23) and "the cost of sin is death." (6:23) Then it moves into the good news "But God demonstrates his own love for us in this: While we were still sinners, Christ died for us." (5:8) Finally, it ends with a decision. "If you declare with your mouth, 'Jesus is Lord,' and believe in your heart that God raised him from the dead, you will be saved. For it is with your heart that you believe and are justified, and it is with your mouth that you profess your faith and are saved." (10:9-10)

- The ABCs: Reinhard Bonnke said it's critical to stick to the ABCs of the Bible for salvation. LifeWay's Vacation Bible School designates the ABCs for evangelism as: A for Admit to God that you are a sinner, B for Believe in Jesus as God's Son, C for Confess your faith in Jesus Christ as Savior and Lord.

- The Cross Bridge: Billy Graham used the cross as a bridge over a deep chasm separating God and man. On the man's side is sin and death and on the God side is God and the gift of eternal life. The bridge linking the two is the cross. The verse that goes with this illustration is also Romans 6:23, mentioned above.

- The Four: Cru, a ministry in Switzerland, created this tool. It uses four symbols—a heart (for God's love), division symbol (sin has broken us and divided us from God), cross (Jesus defeated evil), and question mark (will you follow Jesus?)—printed on handheld signs to represent four points of the gospel in a clear and easy-to-remember way. I've seen this used often in villages throughout Eastern Europe. Not only does showing these four symbols on cards help in staying focused on the message but also gives a visual for those they are communicating the gospel to.

These are just a few of the many tools created over the years that can aid you in sharing the gospel. Find a strategy that fits your communication and personality the best. Together with the Holy Spirit, these tools should prepare you to clearly communicate the gospel.

I was on a plane from Zürich to Dublin. There was an elderly Swiss gentleman sitting next to me. I had my earbuds in most of the flight, listening to worship music. As we neared the end of the flight, I suddenly felt the Holy Spirit tell me to share the gospel with this gentleman. Excuses about why this was not a good time to share flooded my mind. So, I turned the volume of my worship music up a bit more to make me feel better. Again, it was clear that the Holy Spirit wanted me to share. I had to share. I knew the Holy Spirit was with me and that it was my time to be God's spokesman.

Prepared with a simple tool called The Three Spiritual Laws I had memorized a few days earlier to help explain the victory of Jesus' life, death and resurrection, I was ready. These three simple steps progress from how sin broke the world separating us from God, to how our sin ultimately sends us to hell, then brings the good news. Jesus won. He came to Earth, died, and rose again to restore what was broken so we can have hope for today and all eternity.

Near the end of the flight, I greeted the man, we exchanged names and within a few minutes we were talking about a political scandal that was in the news that morning. The pilot announced on the loudspeaker that we had begun our descent. Now was the time. I was ready to share the gospel.

"Sir, as we've talked it's obvious that our world is pretty messed up, huh?" I asked.

"Very!"

"As a matter of fact, we are all pretty messed up."

The man slowly nodded.

"Is there any hope for mankind?" I questioned.

"I really don't think so," he whispered back.

"Sir, I've got something important to tell you. Our sin is what has broken the world. It has separated us from God and ultimately sends us to hell. This is terribly bad news."

The man just stared at me. No response. I could tell his mind was turning and his heart was pounding.

"But, I have good news. This is why Jesus came." The Holy Spirit took over and filled my mouth with words from heaven for that man at that moment.

As the wheels hit the runway, I finished sharing this good news of Jesus to him. I asked if he'd like to know this Jesus I was speaking about. He did.

As we unbuckled our seatbelts, He looked me in the eyes and asked, "When we get back to Zürich, will you come to my house and tell me more about your Jesus?"

The gospel was proclaimed with simplicity.

A life was changed.

The plane landed.

And, so did I.

LAND THE PLANE

Conversations are like a plane in flight. There's progress. The conversation is going somewhere. There's a destination in the forecast. Landing the plane is the final touchdown of the conversation. It is the closing sentences wrapping up what has been discussed. When it comes to the gospel message, this means giving someone a chance to respond if the Holy Spirit is drawing that individual to repent of their sins and follow Christ. It's the point of decision. And, it's easy to do.

As the conversation is wrapping up, you can end by asking a straightforward question like, "Do you need to get right with God?", "Would you like to repent of your sins?", "Would you like to follow this King?", "What is keeping you from surrendering your life to Jesus?" or "Can I pray with you right now?"

You will be surprised how many people are not only prepared to hear the gospel, but are also ready to begin following Jesus immediately. Always be prepared to reap a harvest from the seeds you sow and the countless seeds sown in the individual prior to you meeting them. This could be their day of salvation.

D.L. Moody told a story when he once shared the gospel at his church in Chicago. Instead of asking people if they'd like to make a decision to follow Christ, he told them to go home and think about what they heard. Before they could gather the following Sunday, the infamous Chicago fire of 1871 blazed through the city that week. Over seventeen thousand buildings were destroyed and many of those very people lost their lives before they made a decision to follow Christ.

You will be surprised how many people are not only prepared to hear the gospel, but are also ready to begin following Jesus immediately.

From that day on, Moody made a commitment to never share the gospel without giving someone an opportunity for a decision to follow Christ. He was reminded of the urgency of the simple, but powerful message he was sharing.

Communicating a clear message is our responsibility in proclaiming the gospel. Jesus set the example for the early believers. Thomas Aquinas and the Middle Ages church followed. And, whether sharing the good news in front of millions of people like Reinhard Bonnke or one-on-one with a neighbor, the gospel continues on today with the simple ABCs of salvation.

A young reporter asked Winston Churchill how he could be a great communicator like Churchill. "When speaking," Churchill responded, "be short, be sincere, and be seated."

I would add one more when you are sharing the gospel: Be simple.

15

THE 1300s–NOT-SO POLITICALLY CORRECT
But … I Don't Want to Offend Anyone

"I want to know one thing—the way to heaven. God Himself has condescended to teach the way...He hath written it down in a Book! O give me that Book! At any price, give me that Book of God!" — *John Wesley*

The gospel was making its way around the world. But, the fourteenth century arrived with a major hurdle. The Black Death (a bubonic plague) would wipe out one third of Europe, while the Hundred Years' War between England and France would devastate the remaining citizens of the two countries. The Friuli earthquake of 1348 in Northern Italy would rock the land. Many people thought that the biblical apocalypse had arrived. But, the greatest threat to the gospel being proclaimed throughout the whole world came not from outside the Church walls but within.

In the centuries leading up to the thirteen hundreds, many church leaders gradually began to think this message of the gospel was about them; what they could get from it. Fame, money, and corruption had slyly entered the Church.

These corrupt leaders proclaimed that salvation could be bought or earned. One could pay the "church" a sum of money to ransom themselves or a loved one from hell. Since the Bible was not available in the modern language, only the church leaders who knew the language could both read it and translate it to the people. As a result, these immoral church leaders could promote their false gospel and get rich and famous in return.

The gospel is for all mankind.

Gold flowed into the church by sinners desperate to buy their way out of hell. The church gained earthly riches, but it lost its heavenly message. Something had to be done.

The previous thousand years of believers had not given their lives for the gospel only to see it diluted by false leaders who wanted to financially benefit off its popularity; or to become admired themselves. Yet, in one of the darkest periods of the gospel's advancement, there was a remnant of believers who would shine brightly with the true gospel message. One of those men would be nicknamed the "Morning Star of the Reformation."

His name was John Wycliff.

Born in Yorkshire, England in 1329, Wycliff was a quiet, yet passionate man. He earned his doctorate in theology at the University of Oxford and later taught at the school. He lived peacefully at the university and slowly built a reputation as one of the leading philosophers and th;eologians of his time. But, as his faith matured, he came to detest the errors and abuses by the other church leaders. Wycliff wasn't interested in stirring up controversy or debates. However, the true gospel had to be known.

Against popular culture, Wycliff began to make radical proclamations that the Bible was the ultimate authority and that Jesus' message for eternal life was a free gift. The heart of the gospel was more valuable to him than trying to be politically correct. The gospel is for all mankind.

"Forasmuch as the Bible contains Christ, that is all that is necessary for salvation, it is necessary for all men, not for priests alone," he would write to the people.

In what was politically incorrect at the time, Wycliff set his heart and energy on the immense task of translating the Bible from Latin into English so that the common man could read the good news for themselves. His task threatened the lucrative business of these corrupt leaders and many in his community. The church leaders attacked him with vehemence, stripped him of his position, and set up groups of priests who were formed to harass him or those who sought to aid him in translating the Bible.

Wycliff remained undaunted.

He had a message that needed to be heard. And, in 1382, his many years of perseverance became a reality. The Bible was translated to the common language and available for the ordinary person to read. The gospel would rapidly pick up its pace once again as it circulated the continent through traveling evangelists sent out by John Wycliff.

Wycliff was convinced that the Bible should be the rule of life, and he imparted this truth to his traveling evangelists. Two by two, believers traveled throughout the land illegally distributing the precious new English Bible. As they entered the towns, they proclaimed the gospel and gave out pages from these handwritten Bibles.

Their enemies nicknamed them Lollards, a term from a word meaning "to mumble." It referred to their practice of reciting Bible verses and saying prayers. Though many people were offended, it didn't stop them. These mumblers took the gospel across Europe. One panic-stricken observer claimed that, "every second man" he met was a Lollard.[1] These fourteenth century believers carried the Bible in their hands and the gospel on their tongues. Nothing could stop them or their message.

Thirty one years after Wycliff's death, the church leaders were still upset at his work. In order to silence the Lollards, these corrupt leaders dug up Wycliff's body and burned his bones in public ridicule. They also persecuted the Lollards in an effort to inhibit others from reading the gospel. But, this only inspired the Lollards and other believers to share even more. The Bible, and specifically the gospel of Jesus, had touched the hearts of so many people. The institutional church was losing wealth, but the kingdom was growing exponentially around the world during this time.

A HOUSE ON FIRE

The gospel of Jesus is offensive. There, I said it. Share it, and watch how people respond. A few of the remarks I've heard: "You're so old school," "Holier than thou," "Stop living in the past," "Get out of here." If getting called a name, being laughed at, or losing your job is all that happens to you, rejoice. We've seen how countless other Christians gave their lives in order for the gospel to be heard. Jesus was laughed at[2] and persecuted. Don't be surprised if it happens to you, too.

But don't let that stop you from sharing. The reality is they just don't understand.

Imagine walking down your street at night. You look over and see a beautiful two-story home. The window shades are opened. Inside, a family of five along with their friends are all sitting down at a large table having a candlelight dinner. The atmosphere is cozy, kids are laughing, and the adults are in a deep conversation. Then you notice something.

As you look at the first floor you notice the entire kitchen is on fire. The fire is rapidly spreading to the living room. Soon, the stairs and the entire second floor will be in flames. The family and friends don't know

You may not be able to bring everyone to Jesus, but you can bring Jesus to everyone.

of the life-threatening situation they are in since the upstairs door is closed and they have no smoke alarm in the house. What do you do?

You would do everything possible to rescue them. It is better to offend them by messing up their cute dinner than it is to ignore the situation because you don't want to bother them. If it's that way in a physical situation, how much more in a spiritual sense where one's entire eternal destiny is on the line? The gospel is a firehose, a warning signal, a lifeline to those who are on the verge of an eternal, consuming fire.

Jude 1:23 says for us to, "save others by snatching them out of the fire."

The Greek word used for "snatching" is *harpadzo*. This word conveys, not a gentle knock on a door of the house on fire so as not to offend someone, but rather an aggressive attempt of rescuing one from a dangerous situation. One Greek expositor says this word portrays the idea of being "grabbed by the back of the neck and snatched out of danger, just in the nick of time." This same word is used in Colossians 1:13 when Paul writes, "For God has *harpadzo* us from the power of darkness and brought us into the kingdom of the Son he loves."

Sharing the gospel is an urgent matter. We need to do everything within our power to snatch people out of the fire. You may not be able to bring everyone to Jesus, but you can bring Jesus to everyone. Without Christ, everyone's house is on fire. But, like the family, it just hasn't become a reality to them yet. We have to rescue them before it does.

Even if they get offended.

ALL ROADS LEAD TO GOD

Tanja and I had just moved into a new neighborhood and had invited our neighbors, Fahad and Salma³, over for coffee to get to know them. As the conversation developed, Fahad brought up religion. Oh, boy. It was clear that Fahad was a devout Muslim through some of his comments, and he could tell we were Christians by our responses. Strangely, Fahad blurted out, "Well, Shawn, aren't you glad that all roads lead to God. You believe that, right?"

Always be on the alert to share the gospel. Most of the conversations I have with others about the gospel happens in ordinary discussions like this one. Neutrality or being politically correct is usually not an option in the kingdom. I desperately did not want to offend my neighbor. Afterall, we were the new family on the street.

1 Thessalonians 2:4 says, "We speak as men approved by God to be entrusted with the gospel. We are not trying to please man but God, who tests our hearts."

God had entrusted me with the gospel, and his approval was more important than Fahad's.

We are not to be God's editors; we are to be his messengers.

"Yes, Fahad, all roads do lead to God." I responded. Fahad smiled in approval as I took a pause. "The Bible says that one day we will all stand before God. But there's only one road that leads to heaven, and it's through faith in Jesus Christ." I took a few minutes quoting scripture verses to explain the ABCs of the gospel.

Fahad got it. He understood.

We became close friends. Although he never said a prayer with me for salvation, every time we met, he would ask me several questions about Jesus and he even began attending a local church. I saw the power of the Word of God changing him as the months went on. When it comes to evangelism and the Bible, being politically correct is not an option. You've got to tell the truth.

HIDE BEHIND THE WORD

We are not to be God's editors; we are to be his messengers. We share his word, not our opinions. Nor do we change scriptures that aren't in popular opinion at the time.

The gospel flies on the wings of grace and truth. We must show the grace of Jesus in our conversations, but we can't walk away from the truth found in the Bible. Otherwise, the gospel crashes before it can fly into the hearts of the unbelievers.

The scriptures must rule in evangelism.

The gospel flies on the wings of grace and truth.

Billy Graham is remembered in many ways. He was the spiritual counsel for many presidents and world leaders. He hosted some of the largest evangelistic events in world history. He lived a life of impeccable character.

While all these aspects are true, the simple authoritative phrase he used thousands of times may be his greatest legacy of all—"The Bible says." Graham's message was never his message. Jesus won. He is the king. We are sinners. Jesus forgives. We get to join his kingdom for eternity. And, we tell others this good news.

Do you see what Billy Graham was doing? He was hiding behind the Bible when evangelizing. These weren't his opinions or thoughts. His goal wasn't to protest the culture but to preach the gospel. He knew that he was simply the messenger of God's word—a spokesman for the king. He effectively ran with the Gospel Baton in hand simply by quoting God's word. You and I need to be like Billy Graham. We must use scriptures and not our opinions. We must use it always. And, we must use all of it. The written word of God, spoken to unbelievers, has all the power necessary for communicating the gospel.

> *"For I am not ashamed of the gospel, because it is the power of God that brings salvation to everyone who believes: first to the Jew, then to the Gentile. For in the gospel the righteousness of God is revealed—a righteousness that is by faith from first to last, just as it is written: "The righteous will live by faith."* — Romans 1:16–17

RHEMA WORD VS WRITTEN WORD

I've picked something up in my time evangelizing. When I use Scripture verses, God will oftentimes speak through me with a personal word from the Bible for the individual or audience. Have you noticed this too?

The Bible uses two different Greek words to refer to the Word of God. One of those is *lógos* and the other is *rhema*. Be ready to use both.

Logos is the written word of God. The Bible.

> "*The farmer sows the* **logos**." — *Mark 4:14*

> "*So the* **logos** *of God spread. The number of disciples in Jerusalem increased rapidly, and a large number of priests became obedient to the faith.*" — *Acts 6:7*

Rhema refers to the instant, personal speaking of God to a specific person or audience for a specific situation from the *logos*. The *logos* is like an ocean of water. The *rhema* is like a cup of water from the ocean. It's specific. Let's look at these couple of verses:

> "*Immediately the rooster crowed the second time. Then Peter remembered the* **rhema** *Jesus had spoken to him: 'Before the rooster crows twice you will disown me three times.' And he broke down and wept.*" — *Mark 14:72*

> *Jesus said, "The* **rhema** *I have spoken to you—they are full of the Spirit and life.*" — *John 6:63*

When we speak the *logos*, it's very possible that God will use you to bring a *rhema* word. And the results can change a city. This happened in 1669 in Frankfurt, Germany.

Every year, Philipp Spener preached the gospel to his small congregation. He sowed many seeds but wasn't seeing much result. Then it happened. As he shared the *logos*, God used a specific text from the Sermon on the Mount as a *rhema* word for the people. That Sunday, a great revival began at his church. Many people were converted and took the gospel around Frankfurt.[4]

Spener started a Bible study in his home with some of the new converts. He began recommending local churches to have Bible study groups in their church where the simplicity of the gospel could be heard and taught. Those who would turn from a life of sin to following Christ, Spener would say they were "converted." To this day, many people still recall the moment they became a follower of Jesus as their conversion testimony or story.

C.O.P.

Here's a simple tip to get your evangelistic motor running. Give a Bible to an unbeliever. This is a great jump start in evangelism. In 1899, three traveling salesmen formed an organization to unite other salesmen in evangelism, and Gideon International was born. They strategically placed Bibles in areas where people, who may have never read the gospel, could have access to it. Inside each Bible were multiple translations of John 3:16. They would get other salesmen in on the opportunity to spread the gospel by helping distribute the Bibles to hotels. Help poured in by ordinary people who wanted the gospel available for travelers.[5]

For over one hundred years, almost every hotel room in America had a Gideon Bible. Only eternity knows how many travelers read the goods news as they stumbled upon one of the Gideon Bibles in their hotel room. You may have been one of them!

When I was twenty one, I was a youth pastor at a small church outside of the Dallas/Fort Worth metroplex. We started the Reality youth group with only four students. After several months, the youth ministry had only a dozen students. I felt like a complete failure. One evening, I asked God how I could be a better spokesman for him in the small town.

I clearly heard his leading, "Give everyone in the neighborhood a Bible."

"But, God. Really?" I grumbled. "Surely there was a more modern, creative way to grow."

But, I obeyed.

We started the Community Outreach Program (c.o.p.). One of the youth leaders painted c.o.p. really big on a wall in our small youth group classroom. We bought hundreds of Bibles and mapped out the neighborhood. Each Saturday, we gathered as a youth ministry and went house-to-house knocking on doors, giving away Bibles, sharing the gospel, and asking the neighbors if they wanted prayer.

Each afternoon when we returned, the testimonies were plenty. Many neighbors were saved, healed, and delivered. Random strangers would give us money to buy more Bibles to reach more homes. Sure, we had our share of slammed doors in our faces, but we were so amazed at how God moves when we move. We were like the seventy-two disciples returning to Jesus after taking his message to villages, rejoicing in the power of his gospel. Our youth ministry may have been small, but the impact for eternity was immeasurable.

God moves when we move.

I look back on this simple form of evangelism and am reminded of the power the Bible plays in evangelism. Martin Luther once said, "the Bible is alive, it speaks to me; it has feet, it runs after men; it has hands, it lays hold of me."

The living Bible is necessary in proclaiming the true gospel of Jesus Christ. The Lollards took the newly translated Bible to the ordinary people across Europe. Many people were offended. It was not politically correct. But, as the Gospel Baton was passed to the next century, the good news of Jesus was quickly finding its way in living rooms around the world.

16

THE 1400s–THEOLOGICAL DIFFERENCES
But … I'm Not Good at Debating

"Do not try to make God's Word relevant. Its relevance is axiomatic … Do not defend God's Word, but testify to it … Trust in the Word. It is a ship loaded to the very limits of its capacity!" — *Dietrich Bonhoeffer*

The Renaissance dawned in the 1400s. Philosophy, science, and art were daily topics of conversation. Michelangelo and Leonardo da Vinci became household names. In France, the Hundred Years' War with England ended in victory, and Joan of Arc became a national hero.

Most importantly, the Bible had been translated into modern languages, making it a major force for the gospel. Common people could read for themselves what people in previous centuries only heard repeated to them. And, with the invention of the Gutenberg printing press in 1439, the Bible quickly became the most precious commodity in houses around the world.

In Italy, a young monk named Girolamo Savonarola earnestly studied the Bible every day. Born into nobility in 1452, Savonarola read Plato and Dante from an early age. His pursuit in philosophy led him to the Bible, and at twenty three years old, he joined the local monastery to find healing from the guilt of his sinful life and to surround himself with other believers.

Instead of finding a brotherhood of Christ with the monks, he found a church full of immorality and wickedness. Savonarola isolated himself and committed his time to prayer and studying the Bible. As he read the scriptures, he became convinced that his city needed to hear the true gospel. He focused his energy on proclaiming the basics of the gospel, rather than debating the church or unbelievers on theological issues.

Savonarola took the gospel to markets and squares in the upper-class Italian city of Florence. He preached God's pending judgement and the need for repentance.[1] Savonarola was not well-received initially—his messages against the sin of greed and love of money did not sit well with the wealthy citizens. However, over time, popular enthusiasm from large crowds that came to hear Savonarola preach eventually set him in as Florence's new ruler.

A spiritual awakening was taking place in Florence.

Savonarola led the city, still preaching the gospel everywhere he went. The citizens of Florence turned from a love of money to a love for Jesus. Bankers and traders returned what they had stolen from others. Instead of celebrating an annual evil festival in 1497, children gathered indecent books and pictures and made bonfires of them in the main square while singing worship songs to Jesus. And, many families had sons who would imitate the life of Savonarola by becoming a monk and preaching the gospel.[2]

Although leaders in the city and church attempted to debate with Savonarola on philosophical and theological issues of the time, he remained focused on the gospel and the need to live a holy life. Unfortunately, as we saw in the last chapter, the gospel is not always popular.

Eventually, his popularity began to fade. Corrupt leaders in the government and the Catholic church in Italy had had enough. When Savonarola would not compromise his message, he was imprisoned and severely tortured. On one day alone, Savonarola was lifted fourteen times several meters up in the air by ropes and dropped.[3] He kept preaching the gospel.

In between his days of being tortured, he wrote meditations on Psalm 32 and 51. In the following century, Martin Luther would publish Savonarola's writings. He called them, "a piece of evangelical testing and Christian piety." Savonarola would not be silenced by torture, and he was finally sentenced to death by burning.

But, by then, another city had heard the good news of Jesus.

I'LL TAKE THE BUS

Have you ever found yourself in a conversation with someone who doesn't feel the same as you about the gospel or hasn't experienced a relationship with God like yours? These believers or unbelievers are generally full of rebuttals, minor theological questions, and reasons they don't believe in God or don't believe in him the same way you do.

The first time this happened to me, I wasn't sure what to do.

At the Brownsville Revival, we would sing *We Will Ride* as somewhat of an anthem for how we wanted to take the gospel around the world with Jesus. In Revelation 19, we read how Jesus will return to earth riding a white horse. Our anthem took this story and put it to lyrics for the current time as if Jesus were riding across our land today on a white horse calling out for people to follow him or, as we would sing, "ride with him." At the chorus of the song, thousands of attendees at the service shouted, "And we say yes, Lord, we'll ride with you!"

As a nineteen-year-old man who loved Jesus, I didn't think much about the song theologically. Sure, it wasn't exactly biblically accurate, but the heart behind the words were pure. We will ride with you. We meant it, and surely the other believers in the community felt the same. Right?

The church printed red bumper stickers with bold, white words that read, "YES LORD, WE WILL RIDE WITH YOU!" and the name of the church, Brownsville Assemblies of God, smaller underneath. These stickers were on the backs of cars everywhere around Pensacola. We were proud to publicly display our commitment to Jesus and the gospel.

One day I pulled up to a stop light, and the car in front of me had one of these stickers on his bumper. But as I got closer, to my surprise, I was shocked at what I saw.

It was an exact copy of the Brownsville Revival sticker: red, bold white letters in the same fonts but with another church name written at the bottom. What shocked me was not the church name change but the lyrics change. Instead of "YES LORD, WE WILL RIDE WITH YOU!" the sticker said, "NO THANKS, I'LL TAKE THE BUS!"

He was essentially saying he didn't believe in the gifts of the Holy Spirit and disapproved of the way our church expressed our zeal for Christ in worship. I couldn't believe it. It felt like a snarky slap, a pointed jab over a theological difference. When the light turned green, I raced around the car and rolled down my window. "What's wrong with you? What's up with the bumper sticker?" I shouted. In a brief dialogue back and forth, we argued with each other. I would have continued arguing had it not been for the car in front of me stopping, almost causing me to crash. He raced on while I sat stuck behind the car.

I learned something that day that is critical to evangelism. Neither of us gained any ground. We just solidified a wedge between believers rather than uniting in fellowship. Debating, theological differences, and arguments are sure ways to wreck a conversation about the gospel.

WHAT COULD'VE BEEN THE STORY?

It's the unfortunate reality that many of the greatest revivals, where thousands of people were coming to Christ, have ended because of theological arguments instead of a simple declaration of the gospel.

China in the 1500s is a great example of this. If it hadn't been for squabbles over secondary theological issues, I wonder what the story of China could've been and what the country would be like today.

In 1583, a mathematician and missionary named Matthew Ricci was granted the rare permission of residency by the Ming Dynasty in the tightly closed country of China. He settled in the capital of Peking.

To gain favor with the emperor, Ricci gave him two clocks. When the clocks ran down, the Chinese experts had no way of knowing how to restart them. Ricci's skill in keeping them working gained him favor with the emperor, and he was allowed to remain in Peking even though it was clear he had a greater agenda than fixing clocks. Ricci, the missionary, was focused on telling others about Jesus. Within ten years, a church he started with new converts was running more than two thousand people.

Ricci died in 1610, and Adam Schall, his successor, carried on the work. He built public churches and gained religious freedom for believers throughout the empire in 1657. Schall would not accept that the Chinese were atheist. Rather, he saw them as searching for the God of the Bible. He taught that the "Lord of the Heaven" that many Chinese spoke of and revered, was the God of the Bible.

Through this unique method of sharing the good news, the Chinese people understood the gospel, and China was quickly becoming evangelized. By the time of Schall's death in 1666, there were almost 270,000 Christians in China.

Unfortunately, other missionaries moved into the area and debated the approach Schall used to preach the gospel. Instead of helping to disciple the new converts in areas they saw as theological errors growing in the local Chinese churches, these missionaries spent their time quarrelling with the local Chinese people. These missionaries would eventually report to Rome, where two popes debated on the method used by Schall. One pope approved, another disapproved, and by the end of the century, the whole mission in China fell apart, evangelism came to a halt, and these new believers eventually went back to where they came.[4]

What would China's story have been if the pursuit of evangelism remained as high of a priority as debating with believers and non-believers? What could be the story of China today? Instead of believers having to live out their faith in underground churches, maybe China would be a public light of the gospel for the rest of the world. Maybe China would be known as a country whose greatest export is not goods, but the good news.

> *Jesus said for us to Go & Tell, not Go & Debate.*

And, if this question can be raised about China, what about us?

What about your story?

What about mine?

I hope that at the end of our lives we don't look back and say, "what could've been the story" and instead say "wow, what a story!" Don't let arguments or trivial debates set back where God is setting up for people to come into the kingdom.

JUST OPEN THE CAGE

I have great news for you. You don't have to know all the rebuttals to theological questions to be effective in evangelism. Jesus said for us to Go & Tell, not Go & Debate. After sharing the gospel, God is big enough to take care of the rest when it comes to converting a soul.

Charles Spurgeon said it best, "The gospel is like a caged lion. It does not need to be defended; it just needs to be let out of its cage." It defends itself.

Remember what the writer of Hebrews said about the Word of God? It is ...

*"Living and active, sharper than any double-edged sword,
it penetrates even to dividing soul and spirit, joints and
marrow; it judges the thoughts and the attitudes of the
heart." — Hebrews 4:12*

Every time you share the gospel of Jesus, through the help of the Holy
Spirit, a living and active organism is implanted in the hearer's heart,
mind, and body. It is sharper than our debates could ever be.

It's been said that the gospel spreads the best, not through debates or
arguments but through wonder. Share the gospel, stand back, and watch
in wonder how a simple message can convert the most complicated sinner.

In 1932, Dietrich Bonhoeffer said, "A truly evangelical sermon must be
like offering a child a fine red apple or offering a thirsty man a cool glass
of water and then saying: 'Do you want it?'" In another conversation,
Bonhoeffer would say, "We must be able to speak about our faith so that
hands will be stretched out toward us faster than we can fill them … Do
not try to make God's Word relevant. Its relevance is axiomatic … Do
not defend God's Word, but testify to it … Trust in the Word. It is a ship
loaded to the very limits of its capacity!"[5]

PERIPHERAL QUESTIONS

I've learned that most of the time, people who want to debate are not
sincerely looking for answers to deep questions they have been wrestling
with in regard to God, eternity, or their existence. Instead, their goal is
simply to prove your message wrong or make you look foolish.

Remember the story of the woman at the well? I don't know if she was
exactly trying to prove Jesus' message wrong, but with the good news
standing right in front of her, she randomly begins a debate with Jesus.

"Our ancestors worshiped on this mountain," she said, "but you
Jews claim that the place where we must worship is in Jerusalem."[6] Yet,
Jesus refused to be sidetracked into a debate about religion. He briefly
responded to her inquiry and then dropped the best news she had ever
heard. He was the Messiah.

Evangelist Daniel Kolenda tells a story of a friend who was sharing
the gospel with a group of college students. One girl he met, who was
studying biology, became antagonistic towards the group. She started

pushing evolution to win a debate about the existence of God. Undaunted by her aggression, his friend responded, "Wow, you're smart. I wish God had given me a mind like yours. Can I ask you a question? Do you have any pain in your body?"

"Yes," she said. He prayed for her, and she was healed on the spot. He went on to lead that young woman to Jesus. At the end he asked, "Now can you explain to me what just happened?"

"No," she said.

If his friend had redirected his energy and focus to debate creationism versus evolution, the young college student would have probably made a fool of the group. Instead of trying to win a debate, he stayed focused, and in love was able to lead her to Christ.[7]

Have you ever been in a conversation about the gospel and had to purposefully keep the attention on the end goal of sowing the gospel and not be sucked into a debate?

In the past, when confronted with tough questions while evangelizing, I would often snap back with my thoughts. I would debate with strangers beside me while standing in lines, shopping at grocery stores, walking through a park, and even driving a car. I didn't have the wisdom to gently respond like the story above. My debates after sharing the gospel were a direct result of me not wanting to look crazy. Now, I try not to let these conversations sidetrack me. I've learned that most of the questions asked are questions that are answered in discipleship and spiritual growth, not in the initial step toward salvation.

But, what about when someone asks those hard questions and are sincerely inquiring? They are not looking for a debate, but curiously hopeful we have an answer. I have two things I often fall back on to avoid a debate but to also quickly answer their question like Jesus did for the woman at the well.

The lesser response I use is just to mention that I don't have all the answers. I remind them of a thought from British philosopher G.K. Chesterton.

Chesterton says that as an unbeliever, there are a bunch of peripheral joys through life; marriage, the birth of a child, a job promotion, etc. But there is an ultimate question; what is the meaning to life?

On the other hand, this is completely flipped with a believer. The ultimate question of life is answered. However, there are peripheral questions that may be left unanswered; why did my friend die, why is there suffering in the world, why did I lose that job?

I remind them that as a follower of Jesus, I have questions, but ultimate joy. My king is alive, and I will be with him for all eternity. However, an unbeliever will have many joys but live with an ultimate question. And, that ultimate question is only answered by the gospel of Jesus Christ.

My more frequent response to hard questions comes directly from the Bible. I just quote scripture verses that the Holy Spirit puts on my heart. I've seen how the *rhema* word of God has directly answered hard questions that have bothered an individual for years.

The Bible has a scripture verse to answer almost any of life's tough questions. During a sermon in Washington, D.C. in 1970, Billy Graham said, "The Bible is the only book that fully answers the ultimate questions that youth are asking: Who am I? Where did I come from? Where am I going? What is the purpose and meaning of my existence?"

As we've already mentioned in the previous chapter, use the Bible.

That's why we all need to …

BE LIKE A COW

Have you ever taken time to just watch a cow? They do something unique. While standing up, without ever leaning down to eat food, they will suddenly begin chewing. It's as if they magically make food appear in their mouths out of nowhere. The next time you see a cow, just wait, and you will probably witness this for yourself. There's a reason for this.

A cow has four stomachs that are used as a unique way of breaking down its food. When a cow first eats from a field, it chews the food just enough to swallow. The unchewed food travels down to the first two stomachs where it is stored until later. When a cow is full from this initial eating progress, she rests.

Later, the cow coughs up some of the unchewed food called cud. This time, she completely chews the cud and swallows it again. The cud goes to the third and fourth stomachs where it is fully digested. Some of the digested food enters the bloodstream, travels to the udder, and is made into milk while the rest goes towards the cow's nourishment.

What does that have to do with evangelism? I'm glad you asked.

Throughout the Scriptures, we are encouraged to meditate on God's word throughout the day. "This Book of the Law shall not depart from your mouth, but you shall meditate on it day and night" (Joshua 1:8) and "I will meditate on your precepts and fix my eyes on your ways" (Psalm 119:15), to name a few.

Peripheral questions are sure to come. But, we have the answer to the greatest questions our world needs.

When you hear the word meditate, do you think of a person sitting on the ground with their legs crossed, arms resting on their knees, palms facing upward, and humming. This isn't what God had in mind when he encourages us to meditate on his word throughout the day.

The Hebrew word used for meditate is *hâgâh*. One of the words used to define meditate is the word "ruminate." Ruminate means to think deeply about something, to go over in the mind repeatedly, and often casually or slowly. It also means to chew repeatedly for an extended period; to chew again what has been chewed slightly and swallowed. Just like a cow chews the cud.

We are to be with the Scripture verses like a cow is with her food; eating it, bringing it back up, and chewing on it throughout the day. It's not about how much of the scripture we go through that matters, it's about how much of it goes through us. The Bible is not just about information, it's about transformation. Hide the word in your heart. Memorize it. Chew on it. Again, and again, and again.

Just as a cow doesn't magically put food in its mouth, so the word of God doesn't supernaturally begin to come out of ours. We must put it in us and meditate on it throughout our day. We must be like cows. And, at the right time, God will bring to our mouth the *rhema* Scripture verses we need when sharing the gospel.

Bring the gospel and keep your debates to yourself. When confronted, if prompted by the Holy Spirit, use Scriptures and watch the Holy Spirit defend it. You may be accepted by those you preach to or, like Savonarola, you may be persecuted. Peripheral questions are sure to come. But, we have the answer to the greatest questions our world needs.

The fourteenth century wrapped up with another martyr being welcomed into heaven. On May 23, 1498, tied to a pole in the Piazza della Signoria square in Florence, the story of Savonarola came to an end. As his body was caught on fire, with one final word to the audience, Savonarola shouted out to the crowds, "Should I not willingly die for his sake who willingly died for me, a sinful man?"

And, just like that, the Gospel Baton was passed on. There would be no debate about it, the gospel was sweeping across the world.

17

THE 1500s–COURAGE

But ... It's Not Normal in My Circles of Life

"True boldness for Christ transcends all; it is indifferent to the displeasure of either friends or foes. Boldness enables Christians to forsake all rather than Christ, and to prefer to offend all rather than to offend Him." — Jonathan Edwards, eighteenth century evangelist

The date was October 31, 1517. A day that forever changed the course of history. One act of boldness brought such a spiritual awakening throughout the world that its effects would be felt more than five hundred years later.

But, first, let's back up.

By the beginning of the sixteenth century, the true gospel of Jesus had been polluted by many corrupt church leaders who taught that salvation could be bought with money. An individual would be given a certificate— or indulgence as it was called—authorized by the pope, certifying the individual had purchased forgiveness for themselves or a friend. Due to the sparse amount of Bibles available and the rampant illiteracy, corrupt leaders easily took financial advantage of individuals who wanted to save themselves and family members from an eternity in hell. Dishonest leaders gained recognition that fed their pride and power by using the money to construct great cathedrals.

John Tetzel, one of the leaders in the Catholic Church, was preaching throughout Germany on behalf of the pope. To raise money for St. Peter's Basilica, a new building project in Rome, Tetzel advertised these indulgence certificates. He started a catchy slogan to remind the people that these indulgences could even be bought to rescue someone who had already died from purgatory. "As soon as the coin in the coffer rings," went his jingle, "the soul from purgatory springs." The money flowed in like a river.

This corruption had to stop.

A few years earlier, in 1505, a young monk in Germany named Martin Luther had caught the attention of his superiors. Within three years, Luther would be giving lectures on the Bible as a professor at the University of Wittenberg. It was here where Luther would also earn his Doctorate. Luther was both delighted yet dismayed the more he studied and taught the Bible. He was delighted to read and understand the gospel message. However, he was dismayed that so many leaders in the church were preaching a false gospel—an eternal salvation that was earned from good works and money.

Early that Saturday morning in Germany in October 1517, the burly thirty-three-year-old Martin Luther boldly declared to the leaders and his community the errors found in their false gospel. He wrote up ninety-five points, or theses, of errors that were contrary to what the Bible said regarding salvation and the sale of indulgences for forgiveness of sins. Luther knew it was imperative that the real gospel be made known.

Luther took these Ninety-five Theses he had written on a piece of paper and nailed it to the front door of the Castle Church in Wittenberg, Germany. When the people came to services that morning, they were confronted with this letter. The false gospel had now been openly exposed, and the true gospel found in the Bible would soon be declared.

Luther had no thoughts of starting a religious revolution, nor did he think his actions would catapult the obscure but brilliant scholar-monk into a position of prominence. He only wanted to protest the sale of indulgences so that the true gospel could be known. He had hoped that his Ninety-five Theses would open a scholarly debate on the validity of indulgences and the propriety of their sale by the church. Little did Luther know at the time, a reformation and revolution had begun. However, the sound of the hammer that day would resound around the world and throughout the centuries ahead.

Looking back on Martin Luther's actions may not seem that bold. But, at the time, it must have been immensely terrifying. Luther knew it could not only cost him his livelihood and reputation, but also his life. His strength was in his faith knowing that God was with him. This was not only the secret of his own personal courage, but it was also the secret of his great power as a religious leader.

His actions that day are a reminder that the Gospel Baton has been and always will be one that is carried by bold and courageous men and women.

PEP TALKS AND HIS PRESENCE

What do you think the most repeated phrase in the Bible is? Here are a few hints. It is a command. It is mentioned in the Bible in its various phrases more than a hundred times. And, when the command is obeyed, several times the scripture verse is followed by an action that God is or will be taking. Any ideas? The answer is … drumroll …

The most repeated phrase in the Bible is the command to not be afraid.

"Do not be afraid" or "Do not fear" or "Fear not."

That's right. The most repeated phrase in the Bible is the command to not be afraid. This isn't saying we won't face scary situations and circumstances. But rather, we are not to be scared of them. Why? Because, if you are a believer, God is with you!

> *"So do not fear, for I am with you; do not be dismayed, for I am your God. I will strengthen you and help you; I will uphold you with my righteous right hand." — Isaiah 41:10*

When I was a boy, my parents took us to haunted houses. Don't ask me why, but they did. As we got closer to the entrance to the haunted house, I would always want to turn around and run the opposite direction. It was way too scary. My dad would turn to me and say, "It's going to be alright. Be brave. Be courageous." His pep talks were comforting words. But, his presence was what led me on.

Once we entered the haunted house, I would walk behind my dad, grabbing onto his belt loops, burying my head into his back, and squeezing my eyes shut. As we slowly walked through the haunted house, I would repeat his pep talk over and over through my head. Finally, after several minutes, it was over and we were out.

I made it. My friends would tell me how brave I was. Little did they know, if it hadn't been for my dad's words and presence, there's no way I would have done it alone.

Encourage means to be filled with courage.

Every person mentioned in the Bible was ... a person. Normal people just like you and me. Men and women who, oftentimes, needed a good pep talk from their friends and their heavenly Father.

Remember when Moses, the great leader of Israel, was about to pass away? It was time for him to hand over his leadership to his successor. He called together all of the Israelites. According to Exodus 12:37, there were more than six hundred thousand men, not including women and children. It's safe to say over one million people watched as Moses passed on his leadership to Joshua.

Can you imagine what it must have felt like that day for Joshua? Your predecessor had led the entire nation out of slavery, backed by miracles from God. There were the plagues, the pillar of fire, the splitting of the Red Sea, rocks turned into supernatural water faucets, and the manna from heaven, to name a few.

Joshua must have stood on that platform in front of all Israel shaking in his sandals. It's very possible he was afraid and discouraged because both Moses and God felt it necessary to encourage him. Encourage means to be filled with courage. And, Joshua needed it. Look what Moses told him on that day:

> *"Then Moses summoned Joshua and said to him in the presence of all Israel, "Be **strong and courageous**, for you must go with this people into the land that the Lord swore to their ancestors to give them, and you must divide it among them as their inheritance. The Lord himself goes before you and will be with you; he will never leave you nor forsake you. Do not be afraid; do not be discouraged."*
> *— Deuteronomy 31:7–8 (emphasis added)*

Then, the day Joshua became the leader, God infused courage in him as well:

> "As I was with Moses, so **I will be with you; I will never leave you** nor forsake you. Be **strong and courageous**, because you will lead these people to inherit the land I swore to their ancestors to give them.

> "**Be strong and very courageous.** Be careful to obey all the law my servant Moses gave you; do not turn from it to the right or to the left, that you may be successful wherever you go. Keep this Book of the Law always on your lips; meditate on it day and night, so that you may be careful to do everything written in it. Then you will be prosperous and successful. Have I not commanded you? **Be strong and courageous.** Do not be afraid; do not be discouraged, **for the Lord your God will be with you wherever you go.**"
> — Joshua 1:5–9 (emphasis added)

Three times God tells Joshua to be full of courage. And, three times he reminds him why—because "I am with you."

In 1885, Thomas Smith wrote a best-selling handbook called *Successful Advertising*. He says that effective communication has a formula: more frequency = more effective.[1] Twenty five hundred years earlier, God already knew this formula and implanted it when talking to Joshua.

THE EVANGELISM FORMULA

So, what does this have to do with you and evangelism? I'm glad you asked.

Like marketing, evangelism has a formula: "sharing the gospel = courage." Often, our hearts say "go" but our heads say "no." Excuses flood our minds: What if they reject me? What if they think that I'm crazy? What if they ask me hard questions that I can't answer?

Often, our hearts say "go" but our heads say "no."

We will tell ourselves that it's just not the custom to share the gospel where we are. And, of course it is not. That's why we need to share, so that the gospel will become the standard!

It takes courage to share the gospel.

For many people, it's normal to feel your heart pumping, palms sweating, and legs shaking when you are about to bring the gospel to a friend or stranger. But, remember the pep talk Jesus gave us before leaving the earth:

> "Then Jesus came to them and said, "All authority in heaven and on earth has been given to me. Therefore go and make disciples of all nations, baptizing them in the name of the Father and of the Son and of the Holy Spirit, and teaching them to obey everything I have commanded you. And surely I am with you always, to the very end of the age." — Matthew 28:18–20

Be courageous … for I am with you. Does that sound familiar?

In the King James version, this scripture ends with, "and, lo, I am with you always, even unto the end of the world." Lo … surely … I am with you always. When we go, then lo. We have no reason to be afraid because, like Joshua, even though it may seem scary, we have God leading the way. If you are having a hard time believing that God can make you courageous, just take a look back through our history. You come from a spiritual family of audacious courage.

A BOLD LINEAGE

The final verse in Acts introduces us to one of the core attributes of a believer throughout the centuries, starting with Paul:

Those with the Gospel Baton have always been men and women who are bold.

> "He proclaimed the kingdom of God and taught about the Lord Jesus Christ—with all boldness and without hindrance!" — Acts 28:31

Those with the Gospel Baton have always been men and women who are bold. This is our heritage! The Greek word for bold, *parresia*, means to be daring, courageous, and confident. It speaks of acting without fear of the consequences.

I'm always in awe of the boldness of those killed throughout the centuries for bravely sharing the gospel. They were faithful to the words Jesus gave us about evangelizing and the real consequences that could follow.

> *"What I tell you in the dark, speak in the daylight; what is whispered in your ear, proclaim from the roofs. Do not be afraid of those who kill the body but cannot kill the soul. Rather, be afraid of the One who can destroy both the soul and body in hell." — Matthew 10:27–28*

Our brothers and sisters who have been killed for their faith in Jesus are called martyrs, that is "witnesses." Martyrdoms were often witnessed by thousands in amphitheaters, arenas, and city squares. Even the hardest of the Romans were greatly impacted by the boldness of those willing to die for a king and his message. The awe, admiration, and boldness of the martyrs was one of the key reasons for the rapid advancement of the gospel across the Roman Empire. There are a number of cases of conversions of pagans in the very moment of witnessing the condemnation and death of believers.

The martyrs in the first few centuries were persecuted in countless ways. One of the most ruthless Roman emperors, Decius, so badly wanted to discredit the message of Jesus that he would torture believers until they would proclaim, "Caeser is lord."

If the believer would not stop following Christ and sharing the gospel, he would be labeled a "confessor." If he did turn from God to Caesar, he would be classed among the "lapsed," the fallen ones.

Unfortunately, martyrdom didn't end with the fall of the Roman Empire. Over two thousand years, hundreds of thousands of believers continue to boldly lay their lives down. Their courage is contagious.

We can hear this courage in a letter from a young mother who was martyred just a few years after Martin Luther courageously proclaimed the true gospel in Germany. In 1573, the father had already been executed for getting baptized as an adult for his faith. The mother was put in jail long enough to give birth to her girl before she, too, was martyred. Just before her execution, she wrote this letter to the daughter she would never be able to raise:

> *"My dearest child, the true love of God strengthen you in virtue, you who are yet so young, and whom I must leave in this wicked, evil and perverse world.*
>
> *Oh, that it had pleased the Lord that I might have brought you up, but it seems that it is not the Lord's will … Be not ashamed of us; it is the way which the prophets and the apostles went. Your dear father demonstrated with his blood that it is the genuine faith, and I also hope to attest the same with my blood, though flesh and blood must remain on the posts and on the stake, well knowing that we shall meet hereafter."*[2]

Courage.

As a follower of Jesus, you, too, should be bold. Not because of who you are, but because of who is with you and living in you. "Greater is He that is in us than He that is in the world." (1 John 4:4)

THE TOOTHLESS, PRETEND LION

Oh, and one last thing.

Jesus is talked about as the Lion of Judah, bold and powerful. We are to be like him. But, there's another wanna-be lion and his friends who roam around us. He's not bold and powerful, but rather weak and toothless. And, often, we are influenced by him more than our king. I hear believers talk about the devil and demons as some kind of powerful force upon the earth. But, this is far from the truth.

As a follower of Jesus, you, too, should be bold. Not because of who you are, but because of who is with you and living in you.

The devil and his demons are much like those haunted houses I would walk through with my dad. They make a lot of noise and attempt to look scary but have no power over you. The only way they can get to you is by hoping you will believe their lies.

Timothy says the enemy, "goes around like a roaring lion." Notice that he is not a lion, but rather only pretends to be a lion. And, again, if you were to open his mouth, he has no teeth. He is all noise. He roars excuses in your ears and tries to put fear in your heart, both in life and sharing the gospel.

He wants you to be a wimp with no courage. He wants to discourage, or take away your courage. He wants you to be like him—powerless. When Jesus died on the cross, Satan and all the demons lost any amount of power they might have had.

> "Having disarmed the powers and authorities (Satan and his demons), he (Jesus) made a public spectacle of them, triumphing over them by the cross." — Colossians 2:15 (emphasis added)

The Bible goes on to remind us that Satan is a created being and cannot be everywhere at one time, is a withering branch, a liar who knows that his time is short. One day, when we all see Satan get his final death sentence in hell, we will look at each other and shake our heads on how such a poser took away our courage:

> Those who see you stare at you,
>   they ponder your fate:
> "Is this the man who shook the earth
>   and made kingdoms tremble,
> the man who made the world a wilderness,
>   who overthrew its cities
> and would not let his captives go home?"
> — Isaiah 14:16–17

Be bold and courageous for Jesus and his gospel. Don't fall for the soft roars of a toothless, pretend lion.

Be brave.

From the time of the early church, the martyrs, Luther, and up to this present day, we are a people who are called to be bold. Go & Tell others about our king. He is with you.

18

THE 1600s–HOLINESS

But … I've Made Too Many Mistakes

"A true and faithful Christian does not make holy living an accidental thing. It is his great concern. As the business of the soldier is to fight, so the business of the Christian is to be like Christ." — Jonathan Edwards (1703–1758)

In 1608, Hans Lippershey submitted his patent to the government in the Netherlands. He had invented the telescope. The news of this invention quickly made headlines around the world. The Italian engineer, Galileo, was so intrigued by this new apparatus that the following year, he created his own telescope. He would eventually become known as the father of observational astronomy and the father of modern science.

Meanwhile, just twelve years later, the patent office in the Netherlands received another application. Although the inventor was unknown, this new device did not look at lands far away, but rather magnify what had before been hidden right before one's eyes. People could now see germs and diseases that before were unseen and overlooked. The modern microscope had arrived.

These two inventions perfectly reflect this century of believers who had grabbed onto the Gospel Baton. The following hundred years would be highlighted by a people who desired to expedite the global expansion of the gospel by going to distant lands while being personally driven to examine the microscopic details of their everyday walk with God.

In 1620, nine years after King James had authorized a new translation of the English Bible, a hundred passengers boarded the Mayflower to bring the gospel to an unreached land and to build a pure church, untainted by the flaws of the Church of England.

After sailing across the Atlantic, the Mayflower ran ashore on a land later to be named the United States of America. Huddled aboard the ship, forty one men signed the Mayflower Compact, a declaration of commitment to create a government based on scripture and the advancement of the gospel.

Meanwhile, in Europe, many believers who weren't setting off for distant countries had started movements to return to being pure, holy witnesses for Christ. The corruption that Luther and the reformers had exposed in the prior century paved the way for the holiness movement of the seventeenth century. Believers realized that a pure people brought a clear gospel to the lost while a dirty, immoral believer brought a muddied gospel.

In 1641, Richard Baxter became pastor at Kidderminster and quickly earned the nickname "Holy Baxter" for his focus on purity. He reminded the people of Worcestershire, England to keep "heaven in your eye at all times" and to live holy. His book *Saints Everlasting Rest* became a classic, influencing believers for the centuries to come.

George Fox started a holiness movement in 1648 that landed him in jail. When mocked by a judge, Fox said, "tremble at the word of God." The judge replied, "You are the tremblers, the Quakers." The name stuck.[1] Rembrant painted the *Return of the Prodigal Son* in 1662 and John Bunyan wrote *Pilgrim's Progress* in 1678, which went on to be the second most read book in the world only behind the Bible.

A return to holiness was a theme of this century and set the example for future generations of believers.

HOLY, HOLY, HOLY

"Friends, God is calling you to be holy just as he is holy," Steve Hill pleaded with the audience as tears flowed down his cheeks.

Does the word "holy" seem like an odd, religious word to you? In my early years as a believer, I had a hard time grasping the truth of this word. I would sing it in songs, read it in scripture, and hear it in sermons. Even though it's mentioned more than five hundred times in the *Holy* Bible,

I just didn't seem to pay much attention to it. It wasn't until my days serving at the Brownsville Revival in Pensacola, Florida that it sank in.

Day after day, the worship team at the revival would lead the crowd in songs of God's holiness—

"Friends, God is calling you to be holy just as he is holy."

about how God is separated high and above anyone or anything.

"Holy, holy, holy!
Lord God Almighty!
Early in the morning our song shall rise to thee
Holy, holy, holy!
Merciful and mighty
God in three persons, blessed Trinity!"
— *Reginald Heiber, England 1826*

A reverence would sweep the auditorium as people humbly bowed in reverence to the holy God. Then, we would stand in proclamation joining former centuries of believers in faith as we sang:

"All hail the power of Jesus' name!
Let angels prostrate fall
Bring forth the royal diadem
And crown him Lord of all."
— *Edward Perronet, England 1779*

Jesus is set apart—holy—as the King of Kings. The music was followed by a powerful gospel message from evangelist Steve Hill. He would, again, remind the audience of the holiness of God and how we, too, are to be holy. We are not to be sinful, but instead live according to God's Word. Over the next few years of the revival, hundreds of thousands of people made decisions to follow Jesus.

To be holy means, in both the Hebrew and the Greek, to be clean, good, pure, and set apart. God is, by nature, holy. On the other hand, we are called to be holy through our association with God and the lives we live. Holiness is critical in effectively sharing the gospel. After all, "…without holiness, no one will see the Lord." (Hebrews 12:14)

RUN HOLY

We are in a race. The Gospel Baton is in our hands. Let's run to win! This means we must train properly.

Remember what Paul wrote in his first letter to the church in Corinth?

> *Do you not know that in a race all the runners run, but only one gets the prize? Run in such a way as to get the prize. Everyone who competes in the games goes into strict training. They do it to get a crown that will not last, but we do it to get a crown that will last forever." — 1 Corinthians 9:24–25*

There's a reward at the end of our race, and we have a baton to pass to the next century of believers. However, we aren't just supposed to run hard, we are also supposed to run holy.

One of the greatest battles you will face is keeping yourself in the world to be a light while keeping the world out of you. Think of it this way: We are like boats. Boats are made to be in the water, but not for water to be in the boat. We can be holy while living in a sinful world. Jesus did. And, we can too. However, we can't run effectively for a holy God if we let sin live in us.

A person who wants to win the gold medal trains much differently than someone who just wants to compete. Spiritually train to win a heavenly gold medal, the crown of life. This comes by training ourselves to follow the commands of Jesus.

Did you know that evangelism and discipleship go hand in hand? You can't have one without the other. We must disciple those we evangelize. Let's look at discipleship for a moment. Discipleship has one goal in mind. Notice what Jesus tells his disciples with his final words:

One of the greatest battles you will face is keeping yourself in the world to be a light while keeping the world out of you.

"*Therefore go and make disciples of all nations, baptizing them in the name of the Father and of the Son and of the Holy Spirit, **and teaching them to obey everything I have commanded you.**" — Matthew 28:19–20*

You can't be a follower of Jesus only with words, you have to live it out. We have to obey the command of Jesus and teach other new believers to do the same. This is discipleship. And, when a disciple is following the teachings of Jesus, they are living holy.

Holiness within the early believers was one of the reasons for the rapid expansion of the gospel. In Acts 11, Luke documents what was taking place in the church in Antioch (modern day Turkey). He says that, "the hand of the Lord was with them, and a great number became believers and turned to the Lord"[2] and that "it was in Antioch that the disciples were first called Christians."[3]

> *You can't be a follower of Jesus only with words, you have to live it out.*

A Christian at that time, mostly in modern terms, and as mentinoed throughout this book simply means a follower of Christ. For the rest of the New Testament, when a letter was written to the Christians, it would be addressed to the "saints." The Greek word for "saint" is *hagios*—holy.

You and I are supposed to be holy. That's what it means to be a follower of Christ.

In the first couple of centuries, this holy lifestyle of believers attracted the attention of unbelievers. Pagans noticed the difference of the life of a follower of Christ. Believers did not participate in the heathen lifestyles of the time. They refused to attend gladiatorial games and wouldn't work on projects that would be dedicated to pagan gods. They valued all human life. Everywhere the Christian turned, his life and faith was on display because the gospel introduced a revolutionary new way of living. This could be seen in almost every area of life including careers, slaves, children, and sex.

Christians would refuse to work in the schools where textbooks were used to teach of ancient gods and called for observing religious festivals. Others would not work as nurses because people would be required to walk up and down the halls offering incense to the pagan god, Aesculapius, for healing.

Slaves were treated with respect instead of as objects. Children were valued. Unlike his pagan neighbor, the believer refused to take his weak and unwanted children out in the woods and leave them to die or be picked up by robbers. If a Christian woman was married to an unbeliever

It's been said that one of the leading causes of atheism in the world is because of "believers" who proclaim Jesus with their lips but deny him with their lifestyles.

and a girl baby was born, the father might say, "Throw her out," but the mother would refuse.

Sex was to be observed according to the holy scriptures. Sex outside of marriage was forbidden, and marriage was a holy union between a man and a woman. This was contrary to the unholy lifestyles of the unbelievers in the Roman empire.[4]

It was not that believers went about criticizing and condemning unbelievers, nor were they consciously self-righteous and superior. It was simply that the believer was a follower of the commands of Jesus, which was in itself contrary to the "normal" way of living in society.

Athenagoras, philosopher of Athens in the second century, said that there were many believers who were "unable to describe the value of the Bible doctrines in words, but who attested them by their deeds."[5] Simply put, the lives of the believers matched the good news they proclaimed with their mouths. And, people listened.

Have you ever met someone who said they were a follower of Christ, but his or her lifestyle was opposite of the teachings of Jesus? Isn't that puzzling to you? How much more puzzling is it for an unbeliever?

It's been said that one of the leading causes of atheism in the world is because of "believers" who proclaim Jesus with their lips but deny him with their lifestyles. A gospel message brought by such a "believer" has little effect in leading someone to Christ.

Christian missionary E. Stanley Jones asked Muhamid Gandhi, "Mr. Gandhi, though you quote the words of Christ often, why is it that you appear to so adamantly reject becoming his follower?" Gandhi replied, "Oh, I don't reject your Christ. I love your Christ. It is just that so many of you Christians are so unlike your Christ."

A gospel message brought to an unbeliever by a holy follower of Christ is crucial in evangelism. And, it's attractive to an unbeliever. Holiness brings credibility to the message you proclaim.

RUN NAKED

"Train yourself to be goldly (holy)" — 1 Timothy 4:7

Paul gives this special instruction in his first letter to Timothy, the pastor of the largest church in the first century. He's reminding Timothy of the race he's running and the training required to win. Timothy has to train to be holy, or, in some versions, godly.

> *Holiness brings credibility to the message you proclaim.*

The Greek word for exercise is *gumnadzo*. This word was used to describe the professional combat sports of the time. The three main sports of wrestling, boxing, and a type of gladiatorial game called pankration could easily cost an athlete his life if he lost. Winning was critical. In order for these athletes to compete with full strength and agility without having any kind of hindrance, they would both exercise and compete naked.

Yes, you read that right. The word *gumnadzo* is developed from the Greek word, *gumnos*, naked. Paul was telling Timothy that he needed to exercise and compete naked!

Of course, this is a spiritual analogy. Timothy had a message to bring, a baton in his hand. He needed to Go & Tell everyone about Jesus. But, to do it effectively, he couldn't be weighted down with things that kept him from following everything Jesus had commanded. He had to throw off any sin so as not to be weighed down and become ineffective.

We don't know exactly what it was that Timothy may have been carrying for Paul to write such a message. Maybe Timothy was getting prideful or arrogant because of his success? Maybe it was something else? Or, maybe Paul was just reminding Timothy of the weight that sin would bring him and his ministry if he let sin into his life. Either way, Paul, through the Holy Spirit, felt it important to remind Timothy of this critical point.

The writer of Hebrews would echo Paul's words this way:

> *"Therefore, since we are surrounded by such a great cloud of witnesses, let us throw off everything that hinders and the sin that so easily entangles. And let us run with perseverance the race marked out for us."* — Hebrews 12:1

What is keeping you from running the race effectively? Is there a habitual sin in your life that is contrary to God's commands? Is there a secret sin that no one but you and God knows about? Today is the day to cut it off. The secret to being holy is to be holy in secret. You are in the greatest race of your life and those sins only weigh you down from being all God has for you to be.

> *It's said that sin will take you farther than you ever wanted to go, cost you more than you ever wanted to pay, and keep you longer than you ever wanted to stay.*

It's said that sin will take you farther than you ever wanted to go, cost you more than you ever wanted to pay, and keep you longer than you ever wanted to stay. You can't afford to allow sin in your life. It destroys you, keeps you from running the race God has for you, and mutes your message to unbelievers.

Evangelist Billy Sunday (1862–1935) often preached against the sin of drunkenness. He even held an actual funeral service for "John Barleycorn," a symbolic character representing death to drunkenness. Sunday said that for a drunkard, alcohol "eats the carpet off the floors, the clothes off your back, your money out of your bank, food off your table, and shoes off the baby's feet." Basically, sin destroys your life.

Let's cut off, kill, and bury whatever sins that may have entangled around us. We can't be effective with the gospel and unholy at the same time. It's a contradiction. When we live this way, nonbelievers hear us preach the gospel and think it is a joke. Your lifestyle does not match your words. You cannot purposefully live in and approve of sin while also being a follower of Christ. Let me explain.

There's no such thing as a follower of Christ who also is a practicing murderer—a murderer Christian. Or a person who thinks it's fine to be a thief but also calls themselves a Christian—a stealing Christian. Or any other sin. You can't be an evil Christian, a corrupt Christian, a Christian adulterer, a homosexual Christian, a hateful Christian, an idolatrous Christian, an unbelieving Christian, and the list goes on.

There are more than thirty one thousand verses in the Bible, and none of them calls you any of the titles listed. Don't fall for the lies of any culture that says you can be a follower of Christ and actively practice living a life of sin. Our name and our conduct must represent Jesus accordingly.

Have you heard the story of the young man in Alexander the Great's army? I wonder if our king sometimes feels the way King Alexander felt when he encountered the young man.

It was 330 B.C., the young man in Alexander the Great's army was accused of a crime. He was brought in to see Alexander personally.

"Are you guilty of the crime?"

"Yes, King, I am guilty of the crime," responded the young man.

Alexander the Great then asked the young man, "What's your name?"

"My name is also Alexander," the young man replied.

"What?" King Alexander exclaimed. "Change your name or change your conduct!"

You have an amazing race to run. Represent King Jesus properly. You are positioned by God, with baton in hand, to win. The race is yours to lose.

> *The secret to being holy is to be holy in secret.*

DON'T GET DISQUALIFIED

We saw in Chapter Three that we are to preach the gospel. The word for preach, *karusso*, was the action of a herald for the king. As preachers of the gospel, we are spokesmen for the king.

However, there's another job a herald might be hired to do. Similar to the Olympics today, a herald was hired to proclaim at the opening of the races the name of each candidate and the rules of the contest.[6] Back to the Bible.

Paul constantly reminded himself and others about this race they were in. Not only were they heralds but also competitors. How sad it would be to tell others the good news, but disqualify yourself from the race because of your sins.

> *"...Run in such a way as to get the prize. Everyone who competes in the games goes into strict training. They do it to get a crown that will not last; but we do it to get a crown that will last forever. Therefore I do not run like someone running aimlessly; I do not fight like a boxer beating the air. No, I strike a blow to my body and make it my slave so that*

Don't fall for the lies of any culture that says you can be a follower of Christ and actively practice living a life of sin.

after I have preached to others, I myself will not be disqualified for the prize." — 1 Corinthians 9:24–27

When temptation to sin comes, don't fall for the lie of the enemy. His only goal is to disqualify you from fulfilling the race God has for you and your effectiveness for Jesus.

You don't get to choose what you are tempted with, but you do get to choose how you respond. Your God is much bigger than any temptation. Respond rightly, run freely, and watch as God fulfills his purpose in and through your life. Holiness is lived one day at a time, one thought at time, decision by decision.

YOU ARE FORGIVEN

Have you ever been hesitant to share the gospel because you don't want to look like a hypocrite? Maybe the very person you want to share the gospel with knows some of the worst mistakes you've ever made. And, even though the mistakes happened before you became a believer, you still think you've made too many mistakes to be used by God.

The good news is not just good news for others, it's good news for you, too! Jesus won for all mankind. Remember, there are no mistakes or lifestyles too bad that Jesus won't forgive. Our forgiveness is not dependent on our good deeds, but rather upon receiving by faith what Christ did at the cross. The world still thinks that being good saves us. However, the gospel actually states that we are being saved in order to be good, and the two ideas are completely different.

We are all born into sin. There is not an alcoholic gene, a liar gene, a murderer gene, or a sexually immoral gene that we are born with. There's a sin gene. It doesn't matter how you were born or what you've done, you have to be born again. And, this is part of the good news of Jesus.

After becoming a follower of Christ, we leave our old life of sin to be followers of Jesus.

"Do not be deceived: Neither the sexually immoral nor idolaters nor adulterers nor men who have sex with men nor thieves nor the greedy nor drunkards nor slanderers nor swindlers will inherit the kingdom of God. And that is what some of you were. But you were washed, you were sanctified, you were justified in the name of the Lord Jesus Christ and by the Spirit of our God." — 1 Corinthians 6:9–11

You've been forgiven. Now, run holy. Run free of sin that hinders. And be a herald of the gospel with a lifestyle that matches your words.

By the end of the seventeenth century, the gospel had arrived on every continent around the world. China, Mexico, the Philippines, Mozambique, India, and North America were some of the many nations buzzing with believers who not only proclaimed the gospel but also lived holy lives worthy of the call.

The world still thinks that being good saves us. However, the gospel actually states that we are being saved in order to be good.

19

———

THE 1700s–PASSION

But … I Don't Have the Right Personality

"I have but one passion: It is He, it is He alone. The world is the field and the field is the world; and henceforth that country shall be my home where I can be most used in winning souls for Christ." — *Nicolas Von Zinzendorf (1700–1760)*

The eighteenth century is often referred to as the age of reason and revival. It was a time when vast advancements of science and human reason were quickly replacing biblical faith as the cornerstone of the Western world. Prominent philosophers such as Jean-Jacques Rousseau and Immanuel Kant were shaping minds while scientific discoveries like the steam engine (1712) and thermometer (1714) were revolutionizing modern life. A common life of faith and the simple gospel message were being challenged.

It would seem that this crisis of faith would discourage believers in sharing the gospel. It did the opposite.

Believers around the world turned up the temperature. The fire burning in them for the gospel would be a light to a dimming world. These believers would constantly talk about God, sing about him, write about him, pray, and testify about him. Their passion for Jesus and his gospel would mark this century as not only the age of reason, but also the age of revival. One of the countless stories comes from a man who allowed fellow believers escaping persecution to build themselves a house on the corner of his property in Dresden, Germany.

For five years, three hundred believers slowly made their way to Count Nicolaus von Zinzendorf's estate. They constructed a small village named Hernnhut, which meant, "the Lord's watch." Zinzendorf moved from his house on the estate into the new-found village where he helped set up small groups and Bible studies.

Then, on August 13, 1727, while a few hundred believers residing on the estate of Count Nicolaus von Zinzendorf were reading their Bible and praying together, something supernatural happened. Suddenly, like the day of Pentecost, a fire-like zeal for Jesus swept over the believers. These believers, along with Zinzendorf, became lit by the fire of the Holy Spirit. A passion for prayer and evangelism burned in their hearts.

In the heat of the moment, a twenty-four-hour prayer meeting began that would go on to last for more than a hundred years. A desire to take the gospel to the world became a daily discussion. By 1742, more than seventy men and women from Herrnhut, full of passion for global evangelism, had taken the gospel around the world to countries such as Suriname, South Africa, Guiana, Algeria, Sri Lanka, and Romania.

These ordinary believers, along with Zinzendorf, were often noted by unbelievers for their passion. They not only said what they believed, but passionately believed what they said.

By the time of Zinzendorf's death in 1760, two hundred and twenty six believers had left Herrnhut to preach the gospel around the world, and they had baptized more than three thousand new converts. William Carey, who would be born the following year in 1761 and eventually be known as the father of modern missions, said of these believers, "See what they have done. Can we not follow their example, and in obedience to our Heavenly Master, go out into the world and preach the Gospel to the heathen?"[1]

BETTER THAN AN AIR PURIFIER

Have you ever been asked to attend a meeting to hear about a new multilevel company? You know, get in on the ground floor, assemble your team, and eventually build enough wealth to retire at a young age. Did you go to the meeting and join the movement? If so, why?

I remember one pyramid company I joined in 2004. I was invited to a gathering to hear about a revolutionary new air purifier machine. Even though I had no money or interest in the product, I attended the gathering

as a kind gesture toward a friend who seemed passionate ┊ *Passion is*
about the product. After a short time of appetizers, a very ┊ *attractive.*
energetic guy began his pitch about this new machine.
"Blah, blah, blah," I thought to myself, "hopefully this won't last long."

However, as the presenter progressed, I slowly became mesmerized by the product. This man talked about unseen impurities that floated in the air, the dangers of breathing in dirty air, and the need to ionize (electronically charge) air molecules. This machine would do the job. I couldn't believe I was listening so intently to the speech. It wasn't as much the machine I was interested in, but rather the passion of the presenter. He genuinely believed that this machine would revolutionize the way humans breathe. By the time he had finished his presentation, I was sold. And, so was the machine.

I walked out of the meeting that evening with a seven-hundred-dollar air purifier machine in my arms. I also spent another two hundred dollars for my introductory fee to be a certified seller. Although I wasn't too passionate about the product, I did my due diligence to start building my new company. I called my friends and told them about that machine and how they, too, needed to buy one of these amazing machines. No one listened. No one cared. No one bought any machines from me, and I eventually gave up on the product myself.

Why do you think I bought the product in the first place? It wasn't because I cared about the company or thought I needed the machine before attending the meeting. I bought it because the presenter seemed to genuinely believe in the product himself. He had passion—and it got my attention.

Passion is attractive. Fans are drawn to athletes who play their games with passion. Conferences are built around passionate businessmen who want to share their success stories. And it is passion, or the lack of it, that is noticed by unbelievers when we tell them about Jesus.

> *Jesus told the disciples, "what is whispered in your ear, proclaim from the roofs." — Matthew 10:27*

Let's say you worked at a market selling eggs in the time of Jesus. When the eggs were put on sale, you would want everyone walking by your store to know. Since there were no print ads, electronic billboards, websites, or social media sites to tell of this sale, what do you think you would do? That's right. You would climb onto the top of the store and passionately shout from the rooftops. "Eggs for sale! Hurry! Hurry! This is an amazing deal that won't last long! Eggs for sale!" This is the context in which Jesus tells his disciples to shout from the "rooftops what is whispered in their ears." They have an announcement that everyone needs to hear.

Passion looks different for each person, but it is always noticeable.

The good news, the gospel, is the best kept secret of all time. Passion looks different for each person, but it is always noticeable. You don't have to literally stand on your roof and shout. But if you genuinely believe in the gospel, there will be passion behind what you say and do.

A believer who has no passion when talking about Jesus is often as effective for the advancement of the gospel as a news channel on mute. You may be talking but, most likely, no one is listening. There is no magnetism, nothing that attracts, and plenty to repel. If you do not believe in what you are offering, why would anyone be interested in what you have to give them?

A FLAME FOR YOU

The word enthusiasm comes from the Greek word *enthousiasmos*. This is a compound word formed from the Greek *en* (in) and *theos* (God), meaning "inspired or possessed by God." The best way to gain or regain passion for the gospel is to ask the Holy Spirit to inspire and possess you. As evangelist Reinhard Bonkke would often say, "There is a flame for every person."

Just before Jesus began his itinerant ministry, his cousin, John, was baptizing people in the Jordan river. As he was talking to the crowds he said, "I baptize you with water for repentance. But after me comes one who is more powerful than I, whose sandals I am not worthy to carry. He will baptize you with the Holy Spirit and fire." (Matthew 3:11)

Fire and the Holy Spirit go together. This is one of the benefits the Holy Spirit brings to us as believers.

Remember on the day of Pentecost? A group of one hundred and twenty ordinary believers were praying when the Holy Spirit entered. Luke tells the story in Acts.

> *"On the day of Pentecost all the believers were meeting together in one place. Suddenly, there was a sound from heaven like the roaring of a mighty windstorm, and it filled the house where they were sitting. Then, what looked like flames or tongues of fire appeared and settled on each of them. And everyone present was filled with the Holy Spirit and began speaking in other languages, as the Holy Spirit gave them this ability."* — Acts 2:4–5

Fire represents many things. But it for sure indicates passion. The men and women noted in the passage left that prayer room and passionately proclaimed the gospel for the rest of their lives. People noticed, listened to them, and many became followers of the king as a result.

It's common to hear people say that they don't share the gospel because it's just not their personality. Maybe this is something you've said to yourself. And, it is understandable. I have found myself using this excuse at times. You don't like making noise, drawing attention to yourself, disturbing people, and so on.

The great news is that you don't need the "right" personality to share the gospel. You just need to have passion—a fire burning inside of you.

If we accidently put our hands on a burning hot stove, the fire will quickly change your personality. And, this is what the Holy Spirit will do for you, too. He will infuse you with a fiery passion to share the good news with enthusiasm. You will believe what you say, and unbelievers will take notice.

An Indian proverb says, "snowflakes can't fall on a hot stove." When we are filled with the fire from the Holy Spirit, our cold, passionless presentations become burning words. Every conversation we have about Christ will be like Richard Baxtor said when he was filled with that fire, "I preached as never sure to preach again, and as a dying man to dying men."

I love how Jeremiah describes how the Spirit's presence affected him. He had decided he would stay silent and not talk about God anymore. But, he could not. He wrote of that moment:

> *"But if I say, "I will not mention his word or speak anymore in his name," his word is in my heart like a fire, a fire shut up in my bones. I am weary of holding it in; indeed, I cannot."* — Jeremiah 20:9

The writer of Hebrews said that, like Jeremiah, we all should be servants that are on fire. And, check this out. When we are on fire, God sends angels to fan the fire in our heart even brighter.

> *"In speaking of the angels he says, 'He makes his angels spirits, and his servants (ministers) flames of fire."* — Hebrews 1:7 (emphasis added)

God wants us to be full of passion. He brings the fire; we bring the gospel. And, together, we bring life to a dead world.

AGES OF REVIVAL

Revival simply means to be brought back to life. For believers, it's when we once again regain our passionate love for our savior; when the most important thing in our lives is not our bank accounts, our education, or our leisure activities. We return to him. Jesus pleaded with the believers in Ephesus to revive their love and passion for him again. Otherwise, they would no longer be a light to unbelievers in their area.

> *"You have forsaken the love you had at first. Consider how far you have fallen! Repent and do the things you did at first. If you do not repent, I will come to you and remove your lampstand from its place."* — Revelation 2:4–5

Revival is like a fire. It happens with a spark during prayer by an individual who becomes passionate again in his love for Jesus and, before long, a whole area is influenced for the cause of Christ. The result is always the same—joy with believers and salvations among unbelievers.

It was Issac Watts, who in his passionate love for the king, wrote these lyrics in 1719:

> *Joy to the World; the Lord is come!*
> *Let earth receive her King!*
> *Let every heart prepare Him room,*
> *And Heaven and nature sing.*

God wants us to be full of passion. He brings the fire; we bring the gospel. And, together, we bring life to a dead world.

Joy to the World has been sung through the centuries, bringing joy to believers and the hope of the gospel to the lost.

John Newton, an unbeliever working aboard a slave trade boat, cried out to God to rescue him during a ferocious storm on March 21, 1748. He became passionate for God, constantly reading the Bible and praying. He quit working aboard the boat and in 1764, at the age of thirty nine, became a minister in the Church of England. His passion spilled over into his autobiographical hymn *Amazing Grace*.

In February of 1739, an enthusiastic, fiery twenty-four-year-old wanted to tell as many people about Jesus as possible. Unfortunately, most of the churches in England were not interested in having him preach. So, George Whitefield, decided to stand out in the fields and preach near the coal mines in Kingswood.

On a cold Saturday afternoon, Whitefield invited the people to leave their shacks and come hear him preach at a field called Rose Green. About two hundred people attended the first meeting. Encouraged, Whitefield announced a second open-air meeting several days later, and more than two thousand attended. Attendance increased steadily until more than twenty thousand gathered for each service.

What was it about Whitefield that drew the crowds? Passion.

His passionate messages so moved these hardened coal miners' hearts that everyone could see "the white gutters made by their tears" falling down their cheeks as they emerged from the coal pits. With passion in his voice, Whitefield shared the gospel until his audiences cried with him for forgiveness. "I would give a hundred guineas," said the actor David Garrick, "if I could only say Oh! like Mr. Whitefield."[2]

Whitefield handed the Gospel Baton to John Wesley and then moved to the United States, where he brought the message of Jesus to hundreds of thousands of Americans.

In the meantime, John Wesley was as passionate as Whitefield. A year before Whitefield started preaching near the coal mines, Wesley reluctantly attended a meeting on Aldersgate Street in London on May 24, 1738. A random believer, with a zeal for Jesus, began to read Martin Luther's commentary on Romans. Wesley would later recall, "About a quarter before nine, while he was describing the change which God works in the heart through faith in Christ, I felt my heart strangely warmed." He trusted God for the forgiveness of sins. His warm heart became on fire for Jesus. Everywhere Wesley preached, tens of thousands of people would come out to hear his message.

Legend has it that one time a reporter approached Wesley and asked, "What is your secret? Why do so many people come to hear you preach?" Wesley responded, "I get alone with God in prayer. He sets me on fire. The people come out to watch me burn."

If we just had the passion for Jesus like these men and women … Imagine the revival that could take place among our family and friends if we were as focused as our forefathers.

In his diary on June 28, 1774, Wesley wrote that he traveled a minimum of forty five hundred miles on horseback proclaiming the gospel. As he rode his horse, he prayed and wrote his message for the next gathering of people waiting for him. In Wesley's lifetime, he rode more than two hundred and fifty thousand miles. That is equivalent to ten times around the world![3]

Talk about passion for the gospel!

When John Wesley died in London in 1791, he left behind 79,000 followers in England and 40,000 in the USA.

Charles Wesley, John's brother, also became a believer after hearing the gospel. His passion for Jesus led him to write more than seven thousand songs, including *Jesus Lover of my Soul*, *O for a Thousand Tongues*, and *Hark! The Herald Angels Sing*, which shared the gospel to millions of people around the world.

The Wesleys and Whitefield were just three of the countless believers who passionately brought the good news of Jesus throughout the 1700s.

There were many other prominent leaders, such as Jonathan Edwards, John Brown, and David Brainard. We'll never know how many nameless others there were who were on fire, just like these men. But, heaven does. These men and women were pivotal in the advancement of the gospel.

We could go on and on with examples of believers through the century who were passionate for the gospel to reach their world. Let's look at one last story.

Hundreds of passionate believers in the United States became circuit riders. Although they would make a meager sixty-four dollars per year, they wouldn't let that deter them. They had a message to proclaim. Like John Wesley, they visited unreached towns around the country proclaiming the gospel. The gospel spread like wildfire throughout America.

One circuit rider, Horace Bishop, gives us a glimpse of what being a circuit rider was like from this excerpt from his diary:

> "I preached twenty-eight times a month. I never took breakfast and dinner at the same place except on Friday, which was laundry day in the country ... My wardrobe was one end of my saddlebags; my bookcase the other end ... My 'study' was the shade of any tree on the way to my appointments, where there was grass for my horse ... I slept where it was convenient, on a sheepskin or my Mexican blanket, occasionally on a dirt or a puncheon floor."[4]

Passion has always been an earmark of those who ran effectively with the Gospel Baton. Not just in the 1700s, but throughout every century starting with the first two people who experienced Christ the day of his resurrection.

Those first two witnesses would say after their encounter with Jesus that "their hearts were burning inside of them"[5] and they went to the disciples and told them that Jesus was the risen king. Every effective preacher of the gospel from that time on is often characterized as a man and woman on fire for the advancement of the gospel and love for the king.

Passion. It is not a personality trait, nor is it defined by a specific outward expression. Passion is impossible to define but obvious when someone has it ... or doesn't.

Passion has always been an earmark of those who ran effectively with the Gospel Baton.

Let's not be willing to live without it. All we need to do is to ask the Holy Spirit to fill us with the fire like he has with countless believers throughout the centuries.

And, when you share with passion, be ready to experience an age of revival in the many cosmoses of your life.

20

THE 1800s–MENTORS
But ... I Am Socially Disadvantaged

"Consider how precious a soul must be, when both God and the devil are after it." — Charles Spurgeon (1834–1892)

Let the industrial revolution begin. The means of production transitioned from hand methods to machines and marked the beginning of a new era of productivity. Electricity, chemical manufacturing, iron production, factories, and steam power completely changed the way of life. These new technologies led to an unprecedented rise in the rate of population growth as the world population would hit the one billion mark.

Rockefeller, Carnegie, Beethoven, Darwin, and Dickens became household names, along with Jane Austen, Geronimo, Fyodor Dostoevsky, and Abraham Lincoln. America doubled in size with the Louisiana Purchase in 1803 from France and the purchase of Alaska from Russia in 1867. Population and production were the buzzwords throughout the century.

The exponential growth would not trip up the good news of Jesus from being effective either. The gospel ran toe to toe with the culture.

The message of Jesus was being clearly proclaimed in many countries by prominent voices and minorities. Americans were being exposed to the gospel through the leadership of men like Charles Finney in New York and D. L. Moody in Chicago. India was being reached through the guidance of a foreign couple from America named Adoniram and Ann Judson. William Carey, also a missionary in India, challenged every believer that with God, there are no minorities. His quote, "expect great things from God, do great things for God" became the marching orders for nineteenth century believers.

A white man from the United Kingdom, during the peak of slavery, went to Africa to proclaim the freedom found in the gospel. David Livingston's book *Missionary Travels* became a bestseller in 1857, bringing attention to the gospel work in Africa and the necessity of eradicating slavery; a task begun by William Wilberforce early in the 1800s.

In China, Hudson Taylor and his wife sailed from America to bring the gospel to China, along with fifteen young men and women they mentored. When they arrived in China, they accounted for twenty-five percent of all evangelistic missionaries in China. Against all odds, as minorities, the Taylors established the China Inland Mission (CIM). Hudson's mentorship to these young missionaries and others to come was like a mass production machine sending evangelists throughout China. By the time Taylor died in 1905, there were two hundred and five mission stations, eight hundred forty nine missionaries, and an estimated one hundred twenty five thousand Chinese Christians.[1]

Back in the United Kingdom, Charles Spurgeon preached the gospel in the largest church in the country while William Booth gathered a band of believers, enrolling them in his new Salvation Army. Over sixteen thousand believers, many being minorities, women and children, became part of this Salvation Army taking the gospel to the streets.

One of the greatest stories of the nineteenth century came from someone who no one would have expected. In New York, a six-week-old girl caught an eye infection. Her doctor prescribed a hot mustard compress to fight the infection, but it scarred her eyes. Fanny Crosby would never see again.

Fanny never had any bitterness about her blindness. As a young girl, her mother once asked her if she resented being blind, and she replied, "Mother, if I had the choice, I would still choose to remain blind ... for when I die, the first face I will ever see will be the face of my blessed Savior."

When Fanny became depressed because she couldn't learn and play as other children, her grandma began to mentor her. Grandmother's mentorship of the gospel, language, and songwriting opened the unseen world to Fanny. This mentorship built this blind woman up to eventually lead millions to Christ in a time when women were generally considered second class.

Fanny wrote poetry about her King Jesus and his good news. In 1843, she was invited to recite one of her poems before the United States Congress. At the age of 44, Fanny took many of these poems and turned them into songs. Her career as a songwriter was born. Her first song, *Lord, Please Don't Pass Me By*, was for a prison service to a group of unbelieving inmates. D.L. Moody used many of her songs in his mass evangelistic gatherings.

More than eight thousand of her poems were put to music with a hundred million copies of her songs printed.[2] Many of her songs including *Blessed Assurance* and *To God Be the Glory* are still actively sung around the world to this day.

Fanny, like countless other believers in the nineteenth century, sought to bring others to her savior. They did not allow their social status to keep them from sharing the good news. Instead, they looked for mentors who would train them to fulfill God's purpose with their lives. At the end of her life, many had come to faith in Jesus, and she had come face-to-face with her king. She would write of that moment in a song shortly before her death:

> *"When my lifework is ended and I cross the swelling tide,*
> *When the bright and glorious morning I shall see,*
> *I shall know my Redeemer when I reach the other side,*
> *And His smile will be the first to welcome me."*

ALIEN INVADERS

Aliens. Do you believe in aliens? Have you ever seen an alien? Would you be surprised if I told you that you see an alien every day?

When I first moved to Switzerland, I was sitting around a table with a half dozen Swiss citizens talking about a referendum that was possibly going to be voted on. It had to do with the number of foreigners living in Switzerland and if Switzerland needed to slow down the rate of non-citizens moving to the country.

"There are too many foreigners here," one of the guys said.

"Yeah, too many aliens. Too many minorities," said another.

I agreed and took sides with their opinion.

Then, it dawned on me. None of us realized that I was one of those "minorities," those "aliens" that we all agreed should not be here. The importance of the moment only magnified as the years progressed. As much as I loved the people and beauty of Switzerland, it just wasn't "home." However, having been away from my birth country for so many years, the United States of America wasn't home either.

This life is just a place we are passing through.

Home was no longer a country, a place, or a nationality. Home was where I was headed. Heaven. Sure, Jesus is coming back to this earth to restore it and fulfill his covenant promises made with Israel.[3] This is part of the gospel message. But, it doesn't stop there. The Bible also says that God is preparing a new creation, a new home for all who believe.[4]

This life is just a place we are passing through. Friedrich Nietzsche famously said that life is not a dress rehearsal for eternity. I couldn't disagree more. Let's look at it another way. Life is like being on a journey, a vacation. It's only a temporary tour meant to be lived through faith until our new home is completed. Have you read Hebrews 11? We will look closer at this chapter soon. However, look how believers in God described themselves:

> "All these people were still living by faith when they died. They did not receive the things promised; they only saw them and welcomed them from a distance, admitting that they were **aliens** and **strangers** on earth.
>
> People who say such things show that they are looking for a country of their own. If they had been thinking of the country they had left, they would have had the opportunity to return.
>
> Instead, they were longing for a better country—a heavenly one. Therefore God is not ashamed to be called their God, for he has prepared a city for them." — *Hebrews 11:13–16*

Back to my question. Have you seen an alien? Well, are you a follower of Jesus? If so, look in the mirror. Look at me. The Bible tells us we are aliens. I don't mean those funny green characters flying around in UFOs that seem to only fly near people with cameras that take grainy photos. No, we are aliens of a different kind. Our citizenship is not of this earth as we know it today. If Hebrews doesn't convince you, check out what Peter says.

> *"Beloved, I urge you as **aliens** and **strangers** to abstain from fleshly lusts which wage war against the soul."*
> — *1 Peter 2:11 (NASB)*

Peter reminds us that, as believers, we are all *paroikos*. We are aliens. Even though we all have been given the right to live on this earth, our citizenship, our ultimate home is in heaven. We must learn to live among those in our cosmos without being like them.

And, we aren't just aliens, the other Greek word Peter uses is *parepidemos*. We are aliens and pilgrims. We are temporary travelers who are merely passing through this time on earth until Jesus makes all things new and then takes us to our final destination.

What does this have to do with evangelism? Well, it doesn't matter what our social status is because this place, as it is now, is not our home. To some degree, as a believer, you will never "fit" in this world.

Do you know one trick the enemy tries to pull? I've seen many believers fall victim to it. They allow the lies of the enemy to convince them to see themselves as a minority and use that as an excuse to remain silent. This seemingly negative minority status convinces us that we are less of a person than those around us. What we often forget, though, is that everyone in the world is a minority in some category or another. Let me explain. Move to a foreign country and you will be labeled a minority. Your sex could make you a minority in your field of work or country you live. Your age, skin color, or net worth are often descriptions that box you into a minority status.

Don't allow yourself to focus on how you are a minority, take on a victim mentality, and never fulfill the purpose God has for you. Instead, see yourself as a child of God who is born in his image. When we make it to heaven, there won't be minorities or majorities, we'll all be children of God, living together *Have you seen an alien? Well, are you a follower of Jesus? If so, look in the mirror.*

and worshipping Jesus forever. Let's take as many people with us as we can.

Imagine if Fanny Crosby would have believed the lies as a blind woman in a male dominant time. She may not have been as effective in sharing the gospel. What if David Livingstone believed the lie that his skin color would be a barrier to reaching people of another color? Or if Hudson Taylor would have focused on the social differences in China and stayed home instead of muting the excuses and sailing to China?

Some of the greatest achievements for the gospel have come through the lives of obvious minorities.

Some of the greatest achievements for the gospel have come through the lives of obvious minorities. If you recall, in an age where women were looked down upon, the first evangelists in the Bible after the resurrection of Jesus were women.

I think of Samuel Crowther, an African born in 1809 during the height of the slave trade who would eventually become an ordained minister in England. His translation of the Bible into Yoruba was used to share the gospel to countless Nigerians.

Or what about Elizabeth Fry? She was a woman, who took the gospel into the prisons in England in the early 1800s, bringing hope and reformation within that cosmos.

Even Jesus himself was a minority. Starting with his birth from a virgin and ending with his death being crucified between two thieves. He had limitless excuses to be silent. Thankfully he didn't. He proclaimed the kingdom and proved himself to be the king. He's the greatest example for us all to follow.

Have you allowed the enemy to whisper lies in your ears that your status eliminates you from being a messenger of the gospel? After a few months of living in Europe, I started to think I couldn't evangelize because I was a minority. I couldn't speak the language and felt many people looking down on me. Thankfully, I shook off the lies of the enemy and rose above my situation. You can, too!

Determine today to no longer see yourself as a victim of something you can't control and instead as a child of the king who is on vacation. You are only passing through this broken world on your way to your heavenly home and a restored world full of life. Be an alien while you're here, invading your cosmos with the good news of Jesus.

WE ALL NEED A JOHN

To be truly effective in evangelism, we must do more than just shake off the excuses. We must also find mentors who will inspire and guide us along the way. You need to surround yourself with people who have the same mission in life.

Be around men like D.L. Moody who said, "I look on the world as a wrecked vessel where God has said, 'save all you can.'" Imagine the inspiration to share the gospel that you would gain if you were constantly around people with an attitude for the gospel like Moody!

Find an older man or woman in the faith whom you can follow and will mentor you. After all, as the old adage says, you will never soar with the eagles if you always strut around with the peacocks.

Discipleship and mentorship are similar yet distinct. Jesus commands you to have one, and it is wise to have the other. We must disciple and be discipled. This was a command of Jesus. He tells us to not only, "go into all the world and preach the gospel" but also to "go and make disciples of all nations."[5] Discipleship is paramount in lives as believers.

The word disciple means "learner." In the time of Jesus, teachers would recruit young men to be taught by them. These disciples would become masters, and many would develop their own followings. We must preach the gospel, and we must disciple the new converts by teaching them what is written in the Bible.

Discipleship is broader and more basic than mentoring. Its main focus is getting believers grounded in their faith, living a godly life, equipped for general ministry expressions, and then reproducing it in other reproducing disciples. Without evangelism, there is no one to disciple. But without discipleship, the new converts hardly grow, and the gospel message rarely reproduces. If the life of a believer was divided into two halves, evangelism would be one half and discipleship the other.

> *After all, as the old adage says, you will never soar with the eagles if you always strut around with the peacocks.*

Unlike discipleship, mentorship is not a comm-and of Jesus. However, it is modeled throughout the Bible and beyond. Elisha was mentored by Elijah. Timothy was mentored by Paul.

John mentored Polycarp. Fanny Crosby was mentored by her grandma. The group of believers who went to China were mentored by Hudson Taylor.

And you should have a mentor as well.

A mentor is focused on the practicalities of a specific area in your life and calling. Their goal isn't to teach you Scripture, although that will be a byproduct. Rather, it's to help you live out that faith in your cosmos. Mentors help you silence the excuses of the enemy and faithfully fulfill your specific life calling.

Some would say that mentoring is advanced discipleship. It prepares leaders for mature, capable, and fruitful leadership. A mentor should teach you how to effectively represent the king and his message to the specific area, line of work, or culture you need help with.

I learned that evangelism is sometimes better caught than taught.

When I returned to Dallas, Texas, after graduating college in Florida, I knew that I wanted to reach professional football players with the gospel. Every weekday for a month, I went to the practice facility of the Dallas Cowboys asking for the chaplain's phone number. Every time, I was denied the information. Finally, one Friday afternoon, I walked in. The beautiful, young secretary at the front desk pulled out a piece of paper. "John Weber — Chaplain" was written on it along with his phone number.

I ran to my car, hurried home, and dialed the number. "This is John." "Hello, John, my name is Shawn Brann. I want to help you reach the Dallas Cowboys for Jesus." This one call changed my life. John became a mentor to me in ministry.

He taught me how to preach to athletes, how to share the gospel in locker rooms, and how to talk to famous people. I watched and listened to the way John acted and talked. I learned that evangelism is sometimes better caught than taught. He was one of the most effective and faithful behind-the-scenes examples of Christ I have ever seen.

I was passionate to bring the gospel, but I needed some wisdom on how and when to say it. John's life example taught me a healthy balance avoiding the warning of Proverbs 19:2, "It is not good to have zeal without knowledge."

With his sudden death seven years after that first call, I found myself with the Gospel Baton in hand. It was now my turn to lead. John had set an example for me. Not only was he a spiritual father to me, he was a mentor. I've noticed that most effective evangelists have older, godly mentors in their lives. You should, too!

Mentors focus on a specific topic or subject matter and how to be the best in that particular field. In my life, John was my mentor for sports chaplaincy. I learned more from him in this one field than I could ever have learned in any seminary. We talked a lot about life, the Bible, our struggles, and our joys. But it was John's mentorship in sports chaplaincy and how to bring Jesus to men that I'll never forget. He taught me how to soar with the gospel in the sports world.

What cosmoses are in your life, and do you know anyone who represents Jesus and shares his message that you would like to emulate? If so, do as I did. Be persistent. Get their information. Call them. Help them. And, let them teach you how to effectively evangelize those around you.

If you can't find anyone, research people who made a difference for Jesus and his gospel. Read their biographies. Study their messages. And, let them mentor you from a distance until you can find someone in person.

NO MENTOR, NO PROBLEM?

Well, not really. History has proven that some of the saddest stories throughout the history of the church were a result of men or women who were zealous for God but had no mentors to help guide them.

In 380 A.D., Roman emperor and believer named Theodosius made an imperial command that Christianity would be the state religion of the Roman empire. Ten years later, a charioteer in a Greek city was accused of homosexuality. The charioteer was thrown in prison, but the people pleaded for his release so he could race. The governor refused, so the people murdered the governor and released the prisoner.

When Theodosius heard what the people did, he was enraged. Without mentorship, and full of zeal without knowledge, Theodosius decided he would punish the people. At the next race in the circus at Thessalonica, when all the spectators had found their seats and were ready for the races to begin, the exit gates were closed. Theodosius ordered soldiers to storm the arena with swords in hand. Within three hours, seven thousand spectators lay dead.

Ambrose, the bishop of Milan, Italy, wrote this to Theodosius, "I cannot deny that you have a zeal for the faith and that you fear God, but you have a naturally passionate spirit which becomes ungovernable when you are excited. I call on you to repent … You are a man, and as you have sinned as a man so you must repent. God alone can forgive you, and He forgives only those who repent."[6] Theodosius was zealous but foolish. What if Theodosius had had a godly mentor teaching him how to live out his faith within the government? What could his story have been? Instead, his lack of mentorship brought a negative view of the gospel to the citizens in Thessalonica.

In another story, if you remember back in the 500s, it was the Berbers in North Africa who passionately carried on the gospel during the Bubonic Plague. Unfortunately, the lack of discipleship and mentorship led to a tragic reversal. When the Muslim crusaders came through that region a few hundred years later, these same Berbers switched from faith in Christ to following Islam. This area is still a predominately Muslim region as a result.

We need mentors in our lives.

Proverbs 27:17 says it like this, "As iron sharpens iron so one man sharpens another." Mentors sharpen and shape us. Their wisdom and experience in specific areas can make us all specialists in bringing the gospel. They help us to overcome excuses so that we can live out our God-given destinies and bring the good news.

As the 1800s progressed, like the industrial revolution, it was almost as if the Holy Spirit picked up production on the export of the gospel as well. A rapid advancement of the gospel had begun. It was becoming clear that the gospel, as Jesus prophesied, would indeed go throughout the whole world. The time of the king's return was drawing near.

21

THE 1900s–GLOBALLY MINDED
But … I Don't Know Where to Go

"People who do not know the Lord ask why in the world we waste our lives as missionaries. They forget that they too are expending their lives … and when the bubble has burst, they will have nothing of eternal significance to show for the years they have wasted." — Nate Saint, missionary martyr

It was early afternoon on Sunday, January 8, 1956. Nate Saint, Ed McCully, Peter Fleming, Roger Youderian, and Jim Elliot stood on the beach ready to make their first contact with the Huaorani men, one of the fiercest unreached tribes in the world.

A few years earlier, these five men, along with their wives and children, moved to Equador from the United States to bring the good news to these unreached native Amerindians from the Amazonian Region of Ecuador. The families learned the language and customs of the Huaorani in preparation for the moment when they would finally approach them in person. In order to build trust, the men would fly over the Huaorani's isolated village once a week in their single engine Piper Cruiser plane, dropping tools, food, and other useful items for the tribe.

Over time, the men learned that if they flew in a tight circle, they could lower a bucket on a line. This way they could personally deliver the goods instead of dropping them from the plane. Soon, the Huaorani were responding back by giving the men gifts such as a woven headband, carved wooden combs, two live parrots, and a piece of smoked monkey tail. Now, after all the contacts and preparations had been made, the men were ready to meet the Huaorani in person and share the gospel.

On Tuesday, January 3, 1956, the men left their wives and children at home as they boarded their small plane. Four miles from the Huaorani's village, they located a beach along the Curaray River that would serve as a landing strip and their temporary campsite. The first Huaorani showed up three days later: a man, a woman, and a girl. They stayed for several hours.

Nate gave the man a ride in his airplane. The other five men entertained them by showing them rubber bands, playing with a yo-yo, and making them a hamburger with mustard. The three Indians seemed to really enjoy the mustard. After a few hours, the Huaorani left. It was only a matter of time before the five men would be able to sit with the tribe and share the gospel.

On Saturday, the men waited alone on the beach, praying, talking to each other, taking photos, and writing in their diaries. Then, it happened.

Sunday afternoon, two Huaorani women came out of the trees and waded into the water. This was their sign. The entire Huaorani tribe were ready to meet them.

Or, so they thought.

Jim Elliot and Peter Fleming waded out to meet the women. Unfortunately, the two men were ambushed by a group of Huaorani men. Within seconds, Elliot and Fleming floated in the river, speared to death. The other three men on the beach were then attacked. Saint was speared first and then McCully. Roger Youderian rushed to the plane to radio for help. Before he could make it to the aircraft, he, too, was killed.

The Indians took their bodies and belongings and threw them into the river. They then returned to their village and, anticipating retribution, burned it to the ground and fled into the jungle. Five families lost their husbands and their dads. All because these men had a baton in their hands and a message in their hearts that they knew the Huaorani needed to hear.

The news of the martyrdom quickly spread around the world. *Life Magazine* put the story on the cover of their January 1956 issue, dedicating ten pages to these families. The magazine told of the powerful truth that although the gospel is free to all who believe it, followers of Christ sometimes pay the same price their king did when they desire to share it.

More than a thousand college students volunteered for foreign missions in direct response to the story. In Ecuador alone, Indian attendance at mission schools and church services reached record levels, and the number of conversions skyrocketed. What seemed like a tragedy only pushed the gospel further into unreached corners of the world.[1]

Reaching every nation, tribe, and language with this message was the theme of the believers in the twentieth century.

And the story didn't end there.

Despite what had happened to their men, Elisabeth Elliot (widow of Jim Elliot) and Rachel Saint (sister of Nate Saint) were still determined to reach the killers with the gospel. They stayed near the Huaoranis territory at a site sixty hours away by foot and canoe. In November 1957, they had a breakthrough. Two women from the tribe had found Elisabeth and Rachel. For ten months, the two Huaorani women taught Elisabeth and Rachel the language and culture of their tribe. The tribal women left, only to return three weeks later with an invitation for Elisabeth and Rachel to visit the tribe.

Fearful but full of faith, Elisabeth strapped her three-year-old daughter, Valerie, to her back and along with Rachel, they headed for the village. They arrived on October 8, 1958, on what would have been Jim Elliot's birthday and the couple's fifth wedding anniversary. The women missionaries were welcomed by the Huaorani.

The two women with the baby were invited to live with the tribe. The women accepted the offer and were able to finally share the gospel to the Huaorani. Slowly, one by one, the Huaorani committed to following Christ.

The Huaorani were asked years after the killing of the three men why they didn't kill Rachel, Elizabeth, and Valerie. The Indians said that they realized that the men were indeed their friends after the killings since they were willing to die for them instead of retaliating. Some even said they had heard singing and saw lights in the trees as angels seemed to be welcoming the men to their eternal home.

When the Huaorani heard the message from the women missionaries that Jesus, too, had come to die for them, they quickly believed. They recognized that the message of the five men was the basis of what they had seen enacted on the shore that fateful Sunday morning in January.

If the purpose of moving or visiting somewhere is to bring the gospel, you won't make a mistake, regardless of the outcome.

The Huaorani believed the gospel preached because they had seen the gospel lived.

This small tribe was just one of thousands of remote, unevangelized areas finally getting to hear the gospel for the first time. Reaching every nation, tribe, and language with this message was the theme of the believers in the twentieth century. They were determined that the whole world would indeed hear the gospel!

A CASE OF PBA

When I was working on my MBA, one of my teachers told his class that many business leaders lack success because they have a mental condition called PBA (Paralysis By Analysis). Basically, someone can analyze a situation so much that it paralyses them and they do nothing.

This isn't just a businessman's condition. I think many more believers suffer from this condition. I've sat with so many believers over the years who have told me how they feel God is calling them to leave their comfort zone where they live to visit or move to a new location to share the gospel. Unfortunately, I can only count on one hand the people who actually followed through. Why?

I think it is PBA. They over analyze the situation waiting on God to give them a green light. After all, they don't want to make a mistake. I understand. Maybe this is you. Have you experienced a case of PBA?

Well, I have good news. Here's your sign. GO! Now, you don't have to suffer any longer from PBA. We've seen throughout this book how Jesus sends us into the world (cosmos) to share the gospel. However, there is another verse that speaks of the Great Commission. We saw this verse in the prior chapter where Jesus said: "go and make disciples of all nations."[2]

The Greek word for "nations" found in this verse is not *cosmos*—it is the Greek word *ethnos*. This is an important distinction. *Ethnos* is where we get the English word ethnicity. We are not just called to reach those in our *cosmos*, but also those in different ethnic groups. In other words, we are called to share the gospel to everyone in every location around the world. The gospel is for all mankind.

You don't have to suffer from PBA when it comes to where you should take the gospel. The whole world is your option.

But what if you make a mistake and visit or move to the wrong location? If the purpose of moving or visiting somewhere is to bring the gospel, you won't make a mistake, regardless of the outcome.

Do you remember when Paul and his friends were preaching in Bithynia and a great multitude heard the gospel and started following Jesus? No. Why? Because it never happened. Paul yearned to go to Bithynia to share Jesus, but the Holy Spirit would not let him.

> *"Paul and his companions traveled throughout the region of Phrygia and Galatia, having been kept by the Holy Spirit from preaching the word in the province of Asia. When they came to the border of Mysia, they tried to enter Bithynia, but the Spirit of Jesus would not allow them to. So they passed by Mysia and went down to Troas." — Acts 16:6–8*

Just like Paul, the Holy Spirit will keep you from making a mistake or going to a place you shouldn't be. This message is not for the advancement of your ministry but of his kingdom. He knows who he wants to deliver his message to each ethnic group. And, if it's not you, he will keep you from going.

But, what about Jim Elliot and his friends? If God wanted them there and allowed them to go then, why did they get martyred? This is one of those questions that only God knows the answer to. What is important is that God sees our obedience to his call and he honors it. History has shown us that some of the most disappointing endings in the life of faithful missionaries was the seed that resulted in centuries of fruitful ministry afterwards. Exactly as Tertullian said in the second century, "the blood of the martyrs is the seed of the church."

A MISSILE OR A MISSED OPPORTUNITY

There are basically two approaches to life: playing to win and playing not to lose. Play to win.

There are basically two approaches to life: playing to win and playing not to lose. Play to win.

Many believers get wrapped up in living the "dream" life only to get to the end and realize it was a nightmare. They played it safe. They never told anyone about Jesus so not to offend anyone. They never followed through with that spark from the Holy Spirit regarding a daring step of faith to advance his kingdom. Instead of being globally minded, they lived as though the world revolved around them, only to remember in their last days that everything except what we do for Jesus in this lifetime is temporary.

Jim Elliott wrote in his journal a few years before being martyred that, "He is no fool who gives what he cannot keep to gain that which he cannot lose."

The way we play to win in life is by following the command of Jesus to Go & Tell others the gospel. It's when you set your vision on eternal things that "moths and rust cannot destroy and thieves cannot break in and steal."[3] We win by living for eternal gain and not that which is temporary. It's when we allow him to send us wherever he wants us to go. And to trust him if he keeps us from going where we may want to go.

"He is no fool who gives what he cannot keep to gain that which he cannot lose."

In every generation, there are enough believers to take the gospel to every un-reached person in the world. It is not God who does not call. It is man who does not respond. He's calling.

JUST GO!

Did you know the word missionary and missile come from the same Latin root word, *mittere* "to send"? God is sending you to your cosmos and to different ethnic groups to bring his gospel. Don't stay back. Let God launch you like a missile and explode with the power from the Holy Spirit wherever you land.

Over the exit door of a church I once visited was a sign that said, "You are now entering the mission field." What a great reminder. Sometimes we think that the only way we can share the gospel is by going on a "missions trip" to a foreign country. Missions is not just crossing the sea. Missions is seeing the cross, and then taking that good news to everyone around you.

Our mission is to take the Gospel Baton and Go & Tell everyone in every ethic group in every cosmos about Jesus. We are not to stay at home but … Go! Go across the room at work.

Go across the street.

Go across the city.

Go across the country.

Go across the world.

Just go! Wherever that is, you won't regret it.

We must give our utmost to tell others about Jesus. What good is our faith that gives us eternity with Christ but does not drive us to tell others about this good news?

We win by living for eternal gain and not that which is temporary.

I read a diary entry of a believer from 1506 who pleaded for more people to join him in reaching the unbelievers in Japan. Few answered the call. Yet, he continued calling, "all of Japan will be Christian in the next ten years if we just had more missionaries!"[4] Imagine what Japan could be today if some of the believers in the 1500s would have joined him instead of focusing on their careers.

There are no excuses for not going. Every cosmos and every ethos is waiting on you to come. Don't let excuses hold you back.

In 1792, missionary William Carey wrote *An Enquiry into the Obligation of Christians to Use Means for the Conversion of the Heathen.* In the book, he gives five excuses people in the 1700s used for not allowing the Holy Spirit to send them wherever he wanted to bring the gospel. They were: distance, barbarism, danger, difficulties of support, and language barriers.

Do any of these sound familiar?

Carey went on to say that none of these excuses kept businessmen from going to foreign lands to sell their goods. He would write, "It only requires that we should have as much love to the souls of our fellow-creatures, and fellow sinners, as they have for the profits arising from a few otter skins, and all these difficulties could be easily overcome."[5]

Missions is not just crossing the sea. Missions is seeing the cross, and then taking that good news to everyone around you.

The twentieth century believers did. Men and women like those missionaries in Ecuador did not let excuses hold them back. With the Gospel Baton in hand, they went. And, as they went, the gospel went, too. Time was wrapping up. The gospel was being declared around the world!

22

THE 2000s–AVAILABILITY
But ... I'm Not Able

> *"Anyone who sets out to serve Christ can be sure that many escape routes will appear so that you can relinquish your responsibilities."* — *Chuck Swindoll*

Two thousand years have passed since the king left; only a few more years before his return. This generation of believers lives in a much different world than when Jesus walked those streets in Jerusalem telling his disciples what to look for before his second coming.

Self-driving cars replaced horses, and birds have to share the sky with airplanes. The telephone and social media changed the way man communicates, while the internet made knowledge unlimited. Everything seemed possible—both to unbelievers and believers alike.

Followers of Jesus passionately share the gospel, believing for Jesus' kingdom to come "on earth as it is in heaven." Healings, signs and wonders, and salvation follow those who believe. Though many have fallen away, as Jesus had prophesied would happen, there is still a large remnant who won't let anything hold them back from declaring this good news of Jesus. They run unabandoned and without excuse. Nick is one of them.

Born in Melbourne, Australia, in most ways, Nick was like any other kid. As a teenager, Nick made himself available to God and even founded a small ministry called Life Without Limbs in 2005. Determined to faithfully carry the Gospel Baton to his generation, Nick lived without excuse to see the impossibility of the gospel making its final stretch on the earth. The reach of his new ministry would go places no one could ever have imagined.

In just fifteen years after the founding of Life Without Limbs, Nick would become a sought-after speaker with the opportunity to share Jesus in almost every major global newspaper, appearing on some of the world's most influential talk shows, and having one-on-one meetings with dozens of world leaders and presidents. In such a short span of time, he had already shared the gospel to over seven hundred thirty three million people, with over a million making immediate decisions to become followers of Jesus.[1]

Nick had made himself available, and God had done the rest. Nick must have been a famous athlete or Hollywood celebrity, right? Not even. In fact, Nick was the most unexpected candidate for God to use on such a large scale. If there was anyone who had an excuse not to follow Jesus and share the good news, it would have been Nick. You see, Nick was born a healthy baby boy. However, he was born with a unique challenge. He had no arms or legs. That's right! Not a right arm, a right leg, a left arm, or a left leg.

As a young boy, he faced the typical challenges in school and adolescence anyone would experience if born under such circumstances. He also struggled with depression and loneliness. However, in his early years, Nick became a follower of Jesus. And even though he was born with bad news, he didn't let it keep him from bringing the good news to others.

No arms. No legs. No problem. Nick carried the Gospel Baton and ran his race without excuses. Nick is a perfect example of how believers of this century run, as impossible as it may have seemed, faithfully with the Gospel Baton. As a result, the message of Jesus has finally made its way around the whole world. Jesus' return is soon.

YOUR GREATEST ABILITY

Have you ever believed the lie that you have nothing of significance to offer God for the advancement of his kingdom? No special talents. No unique skills. No gripping testimony of deliverance? When I first became a follower of Jesus as a teenager, I struggled with the excuse that I had nothing unique to give God. I wasn't delivered from a crazy life of drugs, I couldn't sing, I wasn't the most popular kid in school, and I definitely did not like public speaking. So what value did I have for Jesus? But, I desperately wanted to be useful to him.

God is not looking for our ability but our availability.

When my friends were home watching the latest movies and TV shows, I sat for hours in front of my television listening to evangelist Reinhard Bonnke, Billy Graham, and a fiery, Pentecostal pastor named Rod Parsley. My heart would become inflamed with passion for Jesus every time I heard them preach. They were smart, bold, and gifted communicators. Yet for me, I thought I could never be like them even if I tried. And, once, I did try.

The first time I was ever asked to preach was at a small youth group I attended in Irving, Texas. This was my moment. I tried to do my best Rod Parsley impersonation only to make a complete fool of myself. After about three minutes, I had accidently switched the story of Noah with Moses, misquoted two verses, and then I rambled for another fifteen minutes before humbly walking off the platform. It was my first and last time I was asked to preach at the youth group. It was a complete disaster. I felt like I had nothing of significance to offer God for his use.

A couple of months later, I was driving past a nursing home and sensed the Holy Spirit asking me to share the gospel to some of the elderly people in the home. Hesitantly, I pulled into the parking lot, took a deep breath, and got out of my car. Since I knew no one in the nursing home, I walked into the first bedroom I saw.

There was a frail old woman in the room watching TV.

"Excuse me," I said. "We don't know each other, but I'm Shawn and I have something really important I want to share with you."

She smiled, showed me some photos of her children, and then politely listened to my best gospel presentation. The more I shared, the more passionate I became. Something burned in my heart. My words weren't just words, but something I really believed. Something I knew to be true. Jesus loved this lady and wanted her to know him for all eternity; for her to be part of his kingdom.

This time, my three-minute message was much more effective. When I finished, the elderly lady looked me in the eyes and said she wanted to follow Jesus. My heart leaped inside of me. I could barely believe what

We often exchange a temporary fear of man for the eternal treasures of heaven.

I was hearing. I prayed with her, we hugged, we cried, and that was the first and last time I would ever see her.

As I walked out to my car that day, I felt like I had just preached an evangelistic event with millions in attendance. Before driving off, I sat in my car, tears rolling down my cheeks, amazed at what had just happened. It was at that moment when I understood the reality of this simple truth: God is not looking for our ability but our availability.

No matter how gifted you are, how much you know the scriptures, or how much talent you have, you can't be used by God if you are not available. We often have the misconception that to be used by God we must have special abilities or skills. However, being available is more important to God than our talents.

But we have a serious dilemma. The enemy of our faith constantly bombards us with countless excuses for not sharing the good news. He wants us to be unavailable to the Holy Spirit working through us. And, unfortunately, we often allow the enemy's excuses to keep us from being God's representatives in our cosmos. We buy into the lie that the opinions of man are more important than those of our king. We often exchange a temporary fear of man for the eternal treasures of heaven.

Let's live without excuse in sharing the gospel. The opportunity to evangelize is for all who believe. Everyone can and should share the gospel. Even if you have no arms or legs.

> *"The eyes of the Lord search the whole earth in order to strengthen those whose hearts are fully committed to him."*
> — *2 Chronicles 16:9 (NLT)*

At this very moment, God is scanning the earth looking for men and women he can work through; who he can show himself to. He's not looking for gold or silver vessels but for pure vessels. He's not looking for superheroes, but for people whose hearts are committed to him.

And the first step of that commitment is being available.

GOD IS CALLING

We all have that friend we can never get a hold of when we call. You know what I mean. Every time you call, there's no answer. You get a voicemail, "I'm sorry I'm not available to take your call but leave me a message and I'll get back with you as soon as I can." Most of the time, I just hang

He's not looking for superheroes, but for people whose hearts are committed to him.

up. It's incredibly frustrating. Their lack of availability does not negate the fact that you tried calling. For whatever reason, the friend did not take the call.

When Jesus walked those shores of Galilee, he called,

> *"Come follow me, and I will make you fishers of men."*
> *— Matthew 4:19 (ESV)*

Peter, Andrew, James, and John all followed him. But notice something. Jesus never addresses any of the four men specifically by name when he called; not in Matthew, not in Mark, not according to Luke, or in the book of John. He just makes the statement to follow. Why? Because the call was not for Peter or Andrew, Matthew, or Mark, alone. Jesus' call was for everyone on the shore that day. It was for all who would come later. It was for you. It was for me. It's for anyone available.

Have you ever thought about this: most people watch history but very few get to make it? What separates the two? Is it talent? Is it ability? Is it giftings? Usually not. The greatest ability to make history, especially for God's purposes for your life, is your availability. Jesus is not just looking at you, but he's calling.

Will you be available, or will Jesus get an excuse about why you are not available?

Throughout the Bible, we read of the people God used. Abraham. Jacob. Moses. Noah. Samuel. Rebekah. The disciples. Mary. Paul. Even Balaam's donkey. They came from many different backgrounds over thousands of years from a broad spectrum of experiences. The one thing that was consistent to all of them was that they made themselves available for God. They all followed the example of Isaiah in saying, "Here I am!"

How many people over the centuries have missed their opportunity when Jesus was calling? How many still do? Don't let this be said about you. Don't look at your schedule and say to God that you are unavailable. Availability does not mean that you have lots of time on your hands but rather managing your schedule to say "no" to some good things so you can say "yes" to what is best.

Back to those four disciples. I wonder how many people Jesus called that day when Peter, Andrew, James, and John left their nets to follow him?

Maybe there was a young man named Asher who, when Jesus called, said he wasn't available at the time because he needed to finish his lunch. Or maybe there were a couple boys, Michael and Yoel, who thought it was more important to continue playing their watersport instead of answering Jesus? Maybe Miriam said she couldn't follow because she was a minority, didn't have any special talents, or was just too old. Think of the stories that could have been if these other men and women had just answered the call! Instead, we read of James and John, Peter and Andrew who made themselves available, and Jesus made them great for his kingdom.

You don't have to have all the talents or giftings in the world to share the gospel. Just use what God has given you. No one is given everything, but everyone is given something. And one of those "somethings" that everyone has is their availability to God.

Don't miss the call. There are still more people who need to hear the good news. These are the final days.

THE KING IS COMING

For twenty one centuries, believers have been answering the call, grabbing the baton, and running full speed in the race of a lifetime. Men and women, and boys and girls have put every excuse aside and shared the good news in almost every cosmos and ethnos of the world.

Many would fulfill the prophecy Jesus had told Peter[2] that not even the "gates of hell", the *pulai hadou*, could prevail in the advancement of God's kingdom on the Earth. This Jewish expression simply referred to death; the passageway from this life to the next. And Jesus' followers proved this prophecy to be true. Death and the threats of martyrdom could not silence their message. The grave had been conquered. There are millions of untold stories of believers who were killed for this message to go around the world.

Now, the climax of the story of history has arrived. The final stretch of the race is here. The roar of the heavenly crowds is only muted by the barrier between the visible and invisible realms. Those who have gone on before shout for all of us still alive: Run, the king is coming!

The last book of the Bible gives us a glimpse of this final stretch run of history. Revelation is a drama of triumph, not a horror story. It is the story of the followers of Jesus overcoming death, hell, and the grave, having run the greatest race of all time—the goal of delivering the good news to the whole world. And the story of the king coming to rescue mankind—both Jew and Gentile.

It tells of the king who is on the throne. For all eternity, we will sing his song, the song of the Lamb:

> *"Great and marvelous are your deeds, Lord God Almighty. Just and true are your ways, King of the ages."*
> *— Revelation 15:3*

But before we all gather in that heavenly choir loft to forever praise our king, we've got to finish this race. Our work is not complete. The baton hasn't crossed the finish line. Even though we are in the final stretch of the race.

Are you aware that these are the final steps of this gospel race—the end of time?

Throughout the Old Testament and in conversations with the disciples, hints were given to when Jesus would return. Prophecies tell us that just before Jesus' return there will be a major increase of knowledge and people would be moving all over the world.

> *"But you, Daniel, keep this prophecy a secret; seal up the book until the time of the end, when many will rush here and there, and knowledge will increase."* — *Daniel 12:4*

That time has arrived. The internet gave us the information highway where everything we needed to know is a simple click away. In addition, there are more than twenty five thousand research institutions and universities in the world. Never has the world been so educated as we suddenly became in the past hundred years.

Knowledge transferred from one individual to another has also dramatically increased. From the beginning of Genesis until the nineteenth century, men communicated by flashing mirrors or fires from mountaintop to mountaintop; suddenly the telegraph arrived, then the telephone, then the television, and now we can teleport ourselves via face-to-face conference calls around the world in real time.

The invention of the car and planes revolutionized the way people traveled. For six millennia, people relied on walking or horseback as the means of transportation. Now more than three billion people travel by airplane annually, going to any place on the earth in less than a day. While nearly a billion and a half cars traverse the roads worldwide. We've gone from horseback to automobiles to jets to the moon. People are truly going from here to there, to every corner of the world, as Jesus prophesied would happen just before his return.

These are just a few hints. Others include the rebirth of Israel, which just so happened to be nineteen hundred and forty eight years after the birth of Jesus; just like Abraham came nineteen hundred and forty eight years after the first man, Adam. This is not a coincidence. There are hundreds of passages in the Bible that indicate that Israel will once again occupy center stage in world affairs. We are seeing that at this very moment.

Your Bible says that there would be a breakdown of the home and extremely loose morals[3], the world would be under such stress that there would be no apparent way out (Luke 21:25), and there would be a major push for world peace (1 Thessalonians 5:3). There will be a "new social order," the abolition of social injustice, war, poverty, disease, and racism.

In the days before King Jesus returns, Paul told Timothy that the world would hate to hear the truth of God's Word.

> "For the time will come when people will not put up with sound doctrine. Instead, to suit their own desires, they will gather around them a great number of teachers to say what their itching ears want to hear." — 2 Timothy 4:3

This is true today as liberal messages in many once-Christian universities, and even so-called churches teach doctrine apart from the Bible. The Bible is being taught as allegory for living and not the true way of life. Evolution and sexual immorality have supplanted creation and the sanctity of marriage.

In many churches, the gospel has been swapped for social services and preaching has become a profession of unbelievers only proclaiming what society would like to hear. The truth has been replaced to appease the sinful. This isn't surprising to God. He knew this would come in the last days before his return. And these are just a few of the prophecies mentioned in the Bible.

The predictions of these last days occupy approximately one quarter of all the Bible. The Second Coming of Jesus Christ is dealt with in some eighteen hundred passages in the Bible — three hundred and eighteen of these being in the New Testament.[4]

Jesus, himself, pulled his disciples aside and gave them signs that believers should be looking for before his return. He said there would be "wars and rumors of wars ... nations will rise against nation, and kingdom against kingdom."[5] However, this would only be the "birth pains" before his return.

He then said that believers would "be handed over to be persecuted and put to death, and would be hated by all nations because of him."[6] As we saw earlier, this is happening the very moment you are reading this book.

Credible research has reached the shocking conclusion that an estimate of more than a hundred thousand Christians are violently killed because of some relation to their faith every year. Others are subjected to forced displacement, destruction of their places of worship, rape, and abduction of their leaders.[7]

But don't lose heart over all this evil and destruction. Remember: as a believer your short amount of time on this earth is the only hell you will ever experience. For those who don't know Christ, this is their only heaven. We must share the good news and the hope they can have for eternity. In the meantime, Jesus is patiently waiting to return for his people until the whole world has heard and given the opportunity to be part of his kingdom. Once this final accomplishment fully happens, he will return.

> "And this gospel of the kingdom will be preached in the whole world as a testimony to all nations, and then the end will come." — Matthew 24:14

The end comes when the gospel has been preached in the whole world. That moment is upon us. More than two thousand years of faithful believers running with the gospel, making themselves available, and giving their all instead of making excuses have gotten us to where we are at this moment in history. Now, via radio, television, internet, social media, print, and in person, radical believers are running with the Gospel Baton to every corner of every cosmos in every nation of the world.

The heavenly trumpet is soon to sound. The triumphal entry of the king back to the earth is near. Jesus is coming again! The closing words from Jesus in Revelation are echoing throughout the world, louder than ever before.

> *"Look, I am coming soon! My reward is with me, and I will*
> *give to each person according to what they have done."*
> — *Revelation 22:12*

These are the final days. The ending is almost here. Time is running out. The race is coming to an end, and the Gospel Baton is about to cross the finish line.

Many things may have changed since Jesus first gave the Great Commission to those early believers, but a few things have remained the same. The gospel is still good news, Jesus is still calling people, and he's still looking for people who are available to be part of his plan of salvation.

Now the Gospel Baton is getting the final handoff.

23

TODAY–NO EXCUSES
Now It's Your Turn

"Go into all the world and preach the gospel to all creation."
— *Mark 16:15*

This is it. The final exclamation point of history. The completion of Jesus' prophecy is about to be fulfilled. The Gospel Baton is about to cross the finish line. The crowd is standing on their feet. Every tribe, every nation, and every century represented.

There are Sunday school teachers, theologians, moms, and dads. Many are martyrs. Most are unknown to future generations but decorated soldiers in heaven. Others have gained such a reputation on earth for their example of Christ that centuries later people still imitate their faith: Peter, James, John, Paul, Ignatius, Augustine, Patrick, Aquinas, Wycliffe, Luther, Calvin, Edwards, Wesley, Whitefield, Spurgeon, Bonhoeffer, Graham, and Bonnke, to name a few. There are brothers, sisters, businessmen, and housewives. They all have one thing in common—they made Jesus king of their lives.

As the messenger nears the finish line, the enthusiastic crowd chants with all encouragement, "Run!"

Those in the great audience of heaven have finished their part of the race, advancing the Gospel Baton for the future centuries. They look on in full assurance that their running was not in vain. This isn't a time for the final runner to slow down, but to finish strong. This is the Golden Age of the Church. It is the moment every prior generation longed to see fulfilled in their lifetimes. Now it appears that it may have arrived. This might just be the generation to finish the race!

The runner with the honor of potentially crossing the finish line of history with baton in hand is … _____ (you).

CLOSERS

Don't you love the final few minutes of a live sporting event? I remember a baseball game I attended in Texas in 2010. The Rangers were winning a critical game against the New York Yankees. The winning team would be the American League Champions.

For the entire game, the Rangers players had all given their best to win the game. They jumped out to a quick lead and held the momentum throughout the game. Headed into the final inning, the Rangers brought in the team's best closing pitcher to finish the game. After two quick outs, the Yankees were down to their last batter and losing by five runs. Strike one. Strike two. The crowd stood on their feet as the closing pitcher went into his pitching motion. The noise in the stadium was deafening.

This isn't a time for the final runner to slow down, but to finish strong.

The entire Rangers team shouted and looked on in anticipation. It was the players' game to lose … and his to win.

Strike three! He did it. The Texas Rangers beat the New York Yankees and were the champions. The game was over.

So, what's the point?

You are like that closing pitcher. Instead of a baseball game with a ball in hand, you are in a spiritual race with the Gospel Baton in hand. And, the stadium is roaring with anticipation for what is about to happen.

Hebrews 11 is the chapter often referred to as the Hall of Faith—a comparison to a sports Hall of Fame. The writer talks about biblical heroes who lived a life of faith in God. Then, as if he is thinking about you at this very moment, he says this,

> *"Therefore, since we are surrounded by such a great cloud of witnesses…"* — Hebrews 12:1

There is an interesting word the writer mentions in this text—cloud. Did you notice that too? What is he talking about?

The Greek word for cloud in this verse is *nephos*, which is just like clouds that you see in the sky. Artists over the centuries have used this verse to paint the picture of heaven as a place where we all float on clouds. However, the writer of Hebrews was probably thinking of something else.

In ancient Greek, *nephos* was also used to describe the highest seats in a large stadium. Small stadiums wouldn't have cloud seats, but larger stadiums, even to this day, still have these nosebleed or cloud seats.

Perhaps the writer of Hebrews was reminding us that we are in a race being cheered on by a large crowd of people who have gone on before us. Imagine with me for a moment. With eyes and ears of faith, pull back the curtains of eternity and see yourself running on a track with a baton in hand. The crowd surrounds you with the seats reaching to the heavens. It's a full stadium with millions in attendance. The stands are filled with centuries of believers who ran the race of the Great Commission and have faithfully passed on the baton to you.

Now, as you sprint, they shout out to you ...
"Run!"
"Preach the gospel!"
"Finish the race!"

The Church today is the fruit of twenty-one centuries of believers who preached the gospel whether by life or by death.

The track we run on has been blazed by these believers with blood, sweat, and tears. They gave their lives for the advancement of the gospel. They anxiously awaited this moment. And now it is here.

These are the greatest days in church history. We find ourselves at this amazing time in history, not because of our marvelous preaching, creative services, or glorious music. No. The Church today is the fruit of twenty-one centuries of believers who preached the gospel whether by life or by death. And the fruit of future generations, if time continues, will be a direct result of our labor for the gospel now. Therefore, as the writer continued,

> *"... let us throw off everything that hinders and the sin that so easily entangles. And let us run with perseverance the race marked out for us..."* — Hebrews 12:1

You have a responsibility to all those who have gone on before you, those who have yet to come, and from Jesus, himself, to run with all

God has chosen you to be a closer for his kingdom.

perseverance so that the gospel continues its life-changing advancement throughout the world.

As you have previously already read, you must throw off whatever excuses come and any sin that has attached itself to you, making you paralyzed to proclaim the gospel. And, with the Gospel Baton, run the race God has for you. Don't allow the enemy to distract you. Don't run the wrong race. This is about Jesus and his kingdom coming to earth. Stay focused. You've got this.

David Livingstone wrote in his journal of this moment almost two hundred years ago:

> *"We work for a glorious future which we are not destined to see, the Golden Age which has not yet been, but will yet be. We are only morning stars shining in the dark, but the glorious morn will break—the good time is coming yet."*

This is that good time. This is the Golden Age. And the end of the race is near. God has chosen you to be a closer for his kingdom. This isn't a baseball game that has no eternal significance. Eternal destinies are at stake. Bring them the good news. You can do it. You were born for this moment. Be sold out for the advancement of the gospel. Remember that a life that is totally committed to God has nothing to lose, nothing to be afraid of, and nothing to regret.

One of the greatest compliments in the Bible is found in Acts 13:36. It says of David that when he "had served the purpose in his own generation, he fell asleep." I hope that can be said about us all. I hope that our lives are marked with the reality that we fulfilled God's purpose for our lives—not the purposes we wanted, or what culture said we had to do, but God's purpose of fulfilling the Great Commission. My life would be a win if my tombstone said something like this, "Here lies Shawn Brann. He fulfilled God's purpose for his life and then he died." And, the same for you.

What about you? What will be said about you? What will be said of this century of believers?

GOOD NEWS

The gospel is still good news! Just as the sun is old but still necessary for life, so the gospel may be old but its message is as relevant now as the moment Jesus spoke it to the disciples. Jesus is still the hope for our world.

A life that is totally committed to God has nothing to lose, nothing to be afraid of, and nothing to regret.

Go on any news station on the television, radio or internet, and you will be bombarded with bad news. Murder, lies, deception, and sexual immorality flood our airwaves. The world is desperate to hear something different. Have you ever contemplated the sad reality of individuals who have never received the good news and made Jesus king in their lives?

Think about this. I alluded to it in the previous chapter. As a believer, this world and all its troubles are the only hell one will ever face. But, for unbelievers, this is the only heaven—this world is as good as it gets. Let's change that! Let's make hell empty and heaven full![1] You have the good news every person is desiring to hear. Jesus has won. Satan loses. Hate loses. Excuses lose. And, the king is coming again! All we have left to do is proclaim this good news to everyone we see.

In the 1400s Erasmus said, "give light and the darkness will disappear." As you bring the light of the gospel, darkness flees. This is what has been happening for two thousand years. Faith has replaced disbelief. Hope has uprooted despair. And the love from the gospel has silenced the sorrow of individuals being eternally separated from their king.

Now is not the time to slow down or look back. There are still untold millions who have never heard about Jesus. The main goal of every believer from this point forward is to finish the task by bringing the gospel to everyone they know. Let Paul's declaration be ours, "Woe is me if I don't preach the gospel."[2]

Now it's no longer a discussion of if the whole world will hear, it's a matter of who will take the baton and complete this final stretch run of history.

GO & TELL

Twenty-eight centuries have passed since the king asked Isaiah, "whom shall I send? And who will go for us?" Although he knew he was completely unworthy to represent the king to the world, Isaiah would not let any excuse stop him. The eyes of the Lord saw Isaiah's lifted hand and available heart—his ears heard Isaiah's plea, "Here am I, send me!"

In Isaiah 6:9, the king replied: "Go and tell this people ..."

Now the king is asking you. "Whom shall I send? Who will Go & Tell this generation of this good news? Who will be the closer?" All of heaven is cheering you on.

"Give light and the darkness will disappear."

The baton is out.
Grab it and run.
The gospel needs to be heard.

AFTERWORD

Remember the young girl, Maxima, from the story in the Preface? Let's imagine together.

One of these days, the world as we know it will be over. The last grain of sand in the hourglass of time will have dropped.

Revelation 19:9 reveals the great party feast that will take place for all who believed. It's called the Marriage Supper of the Lamb—a party to celebrate our king, his victory, our commitment to him, and the unbroken union we will have with God forever.

Imagine that party. You'll bump into Abraham, David, the disciples, grandmas, grandpas, and loved ones who faithfully followed Christ. The chatter will fill the halls of eternity. Hugs, kisses, and awe will seem unending. No earthly celebration could compare to this dinner.

Imagine yourself at this party. You sit down to eat, and across the table from you sits a young teenage girl. She's radiating joy.

"What's your name?" you ask.

"Maxima," she responds.

"I'm so glad to meet you, Maxima. What's your testimony? Your story?"

She gleefully replies, "I'd love to tell you my story. I was born in 244 A.D. in a small town on the coast of North Africa; it was later referred to as Tunisia.

"Well, I was an average little girl. I loved playing with my dolls, making mud pies with my friends, and doing my best dolphin impersonation in the Mediterranean Sea. Life was simple. I dreamed of getting married and having a family of my own.

"One joyous day, when I was a young girl, I heard the good news about Jesus. It was the best thing I had ever heard. I quickly fell in love with Jesus and told everyone I knew about him. You know, that is what you do when you are in love. Sometimes, my friends had to remind me that I had already shared the gospel with them, but I guess I couldn't help but tell them again and again. Oh, how much I love Jesus.

"Well, when I was fourteen, Emperor Valerian made a law—sacrifice to the Roman gods or die. It was devastating. Many of my friends did. But, me. I couldn't. I loved Jesus too much. Not only did I not follow the emperor's request, I became even more determined to talk about Jesus and his gospel.

"The authorities arrested me and two of my friends. Imagine that. I was only fourteen. I was found guilty of telling people about Jesus and not worshipping Roman gods. These older soldiers stripped us naked, humiliated us, and tortured us in the city square for all to see.

"'Stop talking about Jesus. He's dead. And, you will be soon if you don't stop!' They shouted.

"'He's not dead! He's alive. He won! He's the king and savior of all.' I responded.

"They eventually dragged us into an arena where thousands of people had gathered. My two friends and I were brought into the middle of the arena to the delight of the crowd. They did some cruel things to us that day."

Maxima pauses and looks down at the table. With a deep breath she looks back up. "But, my king was worth it all. I had to get his gospel out to everyone I knew. That's what he wanted us all to do. It was my time in history. All eternity was cheering me on as I ran with the Gospel Baton in hand. Centuries of believers ahead of me needed me to stand strong and share the gospel so they, too, could hear.

"As I heard the roar of the caged lion near the edge of the arena's floor, I pleaded once more to the crowd to listen to my message: 'Jesus is the savior, heaven and earth's victorious King!'

"Oh, how much I wanted my neighbors and friends to know my Jesus.

"They would listen no more. I sat on that arena floor, bloodied and scared beyond imagination. They tied me to a small gallow in the middle of the floor and beat me until I could barely speak. Yet, I somehow had the strength to shout the gospel. I cried out to the crowds, and I whispered to Jesus of my love. I didn't let any excuse hold me back from obeying Jesus and sharing his gospel on that arena floor.

"Out of the corner of my eye, I saw the procurator give the nod to the gladiators by the lion's cage. A cold shiver of fear swept through my body. I knew what was coming.

"The cage door was opened. He ran directly toward me. I squeezed my eyes shut, gripped the ropes that tied me to the gallows, and let out a scream.

"My life ended that day, and I have been waiting for this celebration ever since. Now, here we are."

With the innocence of a child, Maxima leans forward, puts her elbows on the table and rests her chin on her closed fists. A smile sweeps her face as she looks you in the eyes,

"So, what about you? What's your story?" she asks.

I hope you have one.

Go & Tell.
This is _your_ moment to run.

NOTES

Chapter 1

1. "The Love of God" by Frederick M. Lehman, 1917.
2. Si Sheppard, Actium 31B.C., (Oxford: Osprey Publishing Ltd., 2009), 61-86.
3. N.T. Wright, Simply Good News, (New York, NY: Harper Collins, 2015), 55.
4. Matthew 24:14.
5. Reinhard Bonnke, Living a Life of Fire, (Longwood, FL: Harvester Services Inc, 2010), 149.

Chapter 2

1. Acts 1:8.
2. Matthew 4:19.
3. Mathew 4:17.
4. Acts 2:14-39.
5. Judges 3:10.
6. Numbers 27:18.
7. https://billygraham.org/audio/carrying-out-the-great-commission
8. Quote attributed to missionary David Livingstone.
9. Acts 2:41.
10. Acts 9:17.
11. John 16:17.
12. John 1:32.

13. Symbols of the Holy Spirit: Oil (1 Samuel 16:13), a finger (Luke 11:20), water (John 7:37-38), rain (Psalm 72:6), wind (Acts 2:2), a guarantee (2 Corinthians 1:21–22), a seal (Ephesians 1:13), a river (John 7:38), wine (Ephesians 5:18), and a cloud (Luke 1:35).
14. Quote attributed to Charles Spurgeon.

Chapter 3
1. Quote attributed to Leonard Ravenhill.
2. Bruce L. Shelley, Church History in Plain Language; Updated 2nd Edition, (Word Publishing, 1982), 37.
3. Mark 16:15.
4. Rick Renner, Sparkling Gems from the Greek Volume 1, (Teach All Nations, 2003), 469–471.
5. John 10:27.
6. Jesus prayed before daybreak (Mark 1:35), throughout the night (Luke 6:10), in secret (Matthew 14:23), on a mountain (Mark 6:46), in the wilderness (Luke 5:16), before eating (Matthew 15:36), in times of distress (John 12:27), among the people (Matthew 19:13), at the grave of Lazarus (John 11:41), in Gethsemane (Matthew 26:36–44), and even when he was dying on the cross (Matthew 27:46).
7. Luke 11:1.
8. Matthew 6:10.
9. Shelley, 164.
10. Billy Graham interviewed by Greta Van Susteren on Fox News on December 20, 2010. The full interview can be found on YouTube: www.youtube.com/watch?v=GoSHoKnDuoY
11. John Mark Terry, Evangelism, (B&H Publishing Group, 1994), Kindle Edition 30-32.

Chapter 4
1. The stories of martyrs taken from the book: John Foxe, The New Foxe's Book of Martyrs, (Gainesville: Bridge-Logos Publishers, 2001), 11-39.
2. Shelley, 79.

3. This quotation from the bishop is from Gregory of Nyssa and is quoted in W. H. C. Frend, The Early Church (Philadelphia: Lippincott, 1966), 186-187.

Chapter 5

1. Agop Jack Hacikyan, Gabriel Basmajian, Edward S. Franchuk, Nourhan Ouzounian, The Heritage of Armenian Literature: From the oral tradition to the Golden Age, (Detroit: Wayne State University Press, 2000), 256.
2. Ignite Europe has hosted several One Hope events. These are city-wide, open air evangelistic events.
3. Acts 3:6.
4. Acts 4:4.
5. Acts 9:34.
6. Acts 9:36-42.
7. Acts 6:8.
8. Acts 8:39.
9. Acts 5:12.
10. 1 Corinthians 2:4.
11. Romans 15:18-19.
12. Acts 14:8-10.
13. Acts 16:18.
14. Acts 20:9-12.
15. Shelley, 65.
16. Luke 10:9.
17. Luke 10:17.
18. Luke 10:18-21.
19. Luke 10:17.

Chapter 6

1. A. Kenneth Curits, J. Stephen Lang, and Randy Petersen, The 100 Most Important Events in Christian History, (Grand Rapids: Revell Publishing, 1991), 47-48.
2. 1 Peter 1:18-19.
3. Matthew 3:17.
4. 2 Corinthians 2:11.

5. This is a famous prayer that is attributed to Saint Patrick and is also known as "Morning Prayer", "Saint Patrick's Breastplate", or "The Lorica".

6. Romans 8:28.

7. Richard Wurmbrand was the founder of the magazine The Voice of the Martyrs. More of his biography can be found on the founders page of the magazine's website at www.persecution.com.

Chapter 7

1. Matthew 7:28.

2. Luke 5:3.

Chapter 8

1. The details of this woman's life have been partly taken from the book and can be further studied in the book: Kenneth E. Bailey, Jesus Through Middle Eastern Eyes, (Madison, WI: InterVarsity Press), 200-216.

Chapter 9

1. Shelley, 152.

2. This is a true story but fictitious name.

Chapter 10

1. Robert G. Clouse, Richard V. Pierard, and Edwin M. Yamauchi, The Story of the Church, (Moody Press, 2002), 79.

2. Gene Fedele, Heroes of the Faith, (Bridge-Logos, 2003), 64.

3. Curtis, Lang, and Petersen, 67.

4. 1 Corinthians 13:1.

5. Matthew 9:36, 14:14, and 15:32.

6. John 1:40-42.

7. Proverbs 29:11.

8. This story has several versions from various sermons online and is written about at www.spu.edu/depts/uc/response/new/2011-autumn/features/cautionary-portrait.asp

Chapter 11

1. www.billygraham.org/Assets/Media/pdfs/stepstopeace/Testimony_ Article.pdf
2. Hebrews 11:38.

Chapter 12

1. The Bible says in Luke 15:7 that when one sinner repents, there is great joy in heaven.
2. 1 Timothy 1:13.
3. Matthew 13:9-15.
4. Matthew 13:16.

Chapter 13

1. Curtis, Lang, and Petersen, 77.
2. Shelley, 209.
3. John 3:16.
4. Matthew 5:16.
5. 1 Corinthians 9:10.

Chapter 14

1. Fedele, 87.
2. Matthew 3:2.
3. Matthew 4:17.
4. Mark 1:14-15
5. Colossians 4:4.
6. Reinhard Bonnke, Living a Life of Fire: An Autobiography, (Longwood, FL: Harvester Services, 2010), 138.
7. Ephesians 6:14-15.
8. 2 Timothy 4:2.

Chapter 15

1. Shelley, 230.
2. Mark 5:40.
3. This is a true story but fictitious name.
4. Shelley, 326.
5. www.gideons.org/about

Chapter 16

1. E. Michael and Sharon Rusten, The One Year Christian History, (Carol Stream, IL: Tyndale House Publishing, 2003), 268.
2. Curtis, Lang, and Petersen, 93.
3. Fedele, 102.
4. Shelley, 290.
5. Eric Metaxas, Bonhoeffer, (Nashville, TN: Thomas Nelson, 2010), 272.
6. John 4:20.
7. https://www.charismamag.com/spirit/evangelism-missions/20636-the-surprising-simplicity-of-sharing-the-gospel?

Chapter 17

1. Thomas Smith, Successful Advertising, (Smith's Printing and Publishing Agency, 1885).
2. Shelley, 251.

Chapter 18

1. Curtis, Lang, and Petersen, 122.
2. Acts 11:21.
3. Acts 11:26.
4. Shelley, 40.
5. Shelley, 73.
6. James M. Freeman, Manners & Customs of the Bible, (PA: Whitaker House, 1996), 458.

Chapter 19

1. Curtis, Lang, and Petersen, 134.
2. Shelley, 336.
3. Shelley, 337.
4. Ross Phares, Bible in Pocket, Gun in Hand (Lincoln: University of Nebraska Press, 1964), 156.
5. Luke 24:32.

Chapter 20

1. Curtis, Lang, and Petersen, 161.
2. Rusten, 137.
3. Romans 8:18-23, Isaiah 11:6-9, Jeremiah 31:11.
4. Revelation 21:1–27.
5. Matthew 28:19-20.
6. Shelley, 97-98.

Chapter 21

1. Through Gates of Splender, 177-194.
2. Matthew 28:19-20.
3. Matthew 6:20.
4. Shelley, 287.
5. Shelley, 375.

Chapter 22

1. www.lifewithoutlimbs.org/about/nick-biography
2. Matthew 16:18.
3. Luke 17:26-27.
4. New York Times, October 2, 1970 "When Is Christ Coming?; The Twenty Signs of the Bible Give Us a Clue" by Dr. Billy Graham
5. Matthew 24:6-7.
6. Matthew 24:9.
7. Statement by His Excellency Archbishop Silvano M. Tomasi Permanent Observer of the Holy See to the United Nations and Other International Organizations in Geneva 23rd Session of the Human Rights Council Interactive Dialogue on May 27,2013.

Chapter 23

1. Quote attributed to Reinhard Bonnke.
2. 1 Corinthians 9:16.

ABOUT SHAWN BRANN

Shawn has been in full-time ministry for more than 20 years serving in many areas such as youth pastor, college pastor, evangelist, missionary, professional sports chaplain and a church growth consultant. In the late '90s, Shawn went to the Brownsville Revival School of Ministry in Pensacola where he earned an associates degree in ministry and served full-time on the prayer team at the Brownsville Revival. He went on to become a youth pastor in Texas and Iowa. His youth ministry,  Reality, experienced amazing growth—starting with just four students and growing to several hundred students in less than two years, with outreaches topping over a thousand students.

In 2004, Shawn founded Teen Unite, an evangelistic parachurch ministry uniting youth ministries together in cities across America for united evangelistic events. Teen Unite reached thousands of high school students across the United States. Simultaneously, Shawn served as a professional sports chaplain or assisted chaplains for teams such as the Dallas Cowboys, Texas Rangers, Dallas Desperados, Allen Wranglers, Texas Revolution, and several other professional indoor football teams between 2000–2011.

In 2013, Shawn began working on staff at Gateway Church in Southlake, TX as an Associate Pastor and Dean of Students at The King's University. At the same time, Shawn and Tanja started Ignite Europe. Although The King's University was experiencing amazing growth, going from a start-up branch campus to a main campus university with more than five hundred students, Shawn and Tanja made a life move in 2016, leaving everything in Texas to oversee Ignite Europe full time from Zürich, Switzerland.

Shawn has earned several degrees, including an Associates of Practical Ministry, Bachelor of Arts in Biblical Studies, Master in Business Administration (MBA), Master in Practical Theology (MPT), and a Master Degree in Divinity (MDIV). He is also an author and entrepreneur.

ALSO FROM SHAWN ...

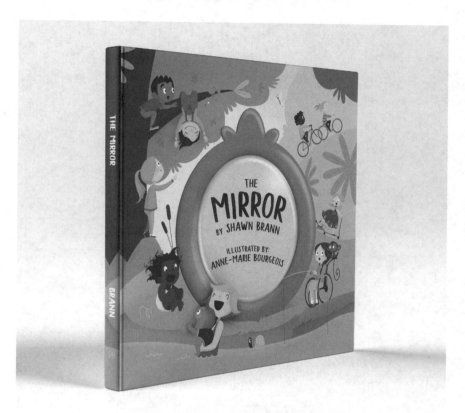

Shawn's best-selling children's book, *The Mirror*, conveys a powerful message that combats the current culture of racism, comparison, bullying, and low self-esteem. It reminds children that God created each of them in his image. And, after God had created all kinds of animals, he wanted to make something more like himself. So, he looked in the mirror and began forming his masterpiece. He would call them people. *The Mirror* gives impressionable little minds the truth that everyone's skin color, personality, and uniqueness are all part of God's perfect creation while celebrating each person's differences.

GET YOUR WHOLE CHURCH OR COMMUNITY EVANGELIZING TOGETHER!

This must-have tool maximizes your Go & Tell experience with practical applications, so you'll be better equipped to share the good news of Jesus!

Go & Tell Workbook

A companion to *Go & Tell,* this interactive workbook is designed to initiate and facilitate discussion and practical application through thought-provoking questions, videos, and bonus material, making it a valuable resource for churches, small groups, youth groups, or even individuals.

GoandTell.online